Entrepreneurial Universities in Regional Innovation

Entrepreneurial Universities in Regional Innovation

Edited by

David Charles

Rhoda Ahoba-Sam

Sergio Manrique

A book from the Marie Skłodowska-Curie RUNIN Project - The Role of Universities in Regional Innovation

This work forms part of the RUNIN project (The Role of Universities in Innovation and Regional Development), which has received funding from the European Union's Horizon 2020 research and innovation programme under Marie Skłodowska-Curie grant agreement No. 722295.

Published by UK Book Publishing

www.ukbookpublishing.com

ISBN: 978-1-914195-64-8

Dedication

During the preparation of this book our colleague and good friend Paul Benneworth passed away suddenly and far too young. We would like to dedicate this book to his memory and with condolences to his wife Leanne and his children Theo and Martha.

Contents

Chapter 6: From Transplantation to Diversification? The University of Stavanger's Role in the Economic Development of Rogaland   171

Utku Ali Rıza Alpaydın, Kwadwo Atta-Owusu and Saeed Moghadam-Saman

Chapter 7: Evolutionary Analysis of a University's Engagement in a Less-Developed Region: The case of the University of Aveiro   219

Liliana Fonseca, Rıdvan Cınar, Artur da Rosa Pires, Carlos Rodrigues

Contributors

Rhoda Ahoba-Sam

Rhoda was a RUNIN research fellow at the University of Lincoln and has a PhD on the 'Microfoundations of Academics Networks: Initiation, Evolution and Context'. She also holds a BSc. in Biochemistry from the University of Ghana and an MSc. in Innovation and Entrepreneurship from the University of Oslo. She has industrial experience working as a supply chain quality specialist in Nestle Ghana. She is a visiting researcher at the University of Lincoln's International Business School and currently works as a business development manager at a startup company, Wattero AS in the Oslo area.

Utku Ali Rıza Alpaydın

Utku was a RUNIN research fellow at the University of Stavanger where his PhD topic was on 'University-industry collaborations (UICs): A matter of proximity dimensions?' He also has an M.A. and B.Sc. in International Relations from Bilkent University and Middle East Technical University (METU), Turkey respectively. His professional experience is as a senior expert on regional development and planning, project management, grant administration and international cooperation. He currently works at the Silkroad Development Agency in Turkey as the head of programme management unit

Kwadwo Atta-Owusu

Kwadwo was a RUNIN researcher at the University of Stavanger (UiS). His PhD investigated how individual and contextual factors influence academic engagement in regions. Prior to joining the RUNIN Project, he has worked as a research assistant for the HURMOS Project at the University of Oulu. He holds a MSc in International Business Management from the University of Oulu and a BSc in Business Administration from the Ghana Baptist University College. He is presently a research fellow at the Centre for Innovation Research at the UiS Business School.

Paul Benneworth

Paul Benneworth was professor at the University of Applied Sciences of Western Norway and before that was a senior researcher at the Center for Higher Education Policy Studies, University of Twente, the Netherlands. Paul's research focused on the dynamics of innovation and regional development and in particular the ways in which cooperations and coalitions function in supporting regional innovation processes. He was chief scientist of projects for a range of research funders including the European Framework Programme/ERA-NET, research councils in the UK, the Netherlands and Norway as well as a wide range of government and not-for-profit funders. He was the editor of eight scientific works, including three in the RSA Cities & Regions series. He published more than thirty peer-reviewed scientific articles in the last decade, and served as reviewer for a range of journals, research councils and funding agencies internationally.

David Charles

David Charles is Professor of Enterprise and Innovation at Newcastle Business School, and director of the Northumbria Centre for Innovation, Regional Transformation and Entrepreneurship (iNCITE) at Northumbria University. He joined Northumbria in February 2018 from Lincoln where he was deputy head of the Lincoln International Business School. David led the RUNIN activities at Lincoln and remains closely involved with the project and was a supervisor for the two RUNIN fellows there as a visiting professor. He is also a visiting professor at Tampere University. David has a PhD in economic geography from Newcastle University on the location of corporate R&D activity and since then he has mainly worked on regional innovation policy, innovation management, universities and their regional engagement, and urban issues.

Rıdvan Çınar

Rıdvan was a RUNIN research fellow at the University of Aveiro in Portugal, working on how universities located in less-developed regions respond to multiple innovation-related institutional demands. He was a visiting researcher at the University of Twente in the Netherlands and European Consortium of Innovative Universities (ECIU). Currently, he is a PhD candidate in Western Norway University of Applied Sciences working towards finalization of his thesis titled "Transitioning from Entrepreneurial to Engaged University Model: Changing Conceptualization of Innovation, Contributions to Regional Development and the Challenges of Institutional Change". He holds a MSc in Educational Administration and Planning and B.A in English Language Teaching from the Middle East Technical University (METU) and Akdeniz University, Turkey respectively.

Gerwin Evers

Gerwin Evers was a RUNIN research fellow in the IKE research group at Aalborg University and has a PhD on the 'The role of universities in regional industrial development'. He also holds a MSc. in Innovation Sciences and a BSc. in Science and Innovation Management, both from Utrecht University. Other prior work experience include amongst others a position as junior researcher at the Copernicus Institute of Sustainable Development at Utrecht University. Currently Gerwin works as science and innovation policy consultant at the Amsterdam office of the Technopolis Group.

Rune Dahl Fitjar

Rune Dahl Fitjar is the Pro-Rector for Innovation and Society at the University of Stavanger since August 2019. He has been a Professor of Innovation Studies at the UiS Business School since 1 September 2013 and is affiliated with the Centre for Innovation Research. Fitjar won the University of Stavanger's prize for research excellence in 2013 and for research communication in 2011. He completed his PhD in political science at the London School of Economics in 2007. His research deals with different aspects of regions, including regional development and innovation.

Liliana Fonseca

Liliana is a research assistant at the European Policies Research Centre at the University of Strathclyde (UK) and a PhD candidate in Public Policies and RUNIN research fellow at the University of Aveiro (PT). She was awarded in 2018 the IND+I Science's Industry and Innovation grant for her paper on "Universities in Innovation Policy-Design: a review of the participation of external actors in the policy process for the creation of public value". She has an MSc in Eco-Cities from Cardiff University and a BA in Political Science and International Relations from the New University of Lisbon. Her research interests focus on governance, urban and regional sustainable development and public policies.

Eloïse Germain-Alamartine

Eloïse Germain holds a PhD from Linköping University (Sweden). She participated in the Horizon 2020 project RUNIN (the Role of Universities in Innovation and Regional Development). Her dissertation deals with PhD education and the model of the entrepreneurial university, and her research interests encompass highly-skilled workers and entrepreneurial ecosystems. She has a background in IT-engineering and in business administration, and is currently working at CEA (France) as an administrative coordinator for two Horizon 2020 projects involving industrial partners, research institutes and universities on the development of innovative energy storage systems.

David Fernández Guerrero

David is a researcher at the Centre for Agro-Food Economics and Development (CREDA), in Castelldefels (Spain). He was previously a RUNIN research fellow at Aalborg University, and has a PhD on 'the role of different factors in industry-university collaboration, in different types of regions'. He also holds an MSc in Sociology from the University of Amsterdam, where he graduated cum laude, and a Master's in Journalism from the Escuela de Periodismo UAM-El País.

Sofya Kopelyan

Sofya was a RUNIN research fellow at the University of Twente where her PhD topic was on 'University governance in the times of 'mission stretch': Implications for the regional mission'. She is also a graduate of the Erasmus Mundus Master course in Research and Innovation in Higher Education (MaRIHE) and holds a joint MSc degree in Administrative Sciences from the University of Tampere and Danube University Krems. She also obtained a Specialist degree with honours in Culturology from the Russian State University for the Humanities and has professional experience as lecturer and academic administrator. She currently works as project manager at the University of Twente.

Sergio Manrique

Sergio was a RUNIN research fellow at Universitat Autònoma de Barcelona (UAB) in Spain with secondment periods at University of Stavanger Business School (Norway), and is finalising a PhD on 'Assessing the Impact of University-Firm Collaboration on Firm Performance and Regional Development'. He holds a M.Sc. in management, organisation and business economics from UAB. Industrial engineer (B.Sc.) and specialist in managerial and organisational control systems from Universidad de los Andes (Bogotá, Colombia), he is certified as Professional Scrum Master, Green Belt in Lean Six Sigma methodology and internal auditor in ISO 9001. Past work experience as class assistant and process engineer in the academic sector, and as planning intern and routing professional in the private sector in Colombia. He is currently based in Colombia and Spain, and works as project manager in the IT consultancy sector.

Huong Nguyen

Huong Nguyen is a RUNIN research fellow at the Universitat Autònoma de Barcelona and an editor of RUNIN Working Paper Series. Huong's research is focused on the role of citizens and users in innovation and regional development through the Quadruple Helix partnerships with various actors from university, government and industry. She holds master and bachelor's degrees in business administration from Umeå University and Foreign Trade University, respectively. Before transferring to academia, Huong spent several years working as a senior tax consultant at PricewaterhouseCoopers (Vietnam) Ltd.

Lisa Nieth

Lisa was a RUNIN research fellow at the University of Twente and Region of Twente. In August 2020, she completed her PhD on 'Universities as institutional entrepreneurs in knowledge-based regional development'. She currently works as a Senior Consultant for the German branch of the Technopolis Group. Prior to her PhD, Lisa worked in project management and consultancy with a focus on innovation, clusters, and startup support at the German-Chilean Chamber of Commerce (2014-2017). She has a double degree (BA & MA) in International Management and Intercultural Studies from the University of Stirling and Passau.

Carlos Rodrigues

Carlos Rodrigues is assistant professor at the Department of Social, Political and Territorial Sciences (DCSPT) of the University of Aveiro (UA). His research and teaching activities are focused on territorial innovation systems, higher education studies, regional policy and sports. Besides Europe, his research 'geography' includes China, Africa and Latin America. Carlos has participated in several national and international research projects. In addition, he has a long experience of collaboration with the public sector and industry. Currently, he is the head of the DCSPT, member of the coordination of the Research Unit on Governance, Competitiveness and Public Policies, and coordinator of Chinese Studies.

Artur da Rosa Pires

Artur Rosa Pires is Full Professor at the Department of Social, Political and Territorial Sciences, University of Aveiro, Portugal. He has as a PhD in Urban and Regional Planning, University of Wales, Cardiff (1987) and his main research and teaching interests are on Spatial Development and Innovation Policy, Spatial

Strategic Planning, Sustainable Development, Rural Development, Governance and Local Government, and Planning Theory. He is member of the research unit on Governance, Competitiveness and Public Policies (GOVCOPP) and has developed an extensive research and professional work, including the coordination of national and international research projects. In addition to his academic activities, he was Vice President of the Regional Commission for Coordination and Development, Centro Region (2003-2005), Secretary of State for the Environment and Spatial Planning (Portuguese XV Constitutional Government, 2004) and Adviser to the Portuguese President of the Republic for Science and the Environment (2009-2011). He was also Pro-Rector of the University of Aveiro responsible for the "cooperation with the Region" (2008-2012). He has cooperated with the European Commission, through the S3 Platform, in the field of research and innovation strategies for smart specialisation (RIS3), namely in the design and implementation of such strategies in rural and peripheral areas.

Maria Salomaa

Maria was a RUNIN research fellow at the University of Lincoln where she completed her PhD entitled 'University Third Mission in Rural Regions: A comparative analysis on university engagement through the Structural Funds programmes in the UK, Finland and Portugal'. She also holds Masters degrees in Administration and Management of Higher Education and Theatre and Drama Research both from the Tampere University. Maria has previously worked in project management in the higher education sector mainly focusing on FP7 and H2020 projects. She has also worked with national and international R&D projects in the field of culture (2007-2015). She is a visiting research fellow at the Lincoln International Business School, and she currently works at the Tampere University of Applied Sciences as a RDI specialist.

Saeed Moghadam Saman

Saeed was a RUNIN research fellow at the University of Stavanger where he conducted his PhD in Innovation Studies, and his PhD topic was on 'Intersectoral collaborations of doctoral researchers and generic skills acquisition'. Saeed has an MSc. in Industrial Management with specialisation in Logistics from University of Borås, Sweden, and BSc. in Industrial Engineering with specialisation in Systems Analysis and Planning from Azad University, Tehran, Iran. Before doing his PhD studies, he has worked as consultant industrial engineer (feasibility studies and quality management systems) and seaborn logistics intern in Iran, and as researcher at the Centre for Innovation Studies, University of Economics and Management, Prague, The Czech Republic. Currently, he works as research fellow at the Mohn Centre for Innovation and Regional Development, Western Norway University of Applied Sciences, Bergen, Norway.

Preface

Rune Dahl Fitjar

This book is the result of a European Union funded Marie Skłodowska-Curie Actions Innovative Training Network on the Role of Universities in Innovation and Regional Development (RUNIN). The network received funding from 2016 to 2020 and supported 14 early-career researchers who undertook their doctoral training in the network. It builds on the collaboration between the universities in the European Consortium for Innovative Universities (ECIU), of which six of the participant teams are members. The universities in the ECIU share an ambition to promote innovation and to work closely with their regions. The RUNIN programme brings together scholars working on higher education, innovation and regions in order to study how the universities realise this ambition. The project aims to provide new knowledge for other universities and policy-makers on how universities can contribute to innovation in their regions. The programme includes a university and a regional development agency in each region as partners in order to examine the relationship between universities and their regions from both perspectives.

The programme involved international mobility both before and during the programme. All early-career researchers moved from abroad to the university and region in which they were employed. The 14 researchers in the programme came from 12 different countries on four continents. They could thus bring an outsider's perspective on the universities and the regions. This book presents those perspectives. It includes seven case studies authored by the early-career researchers working at each university, in which they analyse the relationship between the university and its surrounding region.

The case studies show the wide array of roles which universities can take in their regions. Even though the universities share the same ambition and, as members of the ECIU, have similar profiles, the regional and national contexts in which they find themselves have implications for the types of activities which they do, the effects of these activities, and the way in which they are received both at the university and in the surrounding region.

Work on this book started during the first training week of the project, hosted by the University of Lincoln in March 2017, when the researchers had started their PhDs only weeks or even days before. It ends as the programme draws to a conclusion, following an extensive programme of training weeks in all seven regions, several conference special sessions, joint publications, exchanges and successful PhD defences. It has been an honour to work with such a great group of promising researchers and inspiring supervisors through the process. The scholars in the RUNIN programme share an interest in studying universities and regions, but also in actively engaging with stakeholders, in communicating their research in new ways, and in contributing to the betterment of society. During the course of the programme, the network has evolved into deep collaboration and close friendships, where all participants have contributed to a supportive atmosphere.

We hope this book will reflect that collaboration and will be of use to university managers, policymakers, academics and students who want to know how universities can contribute to their regions. The universities and regions presented here are all, in their unique ways, interesting examples of the multi-faceted nature of this relationship.

4

Chapter 1

Introduction

David Charles, Rhoda Ahoba-Sam, Sergio Manrique

Universities have a special role, some would say a unique role, in their cities and regions in meeting a diverse set of needs, and, in doing so, contributing to the economic and social development of those cities and regions (Goddard et al 1994; Arbo and Benneworth, 2007; Goddard and Vallance, 2014). Whilst the primary missions of a university are to engage in teaching and research, the nature of academic scholarship across all areas of knowledge leads to interaction and positive engagement with businesses, government, public services, voluntary and community bodies and individual citizens. No other organisation in the region has quite such a scale and diversity of engagements and impacts, and correspondingly a diverse set of studies have emerged in recent years to explore and evaluate those impacts. This book examines the nature of some of these impacts for a set of European universities in their regional contexts.

From the most simplistic view, universities can be seen as very large organisations which have large positive impacts through their employment and through the expenditure of their students, as revealed through input-output and other economic impact studies (Florax, 1992; McNicoll et al 1997; Drucker and Goldstein, 2007). As some of the largest employers in their cities, universities have significant economic footprints, larger than firms with a similar employment because of the very large number of students and their spending. Yet, this is only part of the role and impact universities have: a static impact, rather than the dynamic effects which come from the iterative and interactive processes of learning and responses to the region's needs. In this way a university can be seen as a 'community of experimentation and innovation' (Breznitz and Feldman, 2012, 139) engaging in a wide range of business, public and civic activities.

Whilst it may be argued that universities have always had a role to play in their regional and national societies, there has never been a time when so much attention has been paid by universities to their civic role. There has also never been a time when universities were so significant in scale, both through the growth in numbers of institutions and through their size, with enrolments reaching half of the age cohort. So, universities are large, ubiquitous and increasingly aware of the need to engage with society. And although universities are increasingly diverse in nature, engagement seems to be a growing tendency among all types, but with some placing a higher importance on the role than others.

This engagement of universities with business, the community and their surrounding cities and regions has stimulated a growth industry of publications in recent years with a host of different conceptualisations and models (Uyarra, 2010) and a wealth of empirical studies, sometimes theoretically driven and sometimes not. Whilst approaches vary in their conceptualisation of the university and its mission, there is much commonality across different conceptualisations, and different perspectives can be

6

seen as overlaying each other in building a picture of the external engagement of the university. Whilst some studies take a narrow focus on university-industry links at the level of individual businesses, a more systemic approach is needed to explore the overall shape of engagement between universities and their regions, moving beyond individual firms to consider the governance of regional innovation systems and wider contributions to the social, cultural and environmental welfare of a region.

Alongside the growth of studies of university engagement and examples of beneficial impacts on local regions there have also been counter voices expressing a sense of concern that perhaps universities have lost their way and that the demands of science policy have pushed universities away from being relevant to the outside world (Calhoun, 2006; Brink, 2018). The need for academics to focus on scientific publication for internal accountability has led to an explosion in journals and a concern that much of this publication is inward looking. This prompts a response arguing for greater emphasis on impactful research, engagement and responsible research and innovation (RRI) (Fitjar et al 2018). A large number of reports internationally have been written calling for greater engagement and for a change in the nature of science institutions (e.g. Kellogg Commission, 2000) yet at the same time there seems to be more engagement than ever before.

Policymakers have been particularly keen to promote regional engagement as part of a 'third mission' sitting alongside the missions of teaching and research. National governments have sought to encourage universities to be more proactive in supporting innovation and in regional engagement through a variety of reports and policy interventions. One aspect of this, much examined in studies of university knowledge exchange with business has been the means by which intellectual property (IP) has been protected and commercialised, in what may be termed the regime of appropriation (Rappert and Webster, 1997). The passing of the Bayh-Dole Act in the US is one example of this, granting certain rights of IP ownership to universities (Mowery and Sampat, 2004). European countries have had a variety of positions on this, some leaving IP ownership to individual professors (Pettersson 2018), some encouraging universities to actively claim and exploit IP (Geuna and Rossi, 2011).

The rise of innovation system approaches to policy has particularly favoured the role of universities as key actors within innovation systems, especially in those cities and regions where research and knowledge infrastructures are otherwise in short supply. Not only are universities important contributors to the development of knowledge and skills, and providers of research resources, but they now exist in almost all regions, so playing a particularly important role in those regions otherwise disadvantaged. Disparities in resource and esteem do however exist within university systems, with many countries still concentrating funding and hence the best researchers in a small number of core institutions, usually in core regions. Thus, the need for universities to have a greater impact in peripheral regions is tempered by the lower level of resource often available to those institutions. This is particularly so in more rural regions where the university presence may just be in the form of small branch campuses (Charles, 2016).

The diverse national efforts have been complemented by the transnational promotion of good practice through the EU and OECD. The EU in particular has promoted university involvement in regional development through its position on higher education modernisation which seeks to "promote the systemic involvement of HEIs in the development of integrated local and regional development plans and target regional support towards HE-business co-operation particularly for the creation of regional hubs of excellence and specialisation" (European Commission 2013, 1). Also the regional policy of the EU has supported the greater involvement of universities in regional development strategies through active involvement of universities in the ERDF and in strategic initiatives such as smart specialisation (Goddard and Kempton, 2011) At the same time the OECD has promoted regional engagement over a long period from the *University and the Community* report of 1982 (OECD, 1982) through several subsequent reports and associated conferences and dissemination processes (OECD, 1999; 2007).

Universities have responded through the identification of innovation, enterprise and regional engagement in their mission statements and in the development of new forms of organisation and activities to underpin that engagement (Clark, 1998). This book examines these strategies and the outcomes for regional innovation in seven European case studies, and seeks to flesh out in detailed case studies some of the issues involved in translating theory into practice. The seven cases contained in this book are fairly diverse in terms of universities and types of regions: most of them would have strong claims to be heavily engaged, and perhaps more so than other universities within the same countries, but equally they tend not to be among the elite research universities in their countries, with the exception of the Autonomous University of Barcelona. For many of the cases the university is also located in a region which is somewhat peripheral and facing economic challenges, against which the university is expected to provide some form of defence.

Engagement comes in many different forms and we have a variety of terms we use to characterise it. We talk of innovative, entrepreneurial or engaged universities, of universities as anchor

9

institutions and new forms of civic university. There is a proliferation of conceptual frameworks applied to the task of analysing the engaged university at different levels of generality, some pertaining to the university sector as a whole, some to specific forms of institution, yet one common aspect is that all universities are to some degree unique. All universities emerge from national higher education systems in the context of their local environment and history, developing from a unique set of circumstances and strategies. These stories and circumstances provide a base for this book, exploring how a set of engaged universities became so and how their story relates to that of their regions.

A brief history of university engagement

Despite the topical nature of the idea of universities benefitting their local communities, and much recent policy and academic development, the concept has had a relatively long gestation, even before most of our case study institutions were founded. Leaving aside the emergence of the 'ancient' universities in the middle ages, the creation of new universities since the 19th century has often been associated with the desire to support regional economies. This was especially the case in the US since the Land Grant colleges were established by the Morrill Act of 1862. Whilst the Morrill Act endowed a set of state colleges with land to finance their operations, their responsibilities to society were based on the principle that 'no part of human life and labor is beneath the notice of the university or without its proper dignity' (McDowell, 2003, 33). The land grants developed agricultural extension programmes to support local farmers, but at the same time were committed to opening their doors to the working classes and extending their interests and engagement well beyond agriculture. The land grants were born as engaged universities and even their most eminent representatives today, such as MIT, retain that ethos.

In the UK the emergence of the civic universities in the provincial cities of England in the 19th century was driven by a need for locally engaged education and research, and often supported by local interests. Prior to 1900, Oxford and Cambridge were not addressing the needs of British industry, and hence the civic universities were created as a response to those needs (Sanderson, 1972). Universities such as Manchester and Liverpool were established with funds from local industrialists, and in many cases the public also, with specific gifts from business leaders for labs related to their business interests (Sanderson, 1972; Whyte, 2015)

Elsewhere in Europe the universities often developed as public institutions with an emphasis on basic research when research was undertaken. Even the German technical universities drifted towards basic research after initially being founded with a mission for engagement (Beise and Stahl, 1998). But, a second tier of higher education in the form of fachhochschulen, universities of applied sciences or polytechnics have emerged in several countries with a much stronger focus on engagement with local industry, even if some, as in the UK and now Norway, shifted to become universities in more recent years.

The growth and spread of universities across Europe in recent decades, into the regions, islands, more rural and peripheral areas, has been driven by local needs for education and engagement, and by the promises of regional impacts. Some countries have seen expansion in the middle years of the twentieth century, in which several of our cases were established, whilst a more recent expansion has taken place in several countries notably Norway, the UK, Spain and Portugal. In Spain for example, since the return of democracy and the creation of regional government, there has been a proliferation of universities: there were by 2010 some 77 universities, 50 of which were public and a total of 232 campuses (Rubiralta and Delgado 2010). These included new universities in

11

the Balearic Islands, Gran Canaria, and small regional cities such as Huelva, Burgos and Elche. Portugal also saw massive expansion since the fall of the Salazar dictatorship in 1974. From just 3 universities in 1974 the number grew to 16 universities and 15 polytechnic institutes by 2007 (Alves et al 2015). Again, the new institutes spread from Bragança in the North to Faro in the South and to the islands of Madeira and the Azores. The idea of creating universities to stimulate regional economies is not new, and continues today to provide a rationale for university expansion with new universities being developed in Europe. Several of the case study universities in this book emerged with the desire to stimulate their regional economies.

The crucial attribute of the university in promoting regional development and innovation is its openness to society and the opportunity for knowledge to spill over into the region, even if not actively disseminated. Jane Jacobs in 1969 suggested that the broader creation and transfer of knowledge in higher education created more growth in the city than the more focused R&D activities of firms. Universities are also seen as magnets for other activities. Clark Kerr in a series of lectures on his notion of the multiversity in 1963 talks of universities being dangled as bait for attracting industry, more attractive than low taxes and cheap labour. He also sketches a picture of agglomerations of research universities as mountain ranges or plateaus on the east and west coasts of the US with high peaks rising up from the plateaus. These ideopolises attracted research centres and a concentration of knowledge industries (Kerr, 2001).

So, as Bonnacorsi (2017) suggests, there is almost perfect agreement since the early 1990s that universities are crucially important sources of human capital and knowledge spillovers for regional economies (OECD, 1999; OECD, 2007). The debate has been about the processes involved in that contribution, and the kinds of knowledge and interactions involved. Whilst the emphasis in the later parts of the twentieth century was primarily on the commercialisation of academic knowledge through science parks and spin off firms (e.g. Etzkowitz, 2002) in the twenty-first century there has been an increasing concern for the greater interaction between universities as institutional actors in innovation systems. Indeed, there has been a growing interest in wider impacts in fields such as culture, sustainability, urban regeneration, and social development (Goddard et al, 1994; Charles and Benneworth, 2001; OECD, 2007). Policymakers sometimes see universities as underutilised resources in regions and expect more from them, and there is also a potential disenchantment as the reality of experience fails to live up to expectations (Bonnacorsi, 2017).

Universities cannot have impacts solely by their own efforts, but need suitable absorptive capacity in their regions to take up and successfully use the knowledge and ideas generated, although in some places universities have sought to create incubators and science parks to kick start local development where capacity is underdeveloped (Breznitz and Feldman, 2012). The retention of graduates in the region is another key measure of the contribution of a university, but this will depend on the nature of the local labour market and its attractiveness compared with other options open to graduates. So, the experience of engagement and impact of each university is likely to be different dependent on the university, its history and characteristics and the nature of the region and its policy environment. Case studies are thus a useful way of exploring these interactions and hence the primary focus of this book: examining in some detail seven universities in their distinctive regional contexts.

Defining the region

In seeking to understand the interactions and impact of the university on its region, a key question is how we define the region. In some cases, especially where the university is funded by a regional government this seems reasonably self-explanatory, but probably for a majority of universities the question is legitimate, but usually not addressed directly in the literature. Normally the assumption is that universities take as their region the officially defined region in which they are based, but this is not always the case and universities may have a distinct concept of a region, which could be embodied in the mission or even the legislation establishing the university.

Goddard et al (1994) identify four ways universities might consider how to define their region in addition to any externally defined administrative region:

- "the relationship between an institution and its physical surroundings as influenced by historical and institutional context
- the different scales at which attributes or impacts of the university should be measured or assessed
- the different geographic scale or territory over which the university provides different types of 'local' service
- the perceptions held by the institution and its management of the local community which is identified in institutional missions." (Goddard et al, 1994, 11)

Most universities have a strong historical relationship with place, and usually focus on their host city, especially where the university is embedded in its urban environment as opposed to being on an out of town campus. Ancient universities may be inseparable from the cities that have grown up around them, whilst some recent universities have been created in response to demands from their host cities. Other universities have been established as regional multi-campus universities to serve a particular regional geography. In these cases the region is determined by the presence of the campus and legal requirements to serve a specific territory, sometimes written into the statutes of establishment (Charles, 2002).

This contrasts with the definition of a service territory over which a university delivers its services, or which is used for the purpose of measuring impact. Many universities now commission impact studies to demonstrate or justify their local importance, and these will apply some definition of the region, sometimes at multiple levels – city and region for example. Often these instrumental definitions overlap with the idea of the service territory, where for example a university with a medical school will have links with a series of regional hospitals, or an education department will link with a school region. External perceptions may also be important with a local population or local policymakers defining 'their university' and making claims for its support.

In the UK, the question as to the region identified by the university has been asked of university managers in a series of surveys over the last couple of decades (see Charles 2003 and Charles et al, 2014). Whilst the administrative region has been important in times of strong regional policy (in England during the 2000s), more recently the tendency has been for universities to define regions according to their own needs as a group of local authorities which may nest within or cross over regional boundaries. This is particularly important for those universities which are located at the edge of regions, seeking to build links with organisations in the adjacent region.

Another key issue is whether universities have satellite campuses outside of conventional regional boundaries. Again, this is less likely to be the case where universities are governed or regulated by regional authorities, as they will tend to operate within a regional system. But in centralised HE systems universities may seek to establish satellite campuses in capital regions to better attract international students or in under-served regions to respond to policy imperatives.

A final dimension is where universities seek to form regional collaborative groupings, associations or networks. Often these will be formed according to formal regional boundaries – such as in the case of regional university associations in the UK in the 2000s, or the Asociación Catalana de Universidades Públicas (ACUP) in Catalonia. In some cases, university regions have crossed boundaries such as the Øresund University: not a university as such but a transborder association of 14 universities in Copenhagen and Southern Sweden. In these associations, and other less formalised collaborations, universities work together on projects of regional interest, scaling up regional activities, often in partnership with other regional organisations. These networks may occupy variable geographies as described by Harrison et al (2016).

However, whilst universities may seek to define their own regions according to their needs, regional bodies also seek to define the universities eligible for support within their economic development programmes. So, in the current smart specialisation strategies of EU regions, universities will be included in the networks of each region, and this may include those that lie across the borders, especially if they have areas of expertise campus which are relevant to a region's smart specialisation strategy. The key point is that university regional geographies are relational and are redefined according to need.

The European Consortium of Innovative Universities

The choice of universities used as case studies in this book is not random, all are part of a joint research project on the role of universities in regional innovation, and all but one are members of the European Consortium of Innovative Universities (ECIU). The project and its origins are explained below, after an initial description of the ECIU.

The ECIU was established in 1997 by a group of universities with common interests and characteristics. The consortium is a 'selected group of entrepreneurial universities dedicated to the development of an innovative culture in their institutions, and to a catalytic role for innovation in industry and society at large.' (ECIU website).

Table 1.1: Current ECIU Members (2021)

Aalborg University*	Dublin City University
Hamburg University of Technology	Institut National des Sciences Appliquées
Kaunas University of Technology	Linköping University*
Tampere University of Technology	Tecnológico de Monterrey
Universitat Autònoma de Barcelona*	University of Aveiro*
University of Stavanger*	Università di Trento
University of Twente*	

*members of the RUNIN project

Whilst there are individual differences between the universities in the consortium, there are a set of commonalities. As a group they tend to be relatively young universities, in spirit if not actually in age, usually established with some form of local mission to support their host region and also to support entrepreneurship and innovation. They typically have strengths in engineering and social sciences being somewhat more applied in nature than classical universities, but they all seek to be research intensive. All

17

have a commitment to develop unconventional forms of teaching and learning with a specific focus on entrepreneurship, and experiment with managerial organisation and structures. Finally, all are highly international in outlook and keen to contribute to higher education policy at a European scale.

The formation of the ECIU was linked to Burton Clark's book on '*Creating Entrepreneurial Universities*' (Clark, 1998), and several of the founding universities (Twente, Joensuu, Warwick and Strathclyde) were case studies in that book. Whilst Clark talks about the entrepreneurial university and stresses the need for an entrepreneurial culture in universities responding to the challenges of the late twentieth century, the board of the new ECIU preferred the term innovative universities (Kekäle, 2007). Clark's work famously identifies five characteristics of the entrepreneurial university on the basis of his case studies

- The strengthened steering core
- The enhanced developmental periphery
- The discretionary funding base
- The stimulated heartland
- The entrepreneurial belief.

Some of these characteristics seem more obvious than others: the entrepreneurial belief and commitment to developing a culture of engagement seems obvious as well as the creation of a developmental periphery of knowledge exchange units such as research centres and technology transfer offices. This would be expected to lead to increasing diversity of funding as well. However, what was perhaps less obvious was the strengthening of the university's ability to steer the institution to meet a more entrepreneurial mission, and the need for investment into the academic heartland – entrepreneurial success here depends on having distinctive academic expertise which can be commercialised, or applied to the solution of complex social problems.

These characteristics have typically been identified by the ECIU members, particularly the idea of a developmental periphery as a set of boundary-spanning functions linking the university to its local region, and in the entrepreneurial belief and commitment to the stimulation of new enterprise. Each of the universities also tends to explore a diversity of external funding sources, whether to support research or enterprise activities, or even as part of the core teaching mission. Each university interprets the entrepreneurial mission in terms of its own institutional and regional context though. The ECIU provides a means for these universities to explore their mission in conjunction with international partners, exchanging experiences, engaging in collaborative projects and presenting a joint position in European policy debates.

Origins of this book

The origins of this book lie in an initiative of the ECIU to build a better understanding of the way in which their member institutions were engaging in the development of their regions. This stimulated a discussion led by Prof Rune Dahl Fitjar of the University of Stavanger in September 2013 and involving representatives of member universities about how a collective research activity might be developed. This took form in a proposal to the EU Marie Skłodovska-Curie programme for an Innovative Training Network on the Role of Universities in Regional Innovation (RUNIN). After three attempts and a small change in membership the proposal was successful and the project commenced in September 2016, with a set of 14 early stage researchers being appointed to the project in early 2017.

The RUNIN project includes six ECIU member universities: Stavanger, Aalborg, Linköping, Twente, Aveiro and Autonomous University of Barcelona. A seventh project partner, Lincoln, was included with similar objectives and interests to the other ECIU members.

The main aim of the RUNIN project has been to create a body of knowledge on how universities can contribute to innovation and development in the regions in which they are located, identifying policies and practices that can be adopted by universities, firms and regional stakeholders to improve levels of regional innovation. We further specified the main research question through exploring in-depth four main channels of interaction between universities and their regions. Firstly, we explored how universities form regional networks with firms and other actors, and how these connections in turn contribute to stimulating the innovative performance of these firms and, as a consequence, to the development of the regions. Secondly, the relationship between universities and firms is shaped by policies and interventions at the regional level (as well as at higher and lower levels of government). Policy-makers may put pressure on universities to engage with regional industry and other stakeholders alongside incentives for firms to interact with universities. However, universities also contribute to shaping policies through collaboration in regional policy networks and through conducting research with implications for policy. Thirdly, universities and firms are also affected by the economic and social characteristics of the places and territories in which they are located, such as the regional economic structures and the position of the region within wider global production networks. University-regional interaction is an interactive process, and universities' network-building activities can also contribute to upgrading the regional economy to the extent that it manages to play a successful role in innovation and regional development in these wider global networks. Finally, the regional networks may lead to changing practices and new modes of governance, both at the universities and within the networks themselves, in order to coordinate the interaction between universities and firms so that it plays a productive role in stimulating regional innovative development.

The specific projects undertaken within the RUNIN network were developed within these four thematic areas, with typically each partner institution hosting projects covering a couple of themes. There was considerable collaboration across the institutions and themes however and in this book the emphasis is placed on the individual universities and their regions, synthesising across themes in order to develop place-based case studies. Thus the specificity of individual universities and their partnerships can be elaborated but also some of the parallels between cases also explored.

The Universities and the structure of the book

The universities in this study are not 'typical' universities, inasmuch as any set of universities could be truly described as typical. A core theme of the book is that each university has its own distinct character and emerges from a particular history in a particular geographical context. There are commonalities that emerge however from this group of universities having been self-identified as innovative and entrepreneurial universities through their membership of ECIU. None of them are old, traditional, universities based in the centre of major cities. They are all relatively young institutions, mostly based in smaller towns and cities. They also tend to do things in a slightly different way than older universities: they seek to be innovative in their actions as well as in the support they offer to industry and their regions. Mostly they are not among the largest institutions in their countries (with one exception), and in most cases were specifically

21

established to address unmet needs in their regions. They all have ambitions to be research intensive, with varying degrees of success so far, but all can demonstrate excellence in at least some fields, and all have legitimate claims to excellence in their engagement with business.

The cases presented in this book are collectively focused on the role universities can play in their respective regions. Individually, they highlight the contextual nuances of challenges faced and identify prospects for improving the instrumental role of universities.

In chapter 2, 'Regional Mission Impossible? Confronting Complexities of University-Regional Engagement in Twente, the Netherlands', Lisa Nieth, Sofya Kopelyan, & Paul Benneworth present the case of Twente University (UT), an institution located in Enschede and with a key role in the growth of innovation and entrepreneurship in Twente region in the Netherlands. In a regional landscape characterised by a strong knowledge infrastructure and high connection among regional actors, UT must address the tensions emerging from the interaction and collaboration of diverse stakeholders. The complexity of regional governance and intermediary structures together with a shortage of institutional entrepreneurs and uncoordinated individual engagement activities within the university, are the main tensions explained by the authors. Such tensions might require interventions aimed at making provision for network and community building.

Eloïse Germain-Alamartine's chapter 3, 'Transitioning from an Economic to a Broader Social Impact - A Case Study of a Swedish University,' characterises the University of Linköping (LiU) in line with the various models of university interaction with business and regions presented by Uyarra (2010). Eloïse particularly emphasises the median placement of LiU between the systemic and engaged university variants and, by exploring the challenges faced with transitioning from one model to another, calls for a strategic adaptation of the university's approach to supporting regional needs in order to make a wider impact.

In chapter 4, 'Balancing Regional Engagement and Internationalisation - The Case of the Autonomous University of Barcelona', Sergio Manrique and Huong T. Nguyen draw our attention to the tensions and opportunities derived from the coexistence of regional engagement and internationalisation within university goals. Using the case of the Autonomous University of Barcelona (UAB) in Spain, the authors exemplify how universities can engage through passive and active roles in the growth of a highly dynamic, economically strong and innovative region. This chapter portrays the development of strategic research communities within UAB as well as the development of projects with social, innovative and sustainable goals, as key initiatives that can serve both the regional and international aims of higher education institutions.

In chapter 5, 'Co-creation of localised capabilities between universities and nascent industries - The case of Aalborg University and the North Denmark region', David Fernández Guerrero and Gerwin Evers take us to the north of Denmark to develop the case of Aalborg University (AAU) and its interaction with the ICT and biomedical industries, two emerging science-based sectors in North Denmark region. Focusing on the development of localised capabilities through university-interaction, the authors explain the differentiated outcomes in terms of competitiveness for the two studied industries after collaborating with AAU, discussing how the feedback loops between university and industry have stimulated industrial development differently.

Chapter 6, 'From Transplantation to Diversification? The University of Stavanger's Role in the Economic Development of Rogaland' by Utku Ali Rıza Alpaydın, Kwadwo Atta-Owusu and Saeed Moghadam-Saman takes us to Norway's oil-rich Rogaland region, where they assess and acknowledge the complementary role of the university and the oil industry in innovation. Further, they present convincing arguments for dialogue, strategies and policies on both regional and national levels in order to manage and diversify the innovation capacity and vision of Rogaland.

In an 'Evolutionary Analysis of a University's Engagement in a Less-Developed Region', Liliana Fonseca, Ridvan Cinar, Artur da Rosa Pires and Carlos Rodrigues employ the case of the University of Aveiro (UA) to examine universities' efforts in stimulating endogenous innovation. UA has made significant contributions towards innovation dynamics in the Aveiro region by attending to R&D needs and facilitating network collaboration between regional actors. The contributions of UA are however not without challenges. Subsequently, the authors highlight and reflect on the existence of certain internal organisational challenges which hinder fruitful collaborations.

Finally, in chapter 8, we move to the United Kingdom where Rhoda Ahoba-Sam, Maria Salomaa and David Charles reflect on the obstructions to regional engagement in 'On overcoming the barriers to regional engagement: Reflections from the University of Lincoln'. By evaluating the university's role in fostering regional economic development, they present a typology of challenges generated from both internal and external sources, and call for a resolute participation of [all] regional stakeholders in addressing, mitigating and overcoming the hurdles to regional development.

Some brief conclusions round off the book. This set of chapters based on cases from the RUNIN project and ECIU universities serve as evidence of the role of universities in innovation and regional development in Europe. We expect that this book will stimulate further interest with academics, practitioners and policy makers, and facilitate potential improvements and developments for growth and innovation in Twente (NL), Östergötland (SE), Barcelona (ES), North Denmark (DK), Rogaland (NO), Centro Region (PT), Lincolnshire (UK) and beyond. With these seven provoking and well-founded case studies of European entrepreneurial universities in regional innovation, we invite you to start the journey.

References

Alves, J., Carvalho, L., Carvalho, R., Correia, F. Cunha, J., Farinha, L., Fernandes, J., Ferreira, M., Lucas, E., Mourato, J., Nicolau, A., Nunes, S., Nunes, S., Oliveira, P., Pereira, C., Pinto S. and Silva, J. (2015). The impact of polytechnic institutes on the local economy, **Tertiary Education and Management**, 21, 81-98.

Arbo, P. and Benneworth, P. (2007). **Understanding the Regional Contribution of Higher Education Institutions: A Literature Review. OECD Education Working Paper**, Paris: OECD.

Beise, M. and Stahl, H. (1998). **Public Research and Industrial Innovations in Germany, ZEW Discussion Paper No. 98-37**, Mannheim: Zentrum für Europäische Wirtschaftsforschung.

Bonaccorsi, A. (2017). Addressing the disenchantment: universities and regional development in peripheral regions, **Journal of Economic Policy Reform**, 20, 293-320.

Breznitz, S.M. and Feldman, M.P. (2012). The engaged university, **Journal of Technology Transfer**, 37, 139-157.

Brink, C. (2018). **The Soul of a University**, Bristol: Bristol University Press.

Calhoun, C. (2006). The University and the Public Good, **Thesis Eleven**, 84, 7-43.

Charles, D. (2003). 'Universities and territorial development: reshaping the regional role of English universities', **Local Economy**, 18, 7-20.

Charles, D. (2016). The rural university campus and rural innovation – conflicts around specialisation and expectations, **Science and Public Policy**, 43, 763-773.

Charles, D. and Benneworth, P. (2001). **The Regional Mission: The Regional Contribution of Higher Education: National Report**, London: Universities UK.

Charles, D., Kitagawa, F. and Uyarra, E. (2014). University engagement: from regionalisation to localisation, **Cambridge Journal of Regions, Economy and Society**, 7, 327-348.

Clark, B. (1998). **Creating Entrepreneurial Universities: Organizational Pathways of Transformation**. Oxford: Pergamon/IAU Press.

Drucker, J. and Goldstein, H. (2007). Assessing the Regional Economic Development Impacts of Universities: A Review of Current Approaches, **International Regional Science Review**, 30, 20-46.

Etzkowitz, H. (2002). **MIT and the Rise of Entrepreneurial Science**, London: Routledge.

European Commission DG for Education and Culture (2013). **Summary and Key Outcomes - Peer Learning Activity "The Regional Knowledge Triangle: Linking Higher Education, Research and Innovation in Support of Regional Development"** Krakow, 16-17 September 2013. Available from http://ec.europa.eu/assets/eac/education/experts-groups/2014-2015/higher/report-regional-knowledge-triangle_en.pdf. (accessed 20/1/2020).

Fitjar, R. D., Benneworth, P. and Asheim, B. T. (2019). Towards regional responsible research and innovation? Integrating RRI and RIS3 in European innovation policy, **Science and Public Policy**, 46, 772–783.

Florax, R.J.G.M. (1992). **The University: A Regional Booster?** Aldershot: Avebury.

Geuna, A. and Rossi, F. (2011). Changes to university IPR regulations in Europe and the impact on academic patenting, **Research Policy**, 40, 1068-1076.

Goddard, J., Charles, D., Pike, A., Potts, G. and Bradley, D. (1994). **Universities and Communities**, London: Committee of Vice-Chancellors and Principals.

Goddard, J. and Vallance, P. (2013): **The University and the City**, London: Routledge.

Goddard, J. and Kempton, L. (2011). **Connecting Universities to Regional Growth: a Practical Guide**, Brussels: European Commission, Regional Policy.

Goddard, J., Kempton, L., Elena-Pérez, S., Hegyi, F.B. and Edwards, J. (2013). **Universities and Smart Specialisation, S3 Policy Brief Series No 03/2013**, Sevilla: European Commission Joint Research Centre.

Harrison, J., Smith, D.P. and Kinton, C. (2016). New institutional geographies of higher education: The rise of transregional university alliances, **Environment and Planning A**, 48, 910-936.

Jacobs, J. (1969). **The Economy of Cities**. London: Jonathan Cape.

Kekäle, J. (2007). Developing an entrepreneurial and innovative university – the case of the University of Joensuu, in L.W. Cooke (ed) **Frontiers in Higher Education**, New York: Nova Science Publishers.

Kellogg Commission (2000). **Renewing the Covenant: Learning, Discovery, and Engagement in a New Age and Different World, 6th report on the Kellogg Commission on the Future of State and Land-Grant Universities**, Washington DC: National Association of State Universities and Land-Grant Colleges.

Kerr, C. (2001). **The Uses of the University** (fifth edition) Cambridge MA: Harvard University Press.

McDowell, G. R. (2003). Engaged Universities: Lessons from the Land-Grant Universities and Extension, **The Annals of the American Academy of Political and Social Science**, 585, 31-50.

McNicoll, I.H., McCluskey, K. and Kelly, U. (1997). **The Impact of Universities and Colleges on the UK Economy**, London: Committee of Vice-Chancellors and Principals.

Mowery, D. C. and Sampat, B. N. (2004). The Bayh-Dole Act of 1980 and University–Industry Technology Transfer: A Model for Other OECD Governments? **The Journal of Technology Transfer** 30, 115-127.

OECD (1982). **The University and the Community: The Problem of Changing Relationships**, Paris: OECD.

OECD (1999). **The Response of Higher Education Institutions to Regional Needs**. Paris: Centre for Educational Research and Innovation, Programme on Institutional Management in Higher Education.

OECD (2007). **Higher Education and Regions: Globally Competitive, Locally Engaged**. Paris: OECD.

Petersson, I. (2018). The Nomos of the University: Introducing the Professor's Privilege in 1940s Sweden, **Minerva**, 56, 381-403.

Rappert, B. and Webster, A. (1997). Regimes of ordering: the commercialization of intellectual property in industrial-academic collaborations, **Technology Analysis and Strategic Management**, 9, 115-130.

Rubiralta, M. and Delgado L. (2010). **Developing International Campuses of Excellence in Spain**, CELE Exchange, Centre for Effective Learning Environments, 2010/04, Paris: OECD Publishing.

Sanderson, M. (1972). **The Universities and British Industry 1850-1970**, London: Routledge and Kegan Paul.

Uyarra, E. (2010). Conceptualizing the Regional Roles of Universities, Implications and Contradictions, **European Planning Studies**, 18, 1227-1246.

Whyte, W. (2015). **Redbrick: A Social and Architectural History of Britain's Civic Universities**, Oxford: Oxford University Press.

Chapter 2

Regional Mission Impossible?

Confronting Complexities of University-Regional Engagement in Twente, the Netherlands

Lisa Nieth, Sofya Kopelyan, & Paul Benneworth.

Due to the increasingly knowledge-based nature of economic development, and with universities representing sources of knowledge capital, regional partners have taken a growing interest in understanding how universities contribute to their regions. At the same time, regional policy makers have an interest in harnessing universities to existing sources of knowledge-based development, to strengthen the overall innovation ecosystem, to support existing clusters, and to stimulate better interaction between actors. However, there has been a criticism of many analyses for assuming this interaction is relatively straightforward to deliver, overlooking the various kinds of ways in which there may be barriers to regional engagement. This chapter is concerned with understanding the ways that these tensions and pressures played out in a single region with a long history of attempting collaboration, namely the region of Twente in the eastern Netherlands.

What makes the region of Twente interesting in the context of this volume is the long history of the university in attempting to stimulate regional development (Garlick et al. 2006). These efforts have apparently brought rewards, with Twente being nominated in 2017 as one of the Netherlands' three most innovative regions (Avrotos 2017). Indeed, it was Burton Clark in 1998 who identified the University of Twente (UT) as one of a handful of universities that had inspired his archetypal entrepreneurial university heuristic in his volume *Creating Entrepreneurial Universities* (Clark 1998). Nevertheless, a study in 2005 identified there were tensions within Twente in terms of university-regional co-operation (Garlick et al. 2006), and these tensions have persisted to this day. This persistence underlines a more general point that, despite the sincerity of all actors involved in seeking to harness the university to underpin and sustain a region's economic performance, particular tensions will substantively undermine these efforts. We therefore contend that policymakers should temper their enthusiasm for the potential of universities to contribute to regional development with the reality that unlocking that potential is not a trivial task.

This chapter considers how the University of Twente has played this engaged university role and sought out close co-operation with stakeholders from the education, government, business, and research sectors in order to better fulfil this role. We provide some background to the emergence of the University of Twente and the evolution of its regional role[1]. We map the key regional stakeholders and identify four forms of tension that exist between the university and regional partners. We then reflect on those

---

1 The chapter is based on an exploratory case study that took place in spring 2017; data were collected in April-June 2017 from primary and secondary sources, including a review of policy and academic literature as well as semi-structured interviews, and academic publications. In total 12 interviews were undertaken from respondents inside (6) and outside of (6) the UT.

findings, highlighting the complexity of institutional arrangements and the difficulties of sustaining knowledge exchange as two overarching causes of those factors. We conclude by arguing that what is necessary is developing new modes of communication between stakeholders. Thus, meaningful signals need to be prioritised over individual needs and expectations, enabling better coordination between regional partners towards the development of collective knowledge exchange assets.

The Region of Twente and the University of Twente

General description and history

Twente is the most urbanised region of the Dutch province of Overijssel located in the East of the Netherlands. It comprises fourteen municipalities with 626,500 inhabitants who are primarily resident in the three cities of Enschede, Hengelo, and Almelo (European Commission 2017). The region shares a border with Germany and is active in the EUREGIO, European Grouping of Territorial Cooperation. The region was originally a poor agricultural region because of its infertile sandy sediments but underwent a boom in textiles in the mid-19th century, driving expansion in related industries including machinery, metal processing, and construction. This 'Golden Age' boom period lasted until the mid-20th century, when a failure to adapt to global market conditions led to a rapid decline in the textiles industry, with regional textiles employment falling from 44,000 (1955) to 8,200 (1980) (Benneworth et al. 2005, p. 32; Garlick et al. 2006).

The Technical University of Twente was created in 1961 as a campus university, located between the region's two largest cities, Enschede and Hengelo (Timmerman and Hospers 2016). As a technical university, with the mission to revitalise the textiles industry in Twente and provide highly skilled technical employees for post-war reconstruction efforts, it initially focused on degrees in mathematics, physics, and engineering. The subject mix expanded over time, and now includes informatics, social and behavioural sciences, and geomatics; today the UT employs 3,000 staff members and has 10,000 students in five faculties.

With the decline and disappearance of textiles from the 1970s, the university faced an existential challenge: as its reason for existence disappeared, it addressed this by seeking to create new businesses to replace those initially lost. This took on a more institutional dimension in the early 1980s when the university became partner in a new Business Technology Centre (BTC), offering graduate support services as well as creating a scheme to support graduate entrepreneurs to create new businesses, the TOP programme, which still exists today. The BTC was situated adjacent to the campus as a partnership between the regional development agency, the UT, and the city's then polytechnic[2]. In 1987, the municipality, university and polytechnic decided to develop land adjacent to the BTC as a science park, and following a review in 2001, the science park and university campus were rebranded as a single site, Kennispark (Knowledge Park). The university also established the Twente Technology Circle in 1990 to help its spin-offs and other small firms sell into the university, and it quickly evolved into a peer support and mentoring network that at present has 150 members (Benneworth et al. 2006). The university formalised its cooperative arrangements with regional stakeholders in 2005, and today, what is called Novel-T is a

---

[2] Alongside the University of Twente, there is a polytechnic offering professional degrees (with 26000 students and 2600 staff members); an arts institute offering musical and graphic design professional degrees (more than 3000 students in Arnhem, Enschede, and Zwolle, and a total of 900 employees, including around 600 lecturers); and two further education colleges, one with a broad subject offer (ROC Twente) and one specific for the agrotech sector (AOC Twente).

foundation drawing on secondees from university, municipality, polytechnic, and province. Novel-T attempts to collectively steer regional high-technology entrepreneurship and technology transfer activities.

A smart campus for a smart region

The UT was originally created as an out-of-town campus university intending to isolate students from the workers' mentality believed to be prevalent in Hengelo and Enschede (Sorgdrager 1981), and this location continues to influence its regional interaction (Benneworth 2014). The region has long been a peripheral region – its remoteness was only really addressed in the late 19th century when the government extended the railways to Enschede as part of nation-building, and because of this peripherality, Twente developed strong functional and cultural linkages with the neighbouring German region of Westmünsterland. With the development of the motorway network in the late 20th century, the region found itself on the axis between Amsterdam and Berlin; and both region and university have sought to improve their connectivity to other regions to stimulate positive growth dynamics.

With the campus, the effect of form on function has been a central planning concern; the initial masterplan took a country estate (Drienerlo) and developed a series of large stand-alone buildings to host intimate communities of staff and students focused on their disciplinary specialisations (Timmerman and Hospers 2016). But more recently, and with the adoption of the Kennispark concept, there has been an emphasis on rebuilding the campus to stimulate interaction rather than isolation – interaction with the wider region (eliminating a viaduct between campus and science park which presented a physical barrier (Benneworth et al. 2011)) and within the campus (concentrating academic activities in a central education and research zone with a to-be built high-rise tower). At

33

the time of writing, the UT plans to bring the only off-campus faculty (which was previously a standalone institution) onto the campus to further stimulate this concentration effect[3].

The UT has also attempted to integrate itself into the region in various different ways, in particular welcoming regional partners to bring their activities onto the campus, leveraging its picturesque location adjacent to water reserves, parks, and recreational zones. The campus hosts career fairs and open days, the Green Vibrations festival, the finish of the Netherland's biggest student sporting event the Batavia Race, and is available for parking when the region's football team, FC Twente, plays home matches at the stadium located in Kennispark (Hengstenberg et al. 2017). From early 2016, the university sought to make this regional role more explicit by branding itself as a 'Living Smart Campus' (University of Twente 2016), a controlled experimental environment where societal challenges are addressed by improving resident welfare. The university now plans to create a regional living laboratory for telemedicine in its redevelopment of the Technical Medicine faculty building: it has created spaces for policymakers to interact with researchers and societal partners (DesignLab), and makes spaces available for starting social entrepreneurs and innovators[4].

The Twente economy and culture

Despite ambitions to improve its overall situation, the Twente Region remains slightly poorer than the average Dutch region; as a peripheral region, it has tended to experience recessions more quickly and recover more slowly. Nevertheless, it was able to bounce back from the global crisis more strongly than the Netherlands as a whole. Although the region has done well to

---

[3] For more information on the UT Campus and its infrastructural development, see (University of Twente, 2017a); University of Twente (2017b)

[4] For an interactive map of the UT campus and its surroundings, see: https://maps.utwente.nl/

create high-technology jobs, the numbers of middle- and low-skilled positions have shrunk, with unemployment rising and labour market participation falling in these sectors (Scholten and Oxener 2016). SMEs remain important for regional employment: 78.3% of employment is in micro, small and medium sized businesses as well as the self-employed, with almost all recent employment growth coming in these four groups (Kennispunt Twente 2016). Around 10% of jobs in Twente are in the "High-Tech Systems and Materials" (HTSM) sector, a sector with a high knowledge intensity, export orientation, and international competitiveness. Additionally, the HTSM sector supports other important sectors including healthcare, production technology, and construction[5].

Twente is politically and socially distinct, in terms of identity and behavioural norms, something that is sometimes linked to the historical tradition of neighbourliness (*noaberschap*) where neighbours would help each other out to share risks around flooding, crop failure, and sickness. The region today is characterised by a very high level of social activity, with large numbers of people engaged in clubs and societies, and a tendency in public life to form new networks, platforms, commissions, and associations to deal with issues that arise; although these associations can be useful, they have a complicating effect on regional governance. At the same time, there was an absence previously of a culture of regional entrepreneurship and growth, with regional employment being dominated historically by large routine manufacturing and engineering operators, and as these have declined, more highly-skilled residents have left the region (Benneworth and Ratinho 2014; Garlick et al. 2006). This common culture is not the same as regional cohesion, and there

---

[5] For more details in English, see www.government.nl/topics/enterprise-and-innovation/contents/encouraging-innovation.

are many regional divisions, including strong village identities, rivalry between Enschede and other cities, a split between east and west, and also between urban and rural interests. These splits are all salient for any knowledge-based development strategy that envisages investing shared resources into the UT's Enschede campus.

Stakeholders in the Twente innovation ecosystem

Innovation inside-out: The place of the university in the regional ecosystem

The UT plays a number of distinct roles in terms of the Twente innovation stakeholder network. Firstly, and what is often most prominent in the literature, is the contribution that is made through the creation of spinoff companies, with the UT having produced over 1,000 companies operational to date, with an average of 9 employees (Meerman 2017). Along with its patenting activity, this spinoff performance saw it ranked as the most entrepreneurial university in the ScienceWorks Dutch rankings in 2013 and 2015. The UT has fair co-publication and co-financing relations inside the Twente innovation network, as one in eleven articles is produced with nearby authors, and around 10% of research funding comes from within the Province. Alongside these valorisation efforts, and arguably in reality more important to the regional knowledge economy, is the role that the university plays in producing highly skilled individuals to support the growth of the region's high technology economy. The region has almost zero unemployment amongst highly educated individuals, particularly in technical occupations, and much of the region's technical workforce was educated at the university.

It is impossible to talk, however, of the role of the university in the regional knowledge economy without pointing to a tension between this regional role and the university's other, broader ambitions. Saxion, the university of applied sciences, is active in the region, and has a specific mission to support regional knowledge-intensive companies, as well as to build networks and clusters to support knowledge exchange between companies. In contrast, the UT has clearly articulated missions that extend beyond the region. From the perspective of the National Ministries, the UT is regarded as a technical university and one of the key suppliers of highly skilled workers for the Dutch labour market. The UT has to compete for employees, students, and research resources even beyond the Netherlands, and therefore has sought to profile itself in recent years as Europe's leading technical university. Alongside that, the university also is mindful of its international position, developing strategic relationships with universities in Indonesia and Brazil, as well as seeking to improve its positioning in key leading international university rankings. It is thus perhaps unsurprising that in recent years there has been a much greater 'brain drain' of UT graduates from the Twente region, with only 20% of graduates remaining, in comparison to Saxion, where 60% remain (by start-up location (Bazen 2016)). The overall benefit of the University of Twente for the Twente regional economy is therefore on average lower than that provided by the Universities of Amsterdam or the Technical University of Eindhoven in their respective regions, primarily because of this weaker regional absorption capacity (Stam et al. 2016).

A final area of contribution, and one which is almost entirely absent from the discourse that is promoted by regional partners regarding the university's regional role, is the contribution made by its social sciences and humanities research to wider regional society. The UT has many activities that help support this,

37

although they do not receive the high-profile coverage that characterises the reporting on nanotechnology companies and investments. The university has a science shop which links societal partners to students looking for projects, and although these are often technical in their nature, they are also an important way for regional voluntary and societal organisations to get into contact with the university and access university knowledge in the absence of their own resources to fund innovation projects. The UT has latterly tried to develop better support for these activities in part though the Living Smart Campus project; one of these projects was an initiative to promote entrepreneurship amongst refugees in the Twente region, providing them with coaching as well as helping them build connections to other social entrepreneurship support organisations in the region. The benefits from these softer knowledge activities (particularly via students) might actually be more evenly distributed in Twente than the benefits of technology innovation.

Innovation outside-in: Actors and governance in the regional ecosystem

Although the University, and to a lesser extent Saxion, are the dominant partners in the regional innovation ecosystem (certainly for example in comparison to universities in Amsterdam or Eindhoven in their regions), there are a few other important actors within the region who play their own roles in shaping the innovation ecosystem. The region hosts a large number of innovation projects, and ranks second only to the Eindhoven region in terms of number of innovation projects in comparison to the number of companies residing in the region (Stam et al. 2016). In the absence of lead companies such as Philips in Eindhoven, the UT and Saxion (despite the latter being primarily interested in more applied research) have become central to these innovation partnership networks, (Saxion 2015; Stam et al. 2016).

The most important regional stakeholders include Kennispark and Novel-T, because of their involvement in the development of the regional innovation infrastructure. In addition to a number of companies that have become important for regional innovation, there are some public sector organisations, for instance the regional Water Boards or the local waste treatment company Twence, that are active in regional innovation. There are three regional hospitals, two generalist and a rehabilitation clinic, that are actively involved with the university but also have their own research, development, and innovation strategies and projects. The aerospace company Thales remains an important investor in R&D, and has been successful in attracting regional subsidies to upgrade its location as a high-technology campus. Some companies have become important investors in innovative enterprises, including Reggeborgh Invest and TKH Group, and some have substantial innovation investments in their own right, such as the brewers Grolsch, sensor manufacturer Sensata Technologies, the Apollo tyre company, and Ten Cate textiles. Last but not least, various innovative small businesses in the region, many of them spin-off companies, have been able to establish themselves as viable middle-sized enterprises with ongoing research programmes, often in collaboration with the UT, including Micronit, Demcon, and Xsens.

Policymakers have been influential in recent years in attempting to improve the functioning of the regional innovation environment. Spurred on by the creation of an innovation platform for the Netherlands in 2004, Twente launched its own innovation platform in 2005, which in turn created a monitoring tool for the region's innovation performance, the Twente Index. The innovation platform was followed by the creation of an investment programme, the Agenda for Twente (Regio Twente n.d), developed by the 14 municipalities to help the Twente region create a high-technology economy comparable with the rest of the

39

Netherlands, by investing selectively in a limited number of transformational projects, and leveraging in matching funding from the Province, Ministry of Economic Affairs, and European Structural Funds. The managing authority for this programme was the Region of Twente which at that time enjoyed special powers as one of six regional authorities in the Netherlands (these powers being rescinded for four of those regions in 2014). As a final complicating factor, a regional board was created in 2014 as a non-statutory body of regional stakeholders intending to formulate a regional development strategy to respond to a strategic project failure (the Twente Airport plan). They also drew up their own action plan, largely in line with the Agenda for Twente, entitled Twente Works!, intending to promote regional economic development and internationalisation with a focus on the HTSM sector, entrepreneurship, and the labour market (Twente Board 2015).

Regional innovation in Twente: Stakeholder tensions

The previous section has made it clear that the story of the development of the regional innovation ecosystem in Twente is a positive story. In the course of three decades, the university has been at the heart of a stakeholder partnership that has reversed the pattern of disinvestment and downgrading, instead attracting outside public and private investment in high technology, and supporting local innovative entrepreneurship. In the course of these efforts some tensions have arisen, and we contend that how these tensions have unfolded and been overcome provides a useful answer to our overall research question of how has this stakeholder partnership been held together. In the next two sections, we therefore quite explicitly dwell on these problems and tensions, and this may give the impression of a negative story. Instead, we argue that this is the strength of the Twente outcome, that despite the tensions, this partnership has developed and attracted investment, and this provides useful insights for research, policy, and practice. It is therefore necessary in these stylised portrayals of tensions not to regard them as criticism of the participants, rather as a way of highlighting the inevitable frictions that arise when trying to bring together these different knowledge 'worlds' (research, business, policy, practice, society).

Misalignment of stakeholder interests and expectations

The first tension present was a misalignment in the regional innovation partnerships around the interests and expectations of partners, which in turn reflects the sheer institutional complexity of the Twente environment as well as tensions within various missions within the university. In terms of the overall institutional complexity, there were many strategic bodies, but their positions were never certain, and therefore local partners were reluctant to align themselves with these regional bodies in case these were disbanded leaving local partners' strategies out of synch with their real regional needs. In these circumstances, what should have been strategic leadership did not take place. Many strategic documents were produced, but they did not provide new ideas for long term change to which many actors were firmly committed, rather they reflected the view of a secretariat assembled to produce a report. This was particularly problematic for the Twente region because it was impossible to have strategic investments in all areas, and without a strong strategic planning body it was impossible to produce consensus on what was vital for the region and invest in a limited number of places and sectors.

This lack of real strategic decision-making was also problematic for the university, because at the same time as trying to resolve its regional, national, European, and international profile, it lacked a clear message from the region regarding the regional priorities for university contributions. The UT's strategic vision towards 2020 had argued that its priority was to become more internationally based whilst focused on regional collaboration, without clearly explaining how any tensions would be addressed. A number of interviewees from outside the university noted that although the university claimed both of these missions were important, it appeared that the UT placed the international dimension ahead of the local dimension, for example with the increasing ubiquity of English as the university's *lingua franca* whilst regional partners' knowledge needs remained resolutely in the Dutch language. All partners recognised the struggles UT faced, as the smallest of the technical universities, to establish itself internationally, and many noted at the same time the difficulties that this created in practice for developing a specifically regional profile. There was a feeling that the UT was set up to deal with large companies with well-articulated research and technology development needs and was rather less accessible for small firms seeking innovation support. Perhaps surprisingly, some interviewees reported a Kennispark shadow effect, in which having an address off the Kennispark signalled to potential partners that the firm was not innovative. Finally, given all these tensions and a lack of clear regional signals regarding what the university should prioritise, there was a sense that when university academics were facing a choice between whether to engage locally or do excellent research internationally, the internal logics would naturally favour excellence over engagement.

Absence of clear intermediaries

A second tension emerged regarding the apparent invisibility of the intermediaries provided by the university to assist regional partners to contact with university researchers. One interviewee often heard people in Twente demanding, "What is the phone number of the university?" highlighting how difficult it was for outsiders to get into contact with the UT. There was a sense that each side had a lacuna as far as the other went, with firms being unable to find the university, and university staff being unaware of the region in terms of developing research projects and teaching curricula. This was at odds with the reality of a wide range of intermediaries developed by the university to build up links with the external environment, including Novel-T, the Strategic Business Development office, the Science Park, DesignLab, along with business development and valorisation managers in research institutes. A key issue was that they do not add up to a whole and have different sets of users: the Science Shop worked primarily with civil society organisations whilst the Strategic Business Development teams were primarily interested in working with large companies who were able to contract with the university.

Each engagement activity had its own natural community, but for any regional partner who approached the university via the wrong community it was impossible for one organisation to refer on to another because of the totally different orientation of these communities. Indeed, this was quite a source of frustration for regional actors, and a number of interviewees argued that the university should create a single point of contact for external partners (without perhaps knowing that the Liaison Group closed by the university in 2001 had been closed precisely because it was unable to provide the necessary coordination effort). This is illustrated by the case of Novel-T which, as it had grown, had attracted a number of different activities that introduced confusion into its potential user base and a divergence of its apparent primary purpose. As one external interviewee noted, "People in Twente don't understand what the university is doing. They are too far away from it. It is difficult for SMEs to go to the UT and ask a question or ask for research".

A final issue here was that other regional partners did not always themselves have contact points which were readily approachable, or with whom it was possible to develop communication and shared agendas. Although each municipality had officers responsible for liaising with regional innovation partnerships, interviewees noted that these officers did not have regional remits, rather their role was to ensure that their municipality received an acceptably high share of the investment benefits, thereby directly undermining the university's needs for a clear regional message about where it might focus its own investments.

Absence of continuity

A third area of tension was the persistent dependence of the regional partnerships on particular highly skilled individuals who understood how to function effectively within the confusing regional environment and nevertheless achieve agreement on concrete investment decisions. The level of institutional denseness in Twente appeared to make successful interaction dependent on regional networks. Those individuals able to navigate between these institutions had suitable personal networks, which they would take with them when they left. In one example, a faculty business liaison individual took a new position outside the university, and this effectively caused much engagement activity in the faculty to grind to a halt. Arguably more pernicious from the perspective of the regional partners was that these temporary hiatuses in activity were interpreted as being acts of bad faith from the university, indicating however unfairly that the university was unwilling to make good on its commitments to regional partners.

This created a sense of nervousness and even distrust amongst regional partners considering whether to try and build up relationships with university partners. As one external stakeholder related: "A problem of the UT [is that] a lot of people are in place for some years, then they take another step, and they are gone. And then you see mostly all the things you have built up gone … [This is] not a knowledge system that keeps the knowledge". The converse of this situation was that funding from the region did not provide the university with incentives to invest long-term in those individuals undertaking engagement. The short-term and applied nature of many of the demands encouraged the university to use funding to hire new staff on short-term contracts to carry out the work. This development had the result that if the project funding was not renewed or alternative consultancy-type funding could not be found, the individuals would move on, taking their knowledge of how to engage and of the specific regional partners needs with them.

Knowledge asymmetry

A final tension that emerged within the system was the knowledge asymmetry that arose from the fact that there were very many different knowledge communities each engaged in their own endeavours, but there was very little common and shared awareness of activities in other knowledge communities. This created frustration amongst university actors in that it was sometimes very difficult for them to move beyond their own knowledge communities, and for outside partners a disbelief at the lack of coordination to build critical mass amongst actors. There was a realisation that this problem was intractable, and that there was no simple solution to build a directory of knowledge services and communities because they were continually in flux and in varying degrees of latency or agency, as university staff carried out their various teaching and research activities. This was also recognised as a problem by regional partners, who reported regarding the university as being "unknowable" in the sense of being impossible to get data that would give insight into the scale of activity. With the UT generating little regionally-specific data for its own institutional research processes, it was very difficult for these partners to make out how the university was performing in terms of its regional mission, and therefore to understand how sincere the university was in terms of its own regional agenda.

There was an issue for the university in that the success of the nanotechnology valorisation activities, culminating in the creation of a large shared-space between companies and universities on the campus, the Nanolab, had created a false understanding of the ease by which valorisation could be delivered. This model of a large central shared space where companies and universities could work together and spontaneously interact, make new contacts, share informal knowledge, and where students could interact with technicians, did not apply to other sectors. One interviewee reported that ICT companies had no need for university space and were dispersed around the region, and this hindered building a shared sense of knowledge within the community spanning between the university, firms, and policymakers. There were also not always companies to partner with particular fields of knowledge within the university, whilst those fields were important for the UT's standing nationally and internationally. Another issue raised by one interviewee was the lack of coverage of the region in the university's newspaper, which made it harder for academics who were not regionally oriented to make sense of the regional environment and therefore to get at how to begin building up their regional networks.

Regional mission impossible? Discussion of stakeholder tensions

These four varieties of problems can be considered as a manifestation of the kinds of tensions that may arise when a university attempts to engage with regional partners. At the same time, they also point to the ways in which four regional subsystems may interact with each other, and to which interventions may be directed. The first subsystem is regional governance, both in the region but also within the university, and the extent to which the two elements are able to connect in more than a superficial way, influencing each other's activities rather than merely remaining restricted to the strategic level. The second subsystem is that of intermediary organisations, which are intended to create simplicity, but which through their interference and interaction can also affect the overall functioning of the system. The third subsystem is the cadre of regional institutional entrepreneurs, who are able to negotiate these complexities, link operational actors across organisations, and deliver real regional projects. The final subsystem are the kinds of hybrid communities within which knowledge exchange takes place, and they need to be effectively aligned and coordinated if this is to produce valuable knowledge spill-overs at the regional level.

The complexity of strategic governance

This case study illustrates very neatly the question of regional governance. Problems emerged when partners were successful in aligning their strategic goals and producing documents that purported to be regional strategy, but whose influence did not extend to regional partners' operational level. This is manifested most clearly with the creation of diverse strategic boards which sought to bring together the key regional actors, but in the end were criticised for their lack of strategic planning and novel thinking as well as short-termism. This was at the same time reinforced by the density of these associative bodies, meaning that when new bodies formed they were still operating in the shadow of prior associations set up for comparable, complementary or competing purposes. There was also a tendency to create new bodies to deal with emergent challenges, so in parallel with the Twente Board, the Province and City created a so-called Top Team to explore creating a knowledge cluster in advanced materials and systems at a former airbase (whose re-development

47

was the whole rationale for the Twente Board's existence). This undermined the strategic commitment of regional partners to singular strategies, and led to a fracturing of interests in a region with a number of existing deep fissures and tensions. Partners found it easy to make grand commitments, with all Twente Board stakeholders agreeing to the vision of Twente becoming an "enterprising high-tech region" (Ondernemende high-tech region), but found it much harder to define that in ways that allowed concrete actions to be chosen (and others to be rejected).

The other element of governance was the decentred nature of UT governance which sought to pursue regional engagement in parallel with national profiling, and European and internal excellence. Sometimes these tensions could easily be reconciled – the UT was able to attract two German research centres (a Max Planck Institute and a Fraunhofer Centre in advanced materials) which were expected both to generate substantial international profile for the university as well as have substantial benefits for Twente's existing advanced materials cluster. But in almost all other areas, these tensions were not easily resolved and made it difficult for the UT to be able to strategically steer its academics towards regional engagement. There were many academics who were involved in a variety of forms of regional engagement, but this often appeared to happen irrespective of university structures. This also made it hard for the university at the strategic level to be able to deliver promises or guarantees about what particular knowledge activities would contribute to the region, which further added to the strategic superficiality of the regional governance processes.

The complexity of intermediary structures

The second element of complexity arose in the sub-system of regional intermediary structures, and particularly as, taken together in combination, they were not able to open the "black box" of the university for regional partners. Stakeholders suggested that there were problems for potential partner companies to approach university researchers, either because of too many or too few access points creating uncertainty. The intractability of this problem is highlighted by the call for a single entry point for regional companies. The university had abolished its Liaison Group in 2001, and moved to decentralised technology transfer officers because the central office proved unable to understand all the different regional activities. At the same time, the UT also has cross cutting activities that are supposed to support all knowledge exchange undertakings, most notably DesignLab, further occluding the issue. The various access points all had their own consistent internal logic in that they made sense for the participating researchers and companies, but when taken in aggregate, they created a confusing situation around the university.

A number of partners outside the university noted the apparent higher approachability of Saxion, the polytechnic, where the most senior researcher posts are associate professors whose primary role is to establish partnership projects and networking activities with regional businesses. Nevertheless, there is a difference between Saxion and the UT in the nature of the knowledge exchanges with firms, with Saxion providing more solutions to business problems and the UT solving business problems by creating new knowledge about those problems. The complexities around the intermediaries reflected in part the needs of firms and academics around the UT to effectively transfer knowledge and develop shared infrastructures. The reality of these knowledge communities was that participation by SMEs was much more demanding, often longer and more expensive, and therefore had the effect of being off-putting for them. Efforts were made to develop innovation vouchers to allow firms to learn about working with UT academics, but the issue persisted in that working with

49

the UT demanded that firms make a substantial ex ante investment before receiving benefits.

The challenge of institutional entrepreneurs

The Twente innovation ecosystem was dependent on a relatively limited number of individuals as institutional entrepreneurs who understood the complexities of strategic governance and intermediary structures, and were able to selectively pull assets, ideas, and funding together to create projects and upgrade the regional innovation ecosystem. These individuals were often successful in achieving the goal of external leverage, linking local projects to external subsidies and investments. One example is the nanotechnology laboratory, constructed in ways that attracted tens of millions of research infrastructure investment from the Dutch government and European Commission. This was achieved because the individuals who created the laboratory had an extensive local network as well as good contacts at the national and European level – not just with policy-makers but also with the academics who ultimately wrote the scientific content for the proposals that attracted these investments. These individuals also had a kind of creativity and dynamism to react to new opportunities and changing circumstances (such as new national governments changing funding programmes).

A substantial amount of the management capacity of the Twente innovation ecosystem was vested as a kind of institutional memory in these institutional entrepreneurs and their personal connections. Nonetheless, these individuals were not always those who participated in the strategic decision making, which tended to be senior managers at a higher level. When the institutional entrepreneurs left, what remained were the projects and structures, and as a result, activities sometimes suffered from a kind of lock-in, as less experienced staff simply continued the known way of working without the sensitivities and contacts to react effectively

50

to changing circumstances. Similarly, this posed substantial problems for the institutions they left, and indeed a number of the organisations, including the university, created special interim positions to encourage people to stay and retain the institutional memory. In those cases where individuals departed from the regional innovation scene, the stasis or the lock-in that emerged was sometimes experienced by other organisations as bad-faith behaviour or a lack of trust which undermined making a smooth transition to new arrangements.

The challenge of knowledge exchange

The fundamental problem that arose in the knowledge exchange sub-system was that the university did not represent a meaningful organisational structure or level for knowledge activities. Following Brewer's (1999, p. 238) aphorism that "the world has problems but universities have departments", knowledge exchange is hampered most notably when there are potential users who could use knowledge from a variety of university researchers, but those researchers were not necessarily already coordinated with each other. Efforts were being made within the UT to exchange and cross-fertilise across what might be regarded as the natural knowledge exchange communities, grouping departments into cognate clusters and aligning research around a few major themes. However, given the challenges around genuinely interdisciplinary ways of working and the evident mismatch between regional engagement at the strategic and individual levels, it was at the time of writing not clear whether all of this organisational change would do anything more than drive symbolic compliance behaviour from researchers

The other element of complexity was that of a mismatch between knowledge supply within the UT and the absorptive capacity within the region which hindered the development of sensible knowledge exchange practices. What might be considered the

51

institutional imagination had been captured by the Nanolab example, where a large physical infrastructure existed that supported teaching and research, stimulated high-technology entrepreneurship and innovation, and offered shared working space for other companies. This heuristic seemed dominant in the minds of some partners, and created unwillingness to think about diversifying the ways of knowledge exchange (for example, through students or through non-contractual relationships). This also had the effect of instilling a sense akin to hopelessness amongst partners who believed there were some areas where no cooperation was possible because of the absence of those interactive possibilities. This in turn reduced a willingness to think creatively about how other kinds of knowledge exchange could be established: even the social sciences knowledge exchange infrastructure, DesignLab, was a large expensive infrastructure that provided a shared working space.

Conclusion

The study we have offered here explores the relationships between key stakeholders in the Twente Region, and the ways in which these partners are able to coordinate action by signalling their needs and expectations through an iterative process of fine-grained learning. The historical development trajectory of the Twente Region makes it a very interesting example for understanding knowledge-based regional development. Its unfavourable geographical position has provided a relatively sparse regional economic development environment within which the University of Twente has been harnessed to a reinvention process. The university has for 30 years been leading in creating an infrastructure in which knowledge is translated and installed into new companies, slowly evolving from a single building, to a science park, to an integrated education, research, and commercial space seeking to stimulate productive interactions between science and society. Nevertheless, this reinvention process has not always gone smoothly, and so there are tensions evident that provide useful insights into some wider issues of how universities can contribute to the redevelopment of less innovative regions. We reiterate here the point that we have dwelled on problems and tensions, but this is not a negative story, rather it is an account of those tensions that arise in holding together a stakeholder network; and in this we have seen that tensions appear to surface in four sub-systems within the overall regional innovation ecosystem. With the caveat that this is a single exploratory study of one region, we nevertheless contend that the story that emerges has a wider salience for understanding how universities can contribute to regional development.

There seems to be an acute need for more communication between the stakeholders in order to clearly define entry points to knowledge institutions, assist with communications below the level of strategy-makers, and better organise the ways that signals over needs are transmitted and received between regional partners. In each of the domains we have highlighted there is a degree of intractability in the problem in that the two sides appear to misunderstand one another in such a manner that undermines building long-term commitments. Our analysis suggests that the key to solving these tensions lies in the coordination of human agents able to find innovative methods of combining diverse interests into common strategies and prevent overlaps of strategic bodies, functions, and actions. More specifically, there are tensions and problems in this coordination related to each of the subsystems we have identified.

First, the plethora of associative forums in Twente makes it hard to determine a genuinely shared agenda with the university, as the university does not hear a clearly articulated set of demands, and regional partners are left feeling uneasy regarding the university's commitment. Second, the university knowledge communities appear as being closed to outsiders, because they are involved in creating fundamental knowledge, and therefore it is difficult for new users to simply join the communities and access ready-made solutions for their problems. Third, although communications and coordination are easy to develop between strategy-makers, there is an absence of what Sotarauta (2017) calls the institutional navigators who are able to find their way through the labyrinth of administrative structures, policy documents, and funding opportunities to create activities linking knowledge producers in the university and knowledge users in the community. Finally, the policy imagination became dominated by a single model of knowledge exchange based around a large infrastructure investment on the university site where these knowledge producers and users would come together with students, to create new kinds of useful knowledge, and that prevented partners from daring to transmit alternative kinds of signals over their needs and expectations.

For each of these tensions there is a common-sense solution, but these actually serve to exacerbate the problem by dulling the transmitted signals and therefore jamming the communications and undermining the coordination. Because of the relative lack of knowledge of each other's capacities, it can be tempting to opt for simplistic solutions that attempt to synchronise, homogenise, and signpost between partners that are very different and have a reason for being very different. That can undermine what we suggest to be necessary for progression, for partners to be working together to create opportunities for institutional navigators and entrepreneurs to develop knowledge exchange projects that mobilise networks that build a more general knowledge exchange capacity for the region. This is perhaps best illustrated by the issue of the dependence of regional efforts on a limited number of these institutional navigators and entrepreneurs, whose institutional knowledge, memory, and contacts facilitate effective knowledge exchanges linking operational employees in different organisations. A more short-term response might be to try to introduce a form of customer relationship manager system, but these generally fail to understand the degree to which these relationships depend on tacit knowledge and social capital. A more long-term approach would be for sufficient continuity of investment to allow community building and the emergence of denser networks with enough trust between partners to create a stronger sense of collectivity.

References

Avrotos (2017). **De Nederlandse Innovatie Prijzen**. www.avrotros.nl/site/over-avrotros/nieuws/artikel/item/avrotros-presenteert-de-nederlandse-innovatie-prijzen/. (Accessed 25 Sep 2017).

Bazen, J. (2016). **Innovation Driven Regional Development, Case Study Region Twente, Eastern Netherlands.** http://kgk.uni-obuda.hu/sites/default/files/Innovation-driven-regional-development.pdf (Accessed 31 Aug 2017).

Benneworth, P. (2014). Decoding university ideals by reading campuses. In Temple, P. (ed) **The Physical University**, London: Routledge, p. 217-242.

Benneworth, P., Charles, D., Groen, A. J. and Hospers, G. J. (2005). **Bringing Cambridge to Consett? Building University-centred Entrepreneurial Networks in Peripheral Regions**: Case study report 2. Twente: the Netherlands. Enschede: University of Twente.

Benneworth, P., Hospers, G. J. and Jongbloed, B. (2006). New economic impulses in old industrial regions: the role of the University of Twente in regional renewal. In Prinz, A., Steenge, A.E. and Schmidt, J. (eds) **Innovation: Technical, Economic and Institutional Aspects**, Berlin: Lit Verlag, p. 1-24.

Benneworth, P., Hospers, G, J., Jongbloed, B., Leiyste, L. and Zomer, A. (2011), The 'Science City' as a System Coupler in Fragmented Strategic Urban Environments? **Built Environment**, 37, 317-335.

Benneworth, P. and Ratinho, T. (2014). Regional innovation culture in the social knowledge economy. In Rutten, R., Benneworth, P., Irawati, D., and Boekema, F. (eds) **The Social Dynamics of Innovation Networks**, Routledge, London, p. 239-256.

Brewer, G. (1999). The challenges of interdisciplinarity. **Policy Sciences** 32, 327–337.

Clark, B. (1998). **Creating Entrepreneurial Universities: Organizational Pathways of Transformation**. New York: Pergamon/ IAU Press.

European Commission (2017). **Region Overijssel**. https://ec.europa.eu/growth/tools-databases/regional-innovation-monitor/base-profile/overijssel. (Accessed 28 Jul 2017).

Garlick, S., Benneworth, P., Puukka, J. and Vaessen, P. (2006). **Supporting the Contribution of Higher Education Institutes to Regional Development - Peer Review Report: Twente in the Netherlands**. Paris: OECD.

Hengstenberg, Y., Eckardt, F. and Benneworth, P. (2017). Reflections from a living smart campus. **Rooilijn**, 50, 44-49.

Kennispunt Twente (2016). **Twente Index 2016**. www.twenteindex.nl. (Accessed 28 Jul 2017).

Meerman, A. (2017). **University of Twente: The Entrepreneurial University of the Netherlands Through High-tech and Human Touch**. https://ub-cooperation.eu/pdf/cases/W_Case_Study_Twente. pdf. (Accessed 07 Apr 2017).

Regio Twente (n.d). **Agenda van Twente**. www.agendavantwente.nl. (Accessed 08 Aug 2017).

Saxion (2015). **Saxion Strategic Plan: 2016-2020**. http://www.saxion.edu/binaries/content/assets/edu/pdf/saxion-strategic-plan-16-20.pdf. (Accessed 31 Aug 2017).

Scholten, C. and Oxener, D. (2016). **Regional Innovation Monitor Plus 2016: Regional Innovation Report Overijssel**. https://ec.europa.eu/

56

growth/tools-databases/regional-innovation-monitor/sites/default/files/
report/2016_RIM%20Plus_Regional%20Innovation%20Report_Overijs
sel.pdf. (Accessed 07 Aug 2018).

Sorgdrager, W. (1981). **Een Experiment in het Bos: De Eerste Jaren van de Technische Hogeschool Twente 1961-1972**. Alphen aan den Rijn: Samson.

Sotarauta, M. (2017). An actor-centric bottom-up view of institutions: Combinatorial knowledge dynamics through the eyes of institutional entrepreneurs and institutional navigators. **Environment and Planning C: Government and Policy**, 35, 584-599.

Stam, E., Romme, A. G. L., Roso, M., van den Toren, J. P. and van der Starre, B. T. (2016). **Knowledge Triangles in the Netherlands: an Entrepreneurial Ecosystem Approach**. Paris: OECD.

Timmerman, P. and Hospers, G.J. (2016). **Campus in Context**. Enschede: Stichting Stad en Regio & Studium Generale UT.

Twente Board (2015). **Twente Board: Economic Development**. www.twenteboard.nl. (Accessed 08 Aug 2017).

University of Twente (2016). **Living Smart Campus**. www.utwente.nl/en/organization/news-agenda/special/2016/living-smart-campus. (Accessed 14 Aug 2017).

University of Twente (2017a). **The Campus of the University of Twente**. www.utwente.nl/en/campus. (Accessed 14 Aug 2017).

University of Twente (2017b). **Long Term Strategy for Housing**. www.utwente.nl/en/lths. (Accessed 14 Aug 2017).

Chapter 3

Transitioning from an Economic to a Broader Social Impact

A Case Study of a Swedish University

Eloïse Germain-Alamartine

Many of the universities that have been created in recent years carry expectations of making a positive impact on the regional economy in addition to other, more traditional missions (Nilsson, 2006). In countries such as Sweden or Denmark, laws define the role of higher education institutes, stating that beyond education and research, a third role for universities is to "co-operate with their surrounding communities" (UKÄ, 2017). Policymakers increasingly demand that universities integrate into their regions, so that they have a positive impact on society.

There are several models of the roles that can be played by universities in their regions (Guerrero et al., 2016; Gunasekara, 2016; Uyarra, 2010); with the entrepreneurial university being a particularly prominent example (Clark, 1998). For the purposes of this chapter, the model of a university is defined as a set of roles – or missions – practiced by the university as an organisation, within itself or in interaction with its economic, social, cultural, geographical, and political environment. A model is thus characterised by mechanisms that define the internal organisation of the university as well as spatial arrangements with its environment. These models are intensively examined in the literature, along with the motivations for the choice of tending toward a particular model. However, the process of transitioning from one model to another seems to be less discussed. Exploring how a university can or should rethink and reorganise itself and its interactions with its environment in order to assume new roles seems nevertheless essential to avoid failure in such a change (Cherwitz & Hartelius, 2006). This chapter explores the transition from one model to another and raises questions that policymakers and university managers should reflect upon more specifically.

Linköping University (LiU) has previously been evoked in the literature as a major actor in a successful Triple Helix collaboration (Svensson et al., 2012) – the collaboration between academia, the public sector, and the private sector (Etzkowitz & Leydesdorff, 2000). Currently, the case appears to present elements not only of the systemic university model but also of the engaged university model (Uyarra, 2010). How the activities and organisation of LiU are evolving is examined by comparison with the characterisation of these models in the literature. LiU seems to be in transition between these two models, towards achieving a broader social impact.

This chapter addresses the problem of transitioning from one university model to another to create a larger impact on the regional economy and society. The following questions examine this issue: *(i)* How does the literature define the roles of universities? *(ii)* Which of these definitions is applicable to LiU? *(iii)* What disparities exist between the case and the theoretical models in the literature? The chapter begins with a brief overview of the literature discussing the roles of universities, with an introduction to the main theoretical models of university regional interaction. A description of the methodological approach adopted in this study follows. After that, the case of LiU is presented in its regional context and is analysed through two main theoretical lenses. The final section discusses how the case and theory differ and argues that the university currently finds itself in a state of transition.

The Roles of Universities: A Brief Literature Overview

The roles of universities in regional development have been debated in the fields of economics, geography, and innovation for some decades. Over the years, the number of universities has increased, and with that the amount of public investment in education (OECD, 2016). At the same time, "interests and expectations placed upon universities have shifted from a more indirect contribution to economic development and innovation […] to a more formal, institutionalised and proactive role" (Uyarra, 2010, p. 1240). Thus, the demands on universities have evolved, and nowadays, the links between universities and their region have diverse configurations.

Uyarra (2010) reviewed the literature on the roles of universities and synthesised the discussions on this subject into five university models: the "knowledge factory", the "relational university", the "entrepreneurial university", the "systemic university", and the "engaged university" (Uyarra, 2010, p. 1230). These models are not thought to be mutually exclusive; they are different analytical frameworks which can be applied in an overlapping manner to match a particular situation. The models seem to be progressive in the sense that each model shares characteristics with the preceding model(s) but has more characteristics and a higher complexity in its interactions with the environment.

Enarson discusses a model of the university as a "knowledge factory" (1973). In this model, the main roles of the university are to teach, to produce research, and to ensure that the research has a "localised impact" (Uyarra, 2010, p.1232), such as through the applied sciences (Youtie & Shapira, 2008). Research contributions are expected to result in scientific and economic outputs for the companies situated near the university geographically (Jaffe et al., 1993). This, in turn, influences new businesses to choose to establish in a university environment (Abramovsky & Simpson, 2011).

Greater collaboration with the private sector gives rise to the relational university model (Uyarra, 2010). Collaboration becomes bidirectional: an example is when governments pressured universities to foster national competitiveness during the economic crisis in the 1980s. Universities approached industry and suggested an exchange – funding of research for innovative knowledge (Uyarra, 2010). These relations can take many forms (Bonaccorsi & Piccaluga, 1994), but informal contacts are recognised as being the most important channel for linkages between a university and the private sphere (Meyer-Krahmer & Schmoch, 1998).

As these collaborations develop a strategic character, universities reorganise according to the entrepreneurial university model (Uyarra, 2010). Collaborations still occur, but knowledge spillovers (Audretsch, 2014) become more institutionalised. Uyarra argues that the majority of studies discussing the entrepreneurial university use data from the United States. Since then, Kalar & Antoncic (2015) have studied several European universities, suggesting that the entrepreneurial model can be applied not only in America but also in Europe. Gibb et al. (2013) discuss the reasons for the necessity of entrepreneurial behaviours in higher education institutions. Fayolle & Redford (2014) also propose a framework that provides inspiration and tools for any university to become entrepreneurial. In their eyes, "universities need to become more entrepreneurial" (Fayolle & Redford, 2014, p. 1) to be able to carry on all their missions, including "the third one, commercialisation of research" (ibid, p.3). However, there is no single model of entrepreneurial university, to the extent that global "challenges, such as massification, resource availability, and external stakeholder engagement [...] will affect higher education institutions in distinctive ways and lead to different reactions" (Gibb et al., 2013, p.3).

The systemic university model (Uyarra, 2010) derives from discussions on policies for regional innovation systems, in which universities participate in as "institutional actors" (Uyarra, 2010, p. 1236). Gunasekara defines regional innovation systems by their "four key elements":

> "... the spatial agglomeration of firms and other organizations in a bounded geographical space, in a single industry, or in complementary industries; the availability of a stock of proximate capital, particularly, human capital; an associative governance regime; and the development of cultural norms of openness to learning, trust and cooperation between firms" (Gunasekara, 2016, p. 139).

In the systemic university model, collaboration is extended: the public sector joins the private sector and academia in fostering economic development. Such a configuration is sometimes called a triple helix collaboration (Etzkowitz, 2003, p. 119).

The fifth model described by Uyarra is the engaged university model (Uyarra, 2010), adding a developmental focus to the actions conducted by the university. The university henceforth has not only an economic impact, but "social, economic, political and

63

civic roles" (Uyarra, 2010, p. 1240) by responding more specifically to the needs of the region, for the public good, in both formal and informal ways (Hartley et al., 2010; Sachs & Clark, 2017). Breznitz & Feldman (2012) rounded out the literature on this model by suggesting a comprehensive list of the missions that engaged universities assume: basic research, teaching, knowledge transfer, policy development, and economic initiatives.

It can be observed in the literature that for some authors, the distinction between entrepreneurial, systemic, and engaged universities seems to be quite small, and sometimes nearly non-existent. For instance, Gibb et al. (2013) feel that there are

> "a variety of ways in which higher education institutions behave entrepreneurial, for example [...] create and nurture synergies between teaching, research and their societal engagement." (p.1)

The analysis of the case of LiU in this chapter, using the different theoretical approaches just described, confirms this claim: the impact of some university activities in the economy and the society can be still quite difficult to measure, for example entrepreneurship education programmes. Even if all graduates having attended such programmes will not engage in entrepreneurial ventures, they might behave entrepreneurially in their respective organisations, developing collaborations, starting new projects, etc.

Methods and Data

The case study of LiU is based on a combination of existing data, publications and web materials with selected interviews. Literature on LiU was found by using the keyword combinations "Linköping University" and "regional development" in databases such as Scopus and Google Scholar. Around 20 additional online resources were also consulted to collect secondary data on the current activities of LiU, or information published by regional stakeholders that permit a better grasp of the context of the case. In particular, the university website provides elements to understand the organisation of the university and the role of its different entities; municipalities' websites provide with regional demographic data and economic data; and Science Parks' websites provide historical insights on these organisations. Five additional interviews were made with key personnel of the university and of the region to supplement the picture of this university since the latest scientific publication to date was in 2012. Interviewees from the university were chosen because of their positions – in the International Affairs and Collaborations Division (IFSA)[6], in LiU Relation[7], in LiU Innovation[8] – that have daily interaction with strategic partners of the university. The interviewee from Region Östergötland was chosen because of his knowledge and overview of the regional projects, partnerships, and stakeholders.

Case data were analysed using the framework provided by Uyarra , in particular her synthetic table (Uyarra, 2010, p. 1230). The first step was to list all the information and events gathered on the case of LiU and to order them in chronological order. The following step consisted in screening the list in order to categorise each element according to the definitions found in Uyarra (2010) and Breznitz & Feldman (2012). The final step was a new analysis of

---

[6] "The International Affairs and Collaborations Division (IFSA) supports faculties and departments in their work with internationalisation, research funding, commissioned education and collaboration" (Linköping University, 2017b).

[7] "LiU Relation is a unit within Linköping University Holding AB with assignments to work with developing collaboration" (Linköping University, 2016b).

[8] "LiU Innovation supports students, researchers and staff at Linköping University to develop ideas from early concept to finished product or service" (Linköping University, 2016c).

the list in order to determine if the majority of the features of the theoretical models could be observed, and if not, to try to understand what was lacking and why.

The Case of Linköping University

LiU was created in the 1960s, initially as a branch of Stockholm University, but soon thereafter as an independent university in 1975, making it the sixth public university in Sweden. Today, LiU has around 4,000 employees and 27,000 students, distributed among its four campuses: two in Linköping, one in Norrköping, and one in Stockholm (Figure 3.1). On the international scene, LiU welcomes about 2,000 students from abroad, has exchange agreements with 500 universities around the world, and was 47th on the 2016 Times Higher Education ranking of the top 150 universities under 50 years old (Linköping University Library, 2016). LiU's fields of excellence are material sciences, IT and hearing (Linköping University, 2018c).

Figure 3.1. Map of LiU campuses (modified, from Linköping University, 2018a)

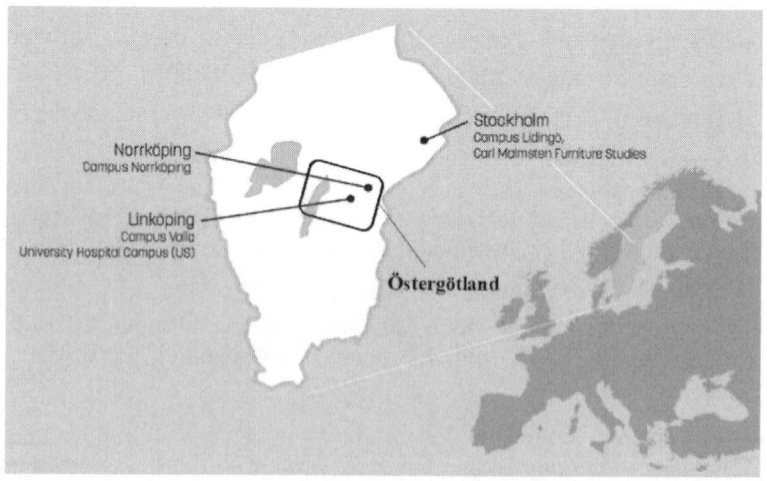

The region for LiU can be defined as the conurbation of Linköping and Norrköping, as these two municipalities comprise the larger part of the population in Östergötland County (Brinkhoff, 2016) (figure 4.1). Östergötland County is situated south of Stockholm in south east Sweden. With around 450,000 inhabitants recorded in 2016 (Statistiska Centralbyrån, 2017), the County represents 4.5% of the Swedish population. The landscape is largely agricultural, although the two main cities – named "twins" by the Östergötland County Administrative Board (Länsstyrelsen Östergötland, 2017) – have attracted important and diverse industrial production throughout history, and in recent years, knowledge-intensive companies. Agriculture, however, remains a dynamic sector in the county but it is closely linked to the regional innovation strategy, witness the recent research grant awarded to the AgTech 2030 project. Both Norrköping and Linköping have good transport links, being situated on the railroad between Stockholm and Malmö and hosting two international airports.

Linköping: "Where ideas become reality"

The 2016 census reports a population of around 153,000 for Linköping, which makes it the fifth largest city in Sweden (Linköping municipality, 2017). Early on, the city was an important place for trading and for religious institutions; it was also one of the first districts in 1627 to establish a gymnasium preparing students for university. Education is thus a distinguishing feature of Linköping, as is research. Besides being chosen to host a branch of Stockholm University in the 1960s, Linköping served in the 1970s as the new location for research institutes such as the Swedish National Road and Transport Research Institute and the Swedish Defence Research Establishment (Klofsten et al., 1999). The area also has a rich military history as a long-term host of garrisons, in particular for the Swedish Air Force; this may be due to its strategic location, at

67

a reasonable distance from the capital and overlooking the Baltic approaches from the east and the south. That might also be one of the reasons why, in the 1940s, Saab AB chose to establish production plants for military aircraft in Linköping (Klofsten et al., 1999). Today, the five biggest employers in Linköping are: the municipality, the region (including hospital employees), Saab AB, LiU, and Ericsson (Linköping Municipality, 2017). So, the administration, the hospital, the university, Saab, and Science Park Mjärdevi (a community of firms, of which Ericsson is a member) are the main entities shaping economic activity in Linköping.

Science Park Mjärdevi was created by Linköping municipality in 1984, on 150 acres adjacent to LiU that the municipality had reserved since 1969 for research, industry, and the housing of "firms with close ties to the university" (Hommen et al., 2006, p. 1339). Mjärdevi grew so quickly that, in 1993, the municipality created a company to manage it (Etzkowitz & Klofsten, 2005). The Science Park has had its difficulties during economic recessions, but overall, the Park has recorded positive results: it evolved from 6 companies hiring 150 persons in 1984 to 260 companies employing around 6,100 people in 2011 (Cadorin et al., 2017). It hosts spin-offs as well as R&D departments of multinational companies, such as Ericsson. One could say that Science Park Mjärdevi embodies the Linköping Municipality motto: "Where ideas become reality".

The Park is close to LiU; not only geographically but in terms of collaboration. The various formal and informal relationships between the University and the Science Park include, for instance, the link between the Foundation for Small Business Development in Linköping (SMIL)[9] with the Centre for Innovation and

---

[9] SMIL is a a club of entrepreneurs from the Linköping area, including from Science Park Mjärdevi.

Entrepreneurship, at LiU (CIE). SMIL is a network of entrepreneurs in Linköping. SMIL members can attend a training programme in entrepreneurship conducted by CIE, which is part of Linköping University. The Shadow Board of Directors at Science Park Mjärdevi is another example: comprising LiU students, the Board is essentially an ambassador for the Science Park with the University. The Shadow Board also meets and brainstorms on issues concerning the operations and management of the Science Park, similar to the ordinary Science Park board (Cadorin et al., 2017). Thus, these links appear to deal not only with technology transfer between the University and the Science Park but also with talent attraction.

Norrköping, Linköping's twin city

For Norrköping, the 2016 census reports a population of around 135,000, which makes the city the 9th largest in Sweden (Norrköping Municipality, 2016). Norrköping preceded Linköping in becoming an industrial region. Due to its situation on Motala Ström, a river system that drains Lake Vättern into the Baltic Sea, Norrköping became home first to mills in the Middle Ages, then to weapons and textile industries in the 17th century, and in the 19th century, the paper industry. In the 1960s, both Philips and Ericsson chose to locate part of their electronic device production to Norrköping. Ten years later, LiU opened Campus Norrköping, attracting a thousand students (Svensson et al., 2012). The labour market worsened in the 1980s and the early 1990s. Although Whirlpool bought one factory from Philips, another was closed down, with Ericsson also deciding to relocate (Svensson et al., 2012). In 1997, LiU decided to expand its campus in Norrköping. The expansion was tightly coordinated with the municipality, which held privileged member status on the strategic committee. At that time, the campus had 500 staff members and 5,000 students. In the 1990s, the public and private sectors in

69

Sweden joined together to create Norrköping Science Park, along with its business incubator.

The expansion of Campus Norrköping occurred at a turning point in the history of Norrköping. Indeed, initiatives from the municipality and local businesses multiplied after the turn of the century to give new energy to the economy and the labour market; but also, in large part, because the regional government realised that the area would lose the talent it was producing if there were no jobs for them after graduation. The decline in talent was considered to be to the detriment of regional development and talent was needed to pull the region out of the economic downturn of the 1980s and 90s.

So, the municipality invested money from the sale of its energy company to create a local foundation for university–industry cooperation for innovation. In addition, two endowed chairs were created: a private local foundation sponsored a professorship in printed electronics and Ericsson, a professorship in communication electronics (Svensson et al., 2012). These moves aimed to foster innovation by improving existing local resources; namely, the know-how in electronics from the Philips-Ericsson era, and the knowledge assimilated, transmitted, and renewed by the University. These efforts paid off: in 2016, the Science Park had 150 companies and 1,000 employees. However, the biggest employers remain the administration, the hospital, the university, and two major paper producers (Norrköping municipality, 2016); this illustrates the unique combination of industry and knowledge that constitutes the Norrköping economy.

Figure 3.2. Comparative chronology of the case

	Region	Linköping	Norrköping	Linköping University
before 1960		1940s: Saab AB builds military aircraft production plants	17th century: weapons and textile industries are important 19th century: paper industry is important	
1960s			Philips and Ericsson locate electronic device production in Norrköping	Linköping University is created, as a branch of Stockholm University
1970s		Linköping is the new location for some national research institutes	Linköping University's Norrköping campus is created	1975: Linköping University receives its status of independent university the Industrial Liaison Office is created
1980s	Regional Development Fund provides state financial support to create the first incubator in Linköping (TeknikByn)	1984: Science Park Mjärdevi and SMIL are created	Philips closes a part of its production in Norrköping	1980: TEMA is created 1981: the Centre for Technology Transfer is created 1986: the Medical School is created Problem-Based Learning is elaborated and tested
1990s	GrowLink is created	1993: Linköping's municipality creates a company to manage Science Park Mjärdevi	Norrköping Science Park is created 1997-99: Ericsson ceases its activity in Norrköping	1993: CIE is created 1995: LiU Holding (with LiU Relation, LiU Innovation, etc.) is created

71

		1999: SMILES is created
2000s	Nokia closes and Ericsson reduces its activities in Mjärdevi	2000: Linköping University's Stockholm campus is opened 2007: LEAD is created 2012: University resource allocation by the government takes into account collaboration
2010s	2016: the East Sweden Business Region is created	2014: LiU has a collaboration policy 2015: Collaboration coordinators' positions are created in each department of LiU

Linköping University

Using Uyarra's framework, LiU could primarily be considered a knowledge factory, to the extent that the knowledge it produces has a localised impact. Saab, for instance, has been involved in the creation of the university, and is still collaborating with the university in research projects. In a study of relations between LiU and SMIL (a club of entrepreneurs from Science Park Mjärdevi aiming to develop business skills), Klofsten & Jones-Evans (1996) evoke LiU as a provider of human, financial, and intangible resources such as structural knowledge and credibility for SMIL, (Laur et al., 2012).

The University has been previously characterised as "entrepreneurial" (Svensson et al., 2012, p. 1) because of its support for entrepreneurship among its students and its academic staff. In 1995, LiU Holding was created, because of a change in the Swedish law that allowed the largest universities of the country to risk the money they receive from public sources through holding companies (Interview, LiU Innovation, 14/03/2018). This holding enabled in particular the creation of the university's innovation office: LiU Innovation. LiU Holding operates as an administrative department of the University but is legally a non-profit private company. Alongside other initiatives dealing with entrepreneurship, such as the creation of a business incubator, is the CIE, and the Entrepreneurship and New Business Development Programme (Etzkowitz & Klofsten, 2005). Since then, entrepreneurship has been taught to students from all types of educational programmes (Linköping University, Communications and Marketing Division, 2016). But entrepreneurship teaching targets not only university students. In 1999, an existing collaboration between LiU and SMIL resulted in SMILES (SMIL Entrepreneurship School), which offers business development and management programmes to local entrepreneurs

(Etzkowitz & Klofsten, 2005). University researchers are also interested in entrepreneurship: Sectra, a medical technology and encrypted communication systems company, is an example of a business created by university researchers that still collaborates with the University.

The literature on the role of LiU in the development of its region mainly concerns its involvement in a Triple Helix collaboration – a collaboration between academia, the public sector (e.g., municipalities and regional agencies), and the private sector (regional businesses; Etzkowitz & Klofsten, 2005; Svensson et al., 2012). University involvement in a Triple Helix collaboration seems to accord with the concept of a systemic university, as defined by Uyarra (2010). Etzkowitz & Klofsten (2005) clearly identify LiU as a key actor in the knowledge-based development of the region. Svensson et al. (2012) also identify the university as essential to the development of a mixed economy based on both knowledge and industry, as in Norrköping Municipality. One can wonder if those Triple Helix collaborations that are successful both in Linköping and Norrköping can be to some extent influenced by what Lämsä (2010) identifies as a Swedish trait of consensus, that tends to ease collaborations.

There are at least three examples of public sector involvement with the university and the private sector to enhance economic development. The first example of public sector involvement embodied by regional organisations occurred in the 1980s when the Regional Development Fund provided state financial support to help the municipality create the first incubator in Linköping (TeknikByn) (Etzkowitz & Klofsten, 2005). This involvement of the public sector fostered the development of spin-offs from the university, thus helping the university, the private sector and regional development. A second example is the initiative of the County to write an application to the Vinnväxt competition

74

sponsored by VINNOVA (the Swedish Innovation Agency) for research funding in the early 2000s (Etzkowitz & Klofsten, 2005). This initiative enabled the participants identified by the County, from academia, the public and the private sector, to benefit from long-term funding to conduct research. Another example of public sector involvement was that Norrköping Municipality was a privileged member of the strategic committee of the University in the expansion of Campus Norrköping and was at the same time involved in creating Norrköping Science Park and its business incubator (Svensson et al., 2012). Currently, the University Board comprises representatives from the university (academic staff and students) and from public and private organisations (for instance, Saab AB and Norrköping Art Museum) (Linköping University, 2016a). As the Board is the highest decision-making authority in the university, all groups and individuals who have dealings with the university may present their opinions and participate in strategic decision-making. The University works also in collaboration with Region Östergötland, that provides funding to regional stakeholders to help them in their activities that support regional growth. A significant part of these funds goes to research projects at LiU or to LiU Holding. For instance, the research project Grönovation (Linköping University, 2018b) is conducting research on agriculture, which is one of the strength areas of the region. At the institutional level, a collaboration agreement was signed both by the university rector and by the president of the region (Interview, Region Östergötland, 22/01/2018), and the creation of a project office at the university is ongoing.

Other elements in the history of LiU and also some characteristics of its current activities are indicative of an engaged university. First of all, a regulation on universities in 2009 encouraged universities to use collaborations with their surroundings to have a societal impact. This expectation became even more important in 2012 when Vetenskapsrådet (the Swedish Research Council) modified the resource allocations to universities to consider the societal impact of research of universities. As a consequence, LiU created organisations such as LiU Relation and LiU Innovation, but also the positions of collaboration coordinators, responsible for developing, documenting and rewarding collaboration at each department and faculty (PhD course, Collaboration as a research skill, 2017/2018). Beyond the involvement in Triple Helix collaborations, the university now partners in a penta helix for instance in the East Sweden Business Region or in HELIX Competence Centre. Penta helix is a collaboration model for regional development through innovation as a "social innovation ecosystem" (Björk et al., 2014, p.27) that includes not only the public and private sectors and academia, as in the triple helix model, but also social entrepreneurs and civil society (Björk et al., 2014). In the penta helix, stakeholders are expected to co-produce knowledge in a model that enhances knowledge exchange and fosters social innovation at a more rapid pace, while strengthening the role of civil society in innovation. Thus, the social, rather than the mere economic, impact is of foremost concern. In such collaborations, the university delivers value to the partners mostly because of its political position perceived as neutral by the other partners. This stance enables the university to act as a mediator, as can be observed in the East Sweden Business Region described later on.

As a member of the East Sweden Business Region, an informal network aimed at fostering the growth and development of innovation in regional companies, LiU exhibits another aspect of an engaged university (Interview, IFSA, 16/05/17). Network members include public organisations, such as the municipality (their business and trade offices); private organisations; and semi-public organisations, such as the Chamber of Commerce. Although it was created in 2016, the East Sweden Business Region has its roots in 1997 under the name GrowLink[10]. In this first phase, LiU created GrowLink in response to the 1992 Swedish Higher Education Act defining the three roles of higher education institutes: research, education, and valorisation (i.e., to spread and utilise knowledge). The University chaired GrowLink throughout the major part of its existence. LiU already had many contacts with the private sector in the region. The idea behind GrowLink was to simplify these contacts and create a platform where organisations – in the beginning, regional public organisations involved in innovation, such as the Science Parks, or VINNOVA – could meet to discuss their projects.

The current (2017) objectives of the East Sweden Business Region are the same as they were in GrowLink. Several working groups focus on themes such as Growth, Development, or Talent Attraction. East Sweden Business Region partners can be inspired and learn about innovation being implemented in other regions of Europe: for instance, in 2017, a visit was organised to Food Valley NL in the Netherlands. The Regional Agency and LiU co-chair East Sweden Business Region, which brings political issues into the network and could, according to one interviewee, lower the participation of network members; this occurred when the Regional Agency was sole chair of GrowLink for 3 years in the 2000s: members asked the University to resume the chair in order to reduce the politics. But measurements of the practical outcomes of the present platform show the network to be successful: there is, for example, the partnership between the Centre for Applied Management for small and medium-sized enterprises (CAM) at LiU and ALMI, an organisation providing loans, venture capital and advisory services to businesses, which arose in the framework of East Sweden Business Region: the CAM–ALMI partnership

---

[10] The name GrowLink comes from "Grow Linköping".

has supported the growth of around 50 small and medium-sized companies, resulting in 400 new jobs and a regional revenue increase of 40% in 3 years (Interview, IFSA, 16/05/17).

Another example of the continuity of university involvement in a penta helix collaboration for regional development is the case of the HELIX Competence Centre. HELIX is a platform where various regional stakeholders can share their concerns and on-going work on working life issues. In the beginning, the HELIX collaboration was known as the HELIX VINN Excellence Centre, which VINNOVA funded for 10 years. The Excellence Centre was a cross-disciplinary research unit focused on sustainable development in organisations (Elg et al., 2016). The aim was to enable a collaboration between researchers, industrial partners, and public organisations in the form of a triple helix collaboration using an interactive research approach. Interactive research begins with the emergence of research questions in discussions between researchers and HELIX partners. The partners then provide researchers access to data, after which the researchers seek the help of the HELIX partners for testing ideas and validating hypotheses and theories. Extensions in funding made it possible to pursue research projects and broaden partnerships in HELIX Competence Centre, which now include labour market organisations and civil society – that is, it is now a penta helix collaboration. "New partners involve actors organising SMEs (SMIL, [...] Coompanion[11]), civil society organisations (SE-

---

[11] "Coompanion gives advisory services to cooperatives of various kinds (mostly small enterprises)" (HELIX Competence Centre, 2017, p.18).

UPP[12], FAMNA[13], Coompanion) and an intermediary organising public authorities (Samordningsförbundet Centrala Östergötland[14])" (HELIX Competence Centre, 2017, p.18).

The specificities of Linköping University: In Transition from an Economic to a Broader Social Impact

Today, LiU seems to fit somewhere between the models of the systemic and the engaged university. Indeed, if we consider the list of missions that an engaged university must undertake according to Breznitz & Feldman (2012), LiU does seem to fulfil a number of these missions. For instance, the activities of the LEAD[15] incubator, which the university owns, appears to fulfil the mission of "business assistance" (Breznitz & Feldman, 2012, p. 147), as well as LiU Innovation. The difference between these two organisations lies in the fact that LiU Innovation focuses on

---

[12] "SE-UPP is a partnership of a broad spectra of organisations including sports organizations and organizations for disabled" (HELIX Competence Centre, 2017, p.18).

[13] "FAMNA is an umbrella organization for idea-driven providers of welfare (without profit distribution)" (HELIX Competence Centre, 2017, p.18).

[14] Samordningsförbundet Centrala Östergötland is the Coordination Association of Central Östergötland. "The Coordination Association is an independent legal entity consisting of its members Kinda, Linköping and Åtvidaberg municipalities, Region Östergötland, Försäkringskassan [Insurance Agency] and Arbetsförmedlingen [Employment Service]. [...] The purpose of the Central Ostergotland Coordination Association is that people should achieve or improve their ability to gain employment" (Samordningsförbunden i Östergötland, 2018; translated with Google Translate).

[15] LEAD is LiU Entrepreneurship and Development: the incubator, owned by both the university and Science Park Mjärdevi.

potential businesses with the University only whereas LEAD supports business ideas from outside the University as well (Interview, LiU Innovation, 14/03/2018). The HELIX Competence Centre and East Sweden Business Regions appear to fulfill the mission of "partnership development" (ibid., p. 151) while the mission of "real estate development" (ibid., p. 153) seems to be included in the present scope of LiU activities, such as with the involvement in the Vallastaden exhibition on urban living (in which LiU is a partner) at the southern end of Campus Valla (Vallastaden, 2017). However, examples of how LiU fulfills the mission of "workforce development" (Breznitz & Feldman, 2012, p. 150) are more difficult to find: although LiU is a teaching organisation and one of the largest employers in Östergötland County, most students leave the region after graduation. A LinkedIn query reveals that among the LiU alumni who have posted a profile, 27% currently work in Linköping, Norrköping, or Östergötland County and 22% in Stockholm and its surroundings (LinkedIn, 2017). As Stockholm itself hosts several higher education institutions, the difference in these rates would be expected to be much larger. Thus, it seems to be difficult to retain students within the region: *"[...] make students stay is the challenge of the University"*, as one Innovation Adviser from the LiU Innovation Office states (Interview, LiU Innovation, 02/05/17).

Figure 3.3. Application of the new roles of the university (Breznitz & Feldman, 2012, p.145)

University role	Program	Characteristics	Examples from the case
Knowledge transfer	Technology commercialization	Patents, licenses, spinout companies transfer knowledge from the university to private sector	Sectra
	Business assistance	Assistance in business education, the writing of business plans, and assistance with facility	Incubator LEAD
Policy development	Economic development and policy research	Research conducted by university faculty and students provided to state and local government/s	Various research projects, such as on crime
	Policy recommendations	Using faculty expertise and research to provide policy recommendations on a variety of issues important to the economic base of the region	Involvement in the RUNIN research project
Economic initiatives	Workforce development	Programs to provide new skills or employment and education in workers' rights and compensation	-
	Partnerships	Connecting different stakeholders to the regions in order to promote local economic success	HELIX Competence Centre; East Sweden Business Region; Collaboration coordinators

81

		in each department
Community development	Improving local business growth and neighbourhoods through entrepreneurship	CAM
Real estate development	Improving both residential and business real estate in adjacent neighbourhood	Involvement in Vallastaden exhibition

Compared with the models proposed by Uyarra (2010), universities are in reality complex, and they tend to be a mix of several characteristics of the different models. Though she points out that "regional-specific determinants" (Uyarra, 2010, p. 1243) make each university case unique, each case will more or less fit one of the models. It is the case for LiU: some elements of LiU seem hardly reproducible. For instance, the favourable period in which the University was founded was during a time in Sweden of government investment in higher education when the labour and accommodation markets were becoming saturated in Stockholm, especially due to the baby boom generation reaching adulthood (Knuthammar & Reksten, 2013). Thus, financial and human resources were available. Needing to develop economically, the city of Linköping took advantage of its geographical location, an easy distance from the Swedish capital, to share in these resources – the University is one result. Other case elements, however, could be considered inspirational and suitable examples for other rural universities wishing to pursue knowledge-based regional development.

An innovative mind-set

Major themes of interdisciplinary research and education have been Ariadne threads woven throughout the strategy of the

University. As early as 1969, at the founding of the university, a Master's programme in Industrial Engineering and Management was being taught (Linköping University, Communications and Marketing Division, 2016). In 1980, five years after LiU achieved accreditation as a university, the Department of Thematic Studies, "Tema" – "a unique academic environment for thematically structured, interdisciplinary and practical societal research" (Linköping University, 2017a) – was founded (Etzkowitz & Klofsten, 2005) and became emblematic of this interdisciplinary approach. In 1998, the Environmental Science Programme for bachelor and master students was launched. This specific interdisciplinary programme was the starting point of the work of Öberg (2009), who was one of the first researchers to reflect on how to assess the quality of interdisciplinary research. Another typical example is the increasing investment in research that occurred in the early 2000s, which brought the Home Communication and Life Sciences Technologies research fields closer; thus, knowledge from IT, electronics, and the life sciences could be combined (Etzkowitz & Klofsten, 2005).

The innovative practice of problem-based learning (PBL) has triggered excellent academic results from students at the medical school, where it was first implemented (Klofsten et al., 1999). The learning process is as follows (Linköping University, Communications and Marketing Division, 2016):

> "In PBL, students face different cases, and have to formulate what they need to know, and search out the knowledge they need. There are no given right or wrong responses, and different sources can contradict each other. The teachers shift from giving answers to asking questions and posing challenges."

Contrary to most other European countries, university employees in Sweden benefit from the 'Professor's Privilege' (Färnstrand

Damsgaard & Thursby, 2012;): the law states that ideas belong to their inventors and not to the organization they are working for (CODEX, 2016). This is another motivating factor for innovation since inventors get not only the authorship but also the royalties of their patents. Inventors also get the freedom to manage them according to their own wishes. For instance, a researcher that developed an invention in the framework of its research at the university, can choose to create their own company to take profit from their invention. In addition to the Professor's Privilege, LiU particularly supports its researchers' entrepreneurial attitude through LiU Innovation, that provides expert advice and practical support, even through financial aid, for commercialisation of research – all for free (Interview, LiU Innovation, 14/03/2018). Events such as Tech Tuesdays at Mjärdevi Science Park, where companies from the Science Park publicly present their activities, allow Swedish entrepreneurs and researchers to share their ideas, and discuss the progress of their work with their peers and with professionals in other fields (Science Park Mjärdevi, 2017). This allows them to inspire others and to improve their own work. Of course, there is always a risk of ideas being stolen since researchers do not have any non-disclosure agreement in their employment contract (Interview, LiU Innovation, 14/03/2018). Yet, combining this ability to share with the multi-disciplinary approaches of the University that include involvement in several networks – local, national and international – seems to show an innovative mind-set that is specific to LiU.

External pressures, however, might be threatening this innovative mind-set (Interview, IFSA, 16/05/17). Nearly the entire generation of entrepreneurs that founded the university has retired, relinquishing their seats to a new, perhaps more risk-averse generation (Interview, IFSA, 16/05/17). In Sweden and more generally in the EU, the increasing importance placed on the impact measurement of university activities is a drag on innovation, as it consumes time, energy and motivation of both faculty and administrative staff (Interview, IFSA, 16/05/17). These are threats to the LiU model that might dissuade the new generation of academics and university staff from aspiring to a new dynamic in the entrepreneurial spirit of the University (Interview, IFSA, 16/05/17). Such great efforts as have been made in the field of quality measurement might weaken the focus on innovative approaches that previously contributed to the success of the university, such as the implementation of PBL. As an interviewee states: *"I come from the field of Quality Management, but I think that this* [quality measurement] *is going too far"* (Interview, IFSA, 16/05/17).

A common objective with regional stakeholders and sense of consensus

From the start, each stakeholder involved in regional development – the municipalities, the region, businesses, and the university – agreed to work for growth and the well-being of society (Interview, IFSA, 16/05/17). This common objective, along with the peculiarly Swedish trait of consensus in decision-making (Lämsä, 2010), is recognised to have spurred regional development. An added value of the University is that it has no political leanings (Interview, IFSA, 16/05/17); thus, the University is especially suited for creating and managing networks in the penta helix collaboration, as well as receiving government funding.

Still today, Saab activities are aligned with those of LiU: for instance, Saab Ventures is a counterpart organisation of LiU Innovation, supporting spin-offs from Saab (Interview, LiU Innovation, 14/03/2018). Saab Ventures and LiU Innovation are quite close: they share the same investment decision board and their members have formal and informal interactions, such as lunch meetings. Other regional collaborations include LiU's

85

involvement in designing the Regional Innovation Strategy, which was drawn up by the LiU Director of Valorization and a Regional Agency representative. LiU, due to its excellent research, was especially suited for participating in implementation of the Smart Specialisation Strategy[16] (Foray, 2015); the University also helped draw up the Regional Development Plan, despite the plan being a political document (Interview, IFSA, 16/05/17). LiU strategy aligns well with these strategies; because the same stakeholders are involved, organisations are able to evolve in the same direction. Thus, the region involves the University in its strategic decisions, granting the University a legitimacy to act for regional development.

LiU seems to be in transition from a Systemic to an Engaged university model. One sign of this is the current evolution from involvement in a triple helix collaboration toward a penta helix collaboration. In addition, the University appears to have taken the lead in the two cases of penta helix collaborations discussed previously – East Sweden Business Region and the HELIX Competence Centre. Through its innovative mind-set, LiU has proven its concern for the public good. Starting in the 1970s, University participation in these collaborations was considered a way of engaging in the region through public awareness. However, such social impact is indirect as it occurs only through the classical education, research, and economic contributions of the systemic university model. The strategic alignment of the university with regional stakeholders still involves only the public

---

[16] Smart Specialisation Strategy is a policy adopted by the EU for regional development. It is a "place-based approach characterized by the identification of strategic areas for intervention based both on the analysis of the strengths and potential of the economy and on an Entrepreneurial Discovery Process (EDP) with stakeholder involvement" (Smart Specialisation Platform, 2019).

and private sectors. The eight strategic partners of LiU Relation are all either from the public or the private sector, so they are members of a triple helix collaboration (Interview, LiU Relation, 12/09/2017). Citizens and social entrepreneurs, and civil society, have not yet been invited to be part of this alignment. Direct social collaboration and impact seem to be a work in progress for LiU.

Conclusion

The overall objective of this case study of LiU was to examine ways of embedding universities in their regions that would create beneficial impacts for the regional economy and society. Five different models of the roles of universities in regional development and their characteristics were discussed: the knowledge factory, the relational university, the entrepreneurial university, the systemic university, and the engaged university. Of these models, the systemic university model seems to fit LiU best, while current university efforts indicate movement toward the engaged university model. Indeed, the involvement of LiU since its creation in a triple helix collaboration has anchored it well in the regional innovation system (Gunasekara, 2016). The evolution of this triple helix collaboration toward a penta helix collaboration with other regional stakeholders such as civil society shows concerns for the social issues of the region that can be interpreted as an emerging orientation toward the engaged university model. Thus, LiU seems to be in transition between these two university models.

Two specificities of Linköping University emerged in particular: an innovative mind-set and an early, solid strategic alignment with regional stakeholders. As both involve collaboration with only the public and the private sectors, they seem to convey the idea that making a direct impact on society is an ongoing task.

This chapter highlights implications for policymakers and university managers in leading a transition process from one university model to another. In particular, the transition implies facing a higher complexity in internal organisation and external collaborations in order to meet higher societal expectations. Such a process needs time and resources. Inviting new stakeholders into collaborations is also necessary. To do that, the right human resources must be found, in order to understand the needs of these stakeholders and reach a consensus. Only after these steps have been taken will a university be able to adapt its strategy to account for regional needs in order to make a direct impact on society.

Acknowledgements

The author thanks the interviewees and reviewers for their time, interest, and precious insights into the study. The author also thanks the HELIX Competence Centre for providing resources.

References

Abramovsky, L., & Simpson, H. (2011). Geographic proximity and firm–university innovation linkages: evidence from Great Britain. **Journal of Economic Geography**, 11, 949-977.

Audretsch, D. B. (2014). From the entrepreneurial university to the university for the entrepreneurial society. **The Journal of Technology Transfer**, 39, 313-321.

Björk, F., Hansson, J., Lundborg, D., & Olofsson, L. E. (2014). **An Ecosystem for Social Innovation in Sweden: A strategic research and innovation agenda**. Lund: Lund University. Retrieved from: https://www.diva-portal.org/smash/get/diva2:1410376/FULLTEXT01 .pdf.

Bonaccorsi, A., & Piccaluga, A. (1994). A theoretical framework for the evaluation of university — industry relationships. **R&D Management**, 24, 229–247.

Breznitz, S. M., & Feldman, M. P. (2012). The engaged university. **The Journal of Technology Transfer**, 37, 139-157.

Brinkhoff T., (2016). **City Population, Sweden: Östergötland**. Retrieved from: https://www.citypopulation.de/php/sweden-ostergotland.php.

Cadorin, E., Johansson, S. G., & Klofsten, M. (2017). Future developments for science parks: Attracting and developing talent. **Industry and Higher Education**, 31, 157-167.

Camagni, R., & Capello, R. (2013). Regional innovation patterns and the EU regional policy reform: Toward smart innovation policies. **Growth and change**, 44, 355-389.

Cherwitz, R. A, & Hartelius, E. J. (2006). Making a "great 'engaged' university" requires rhetoric. In Burke, J.C. **Fixing the Fragmented University: Decentralization with Direction**, Bolton, MA: Anker Publishing Company, 265–288.

Clark, B. R. (1998). The entrepreneurial university: Demand and response. **Tertiary Education & Management**, 4, 5-16.

CODEX, (2016). **Ownership of research results**. Retrieved from: http://www.codex.vr.se/en/agande1.shtml

Elg M., Ellström P.-E., Kock H., Tillmar M., (2016). **Impact Evaluation Report: HELIX VINN Excellence Centre Year 2006-2015**. Linköping: Linköping University Electronic Press, Retrieved from: https://liu.diva-portal.org/smash/get/diva2:970439/FULLTEXT01.pdf

Enarson, H. L. (1973). University or knowledge factory? **The Chronicle of Higher Education**, 7, 36-52

Etzkowitz, H. (2003). Research groups as "quasi-firms": The invention of the entrepreneurial university. **Research Policy**, 32, 109–121.

Etzkowitz, H., & Klofsten, M. (2005). The innovating region: toward a theory of knowledge based regional development. **R&D Management**, 35, 243–255.

Etzkowitz, H., & Leydesdorff, L. (2000). The dynamics of innovation: from National Systems and 'Mode 2' to a Triple Helix of university – industry – government relations. **Research Policy**, 29, 109–123.

Fayolle, A., & Redford, D. T. (2014). **Handbook on the Entrepreneurial University**. Cheltenham, UK: Edward Elgar

Foray, D. (2015). **Smart Specialisation: Opportunities and Challenges for Regional Innovation Policy**. London: Routledge.

Färnstrand Damsgaard, E. & Thursby, M. (2012). **University Entrepreneurship and Professor Privilege. Swedish Entrepreneurship Forum, Working Paper 2012:21**. Retrieved from: http://entreprenorskapsforum.se/wp-content/uploads/2013/03/WP_21.pdf.

Gibb, A. A., Hofer, A. R., & Klofsten, M. (2013). **The entrepreneurial higher education institution: a review of the concept and its relevance today. heinnovate Concept Paper**. Retrieved from: https://heinnovate.eu/sites/default/files/heinnovate_concept_note_june_2014.pdf

Guerrero, M., Urbano, D., Fayolle, A., Klofsten, M., & Mian, S. (2016). Entrepreneurial universities: emerging models in the new social and economic landscape. **Small Business Economics**, 47, 551–563.

Gunasekara, C. (2006). The generative and developmental roles of universities in regional innovation systems. **Science and Public Policy**, 33, 137-150.

Hartley, M., Saltmarsh, J., & Clayton, P. (2010). Is the civic engagement movement changing higher education? **British Journal of Educational Studies**, 58, 391–406.

HELIX Competence Centre. (2017). **Application for Continuation and Development of the HELIX VINN Excellence Centre at Linköping University**. Retrieved from: https://liu.se/-/media/liu/2016/05/30/helix-competence-centre-application.pdf

Hommen, L., Doloreux, D., & Larsson, E. (2006). Emergence and growth of Mjärdevi Science Park in Linköping, Sweden. **European Planning Studies**, 14, 1331–1361.

Jaffe, A. B., Trajtenberg, M., & Henderson, R. (1993). Geographic localization of knowledge spillovers as evidenced by patent citations. **The Quarterly Journal of Economics**, 108(3), 577-598.

Kalar, B., & Antoncic, B. (2015). The entrepreneurial university, academic activities and technology and knowledge transfer in four European countries. **Technovation**, 36, 1–11.

90

Klofsten, M., & Jones-Evans, D. (1996). Stimulation of technology-based small firms - A case study of university-industry cooperation. **Technovation**, 16, 187–193.

Klofsten, M., Jones-Evans, D., & Schärberg, C. (1999). Growing the Linköping technopole—a longitudinal study of triple helix development in Sweden. **The Journal of Technology Transfer**, 24, 125-138.

Knuthammar, C., & Reksten, E. H. (2013). **LiU - Ungt universitet på väg**.

Laur, I., Klofsten, M., & Bienkowska, D. (2012). Catching Regional Development Dreams: A Study of Cluster Initiatives as Intermediaries. **European Planning Studies**, 20, 1909–1921.

LinkedIn (2017). **Linköpings Universitet Alumni**. Retrieved from: https://www.linkedin.com/school/164742/alumni/

Linköping University, Communications and Marketing Division, (2016). **Always an innovator**. Retrieved from: http://old.liu.se/insidan/kommunikationsstod/info/startsida/1.675008/Fickfakta_LiU_eng_2016_web.pdf

Linköping University Library (2016). **University ranking lists**. Retrieved from: http://www.bibl.liu.se/bibliometri/rankinglistor?l=en&sc=true

Linköping University (2016a). **University Board**. Retrieved from: https://liu.se/en/article/university-board

Linköping University (2016b). **LiU Relation**. Retrieved from: https://liu.se/en/article/liu-relation

Linköping University (2016c). **LiU Innovation**. Retrieved from: https://liu.se/en/article/liu-innovation

Linköping University (2017a). **TEMA - Department of Thematic Studies**. Retrieved from: https://www.tema.liu.se/?l=en

Linköping University (2017b). **International Affairs and Collaborations Division (IFSA)**. Retrieved from: https://liu.se/en/organisation/liu/uf/ifsa

Linköping University (2018a). **Campus Valla**. Retrieved from: https://liu.se/en/article/campus-valla

Linköping University (2018b). **Grönovation**. Retrieved from: https://liu.se/forskning/gronovation

Linköping University (2018c). **About Linköping University**. Retrieved from: https://liu.se/en/about-liu

Linköping Municipality (2017). **Facts about Linköping**. Retrieved from: http://www.linkoping.se/contentassets/374bd965f2414e4788575 60637700f49/facts-about-linkoping---september-2016.pdf

Länsstyrelsen Östergötland County (2017). **Home Page: County Administrative Board**. Retrieved from: http://www.lansstyrelsen.se/ Ostergotland/En/Pages/default.aspx

Lämsä, T. (2010). Leadership Styles and Decision-making in Finnish and Swedish Organizations. **Review of International Comparative Management**, 11, 139–149.

Meyer-Krahmer, F., & Schmoch, U. (1998). Science-based technologies: university–industry interactions in four fields. **Research Policy**, 27, 835–851.

Nilsson, J-E. (2006). Regions with Comprehensive Technical Universities: The Case of Aalborg, Luleå and Oulu. In Nilsson, J-E (ed) **The Role of Universities in Regional Innovation Systems: A Nordic Perspective**. Copenhagen: Copenhagen Business School Press.

Norrköping municipality, (2016). **Municipal facts 2015**. Retrieved from: http://www.norrkoping.se/download/18.3ef6b1d158f1bd46e11 d3ad/1489478837194/Norrkoping-i-siffror-

OECD (2016). **Education at a Glance 2016 - OECD Indicators**. Paris: OECD

Öberg, G. (2009). Facilitating interdisciplinary work: Using quality assessment to create common ground. **Higher Education**, 57, 405–415.

Sachs, J., & Clark, L. (2017). **Learning Through Community Engagement: Vision and Practice in Higher Education**. Singapore: Springer.

Samordningsförbunden i Östergötland. (2018). **Om förbundet**. Retrieved from: https://www.samordning.org/centrala-ostergotland/om-forbundet

Science Park Mjärdevi, (2017). **Networking in Mjärdevi Science Park**. Retrieved from: http://mjardevi.se/network/

Smart Specialisation Platform, (2019). **What is Smart Specialisation?** Retrieved from: https://s3platform.jrs.ec.europa.eu/what-is-smart-specialisation-/

Statistiska centralbyrån, (2017). **Population by region, marital status, age and sex. Year 1968-2016**. Retrieved from: http://www.statistikdatabasen.scb.se/pxweb/en/ssd/START__BE__BE0 101__BE0101A/BefolkningNy/?rxid=810d4445-986f-41a7-890c-aaa231c93bff

Svensson, P., Klofsten, M., & Etzkowitz, H. (2012). An Entrepreneurial University Strategy for Renewing a Declining Industrial City: The Norrköping Way. **European Planning Studies**, 20, 505–525.

UKÄ, (2017). **Regulations that govern Higher Education Institutions**. Retrieved from: http://english.uka.se/facts-about-higher-education/overall-responsibilty-and-regulations/regulations-that-govern-higher-education-institutions.html

Uyarra, E. (2010). Conceptualizing the Regional Roles of Universities, Implications and Contradictions. **European Planning Studies**, 18, 1227–1246.

Vallastaden, (2017). **Organisation**. Retrieved from: https://www.vallastaden2017.se/organisation/

Youtie, J., & Shapira, P. (2008). Building an innovation hub: A case study of the transformation of university roles in regional technological and economic development. **Research Policy**, 37, 1188–1204.

Chapter 4

Balancing Regional Engagement and Internationalisation

The Case of the Autonomous University of Barcelona

Sergio Manrique & Huong Thu Nguyen

Universities have been facing new challenges and changes in their role in society and economy, especially in the last decade. In Catalonia, as in most countries and regions, knowledge production relates more and more to economic competitiveness (Solà, Sàez, & Termes, 2010). New demands on higher education and national research institutions emerge as part of their mission in terms of education, research and, particularly, regional development (Perkmann & Walsh, 2007; Göransson & Brundenius, 2011). This third mission affirms a new role for universities in regional innovation systems (Charles, 2006).

The third mission of universities can be considered through two main systemic concepts: the quadruple helix model of innovation (Arnkil *et al.*, 2010) and regional innovation systems (Cooke *et al.*, 1997). The concept of knowledge-based regional development requires the emergence of certain types of activities, actors and collaborative practices (Kolehmainen *et al.*, 2016), in which universities play a crucial role. On the understanding that such development should not be based on a set of traditional top-down policies but on a complex and multi-actor discovery process, the quadruple helix model is proposed as an extension of the triple helix model (universities, governments and industry). The quadruple helix model encourages the collaboration among universities, governments, industry and a wider community of civil society/citizens/users to enhance product and knowledge transfer (Arnkil *et al.*, 2010). It is a general process where the four mentioned stakeholders engage to meet both economic and societal needs in which universities are the main source of new knowledge. The triple helix (Etzkowitz, 2003) is the core model which encourages the collaborations among university, industry and government for innovation purposes (Carayannis & Campbell, 2012). However, this chapter draws on the concept of the quadruple helix, rather than the above traditional model, to be able to observe the relationship of university with a wider community in society. The role of the university in innovation and regional development is also reflected in the regional innovation systems concept. Regional innovation systems are associated with the '*network of institutions in the public and private sectors*' which acts to improve local conditions for technology and knowledge transfer (Freeman, 1987). In this case, the university is considered as a significant actor, even placed at the heart of the region′s economy (Hudson, 2011). The only requirement to define '*region*' in this concept is that it should have an integrated productive arrangement (techno-economic) and an institutional one (political-legal) (Vilalta *et al.*, 2011).

The increasing interest in the role of universities in innovation and regional development has caused a change in the conception of innovation practices in countries and regions. The appearance of new policies involving research and innovation practices is evidence of the interest from regional and local authorities in involving universities and research institutions in the social and economic development of regions. The European Union (EU) has overseen and promoted regional development of EU Member States through two significant and coexisting policies in the budgetary period 2014-2020. First, Cohesion Policy is the core of EU's strategy for territorial development of regions, especially less favoured regions (European Commission, 2014). Different funds in this policy, such as European Regional Development Fund (ERDF), are used to support projects on research and innovation, as well as on SMEs, environment and public administration, among others, aiming to reduce the gaps among European regions in economic, social and territorial terms (Molle, 2008). Second, Horizon 2020, the EU's research and innovation framework programme, provides funding for objectives such as science excellence, industrial leadership and addressing societal challenges through various research and innovation actions (European Commission, 2017). These two policy frameworks are -albeit to varying extents- tools for economic growth and regional development in Europe, recognising research and innovation as a means to this goal, and positioning higher education institutions as key players. In the case of the region of Catalonia in Spain, for instance, the local government has implemented policies and projects aligned with both Cohesion Policy and Horizon 2020, as part of the Research and Innovation Strategy for Smart Specialisation of Catalonia (RIS3CAT) (Generalitat de Catalunya, 2014). This strategic approach towards research and innovation has made Catalonia an attractive region in terms of talent, scientific environment and industrial R&D (Catalonia Trade & Investment, 2018), in contrast with the negative impact of the economic crisis on research and innovation policies (Izsac *et al.*, 2013; Cruz-Castro *et al.*, 2017)

Universities have roles to play in innovation and regional development; at the same time, it should be noted that in a globalised context, universities are also encouraged to implement strategies to promote their international engagement (Van Damme, 2001). A university's internationalisation may be reflected in international contacts among university staff (Smeby & Trondal, 2005), student mobility through schemes such as ERASMUS in Europe (Teichler, 2009) and English as the main medium of instruction (Jenkins, 2011), among others. It is based on the understanding that internationalisation and quality of education and research are complementary (Association of Catalan Public Universities -ACUP-, 2010). This raises the question of whether there are tensions for a university between its internationalisation orientation and its contribution to its region's innovation and development. This chapter explores this phenomenon through a case study of the Autonomous University of Barcelona (Universitat Autònoma de Barcelona in Catalan), hereafter referred as UAB.

UAB is the third largest Catalan university, based on the number of students, located in Barcelona province, Catalonia, Spain (OECD, 2010). This university has become an important actor for its surrounding region and has taken on a mission to support innovation and regional development. Although a key part of the wider Catalan region and its regional research and innovation policy, UAB also strongly identifies with a more local 'region' defined by the university and its partners. This region includes the central section of the B30/AP7 highway, mainly comprising Vallès Occidental county municipalities, which is relevant for UAB due to proximity and collaboration with municipality councils; in addition to Barcelona city, given the historical link between UAB and the city, which is still observed through university-city collaboration and joint research and education projects. UAB also has a strong view on internationalisation presented in its mission, and can be considered as an internationally-oriented university. As a top ranked institution in Spain, UAB has also developed strong collaborations with firms, public institutions and communities, with the aim of creating welfare

98

and development in society. This chapter primarily explores the role of UAB in innovation and regional development, through a study of its initiatives and capabilities (innovation potential), and its collaborations with other stakeholders, such as firms and public bodies. In addition, potential conflicts between these regional mission and international engagements are discussed[17].

This chapter begins with an overview of UAB and its region. Following this it examines current practices in research and innovation at UAB, followed by a summary of UAB's initiatives with influence on regional development and internationalisation. Finally, UAB's engagement in active and passive terms is discussed, and some main conclusions are presented.

Contextualisation

The University

UAB is a young university which celebrated its 50th year anniversary in 2018. It was established in June 1968 when the conception of the

---

[17] This chapter is mainly based on public information from UAB's official sources (e.g., webpage) together with reports from OECD and the Association of Catalan Public Universities (ACUP), and data provided by UAB Data Management Unit. In addition, from the set of interviews conducted in the framework of RUNIN Project at UAB between November 2017 and February 2018, some key players' declarations have been chosen to either contrast or reflect the findings of this case study. This group includes: The R&D head of a firm UAB intensively collaborates with (Interviewee 1), a principal investigator of UAB's collaborative research projects and former directive of UAB's Research Park (Interviewee 2), a staff member at UAB's Strategic Research Communities (Interviewee 3), the Dean of one of UAB's faculties (Interviewee 4), a management member of Computer Vision Centre (Interviewee 5).
Even though this study approaches the role of UAB in innovation and regional development, the single case study approach limits the generalisability of its findings. As indicated by Drucker and Goldstein (2007), regional (economic) effects of a university towards one region cannot be generalised to other universities or regions. As any other regional innovation system, the Catalan one is complex, and this study does not address all the actors, relations and practices that could lead to different reflections on the subject.

university in Europe was evolving due to the nascent access of women and working-class students to higher education institutions (Serra-Ramoneda, 2008). The political context in Spain at that time was different from the rest of Europe after a civil war and almost thirty years of dictatorship. Apart from a massified university system with a high student-staff ratio, there was also a growing demand for democratic values in its classrooms. In this political turmoil with frequent demonstrations and strikes, it was decided to create two new universities located in Madrid and Barcelona as part of an experiment to develop institutions with flexibility and independence. This is the reason why these two universities were labelled with the name "autonomous". The Autonomous University of Barcelona (UAB) and the Autonomous University of Madrid had the possibility of limited self-governance to respond to the new societal demands. UAB started its activities with a small number of students in improvised and limited facilities. Afterwards, a suitable campus site of about 120 hectares, 20 km away from Barcelona city, was acquired by UAB with the support of Barcelona and Sabadell city councils. The autonomous character of the institution, together with the difficulty of developing a new campus within the town, resulted in a location outside, but with a strong link with, the city of Barcelona. The university campus was built from scratch in the Bellaterra district with the four first faculties: Philosophy and Arts, Medicine, Science and Economics, under a model based on the respect for the basic principles of autonomy, student participation and social commitment (UAB, 2017). With many difficulties these principles were translated into: 1) independence in selecting teaching staff; 2) accessible admission of students; 3) freedom for the university to create its own study plans and; 4) freedom to control the University's capital.

After the end of Franco's dictatorship in Spain in the 1970s, UAB created other faculties in different disciplines, and its research activities grew, thanks to collaboration with the Spanish National

Research Council (CSIC) and the Government of Catalonia, among other funding bodies (UAB, 2017). In the 1990s, cultural and social life became stronger in the UAB campus with the inauguration of Vila Universitària as a student village in 1992 and a number of services in Plaça Civica (the University's main square) in 1996. Vila Universitària, with capacity for more than 2,100 people, is a residential complex located in the campus, surrounded by forest and well-connected with Barcelona City. UAB is among the few universities in Spain having the luxury of owning such a complete campus that includes major green areas, sports facilities and students' residences, adjacent to faculties, research centres, firms and funding bodies in the same geographical scope (UAB sphere). The 1990s also brought an increase in social responsibility actions and programmes, as evidence of UAB commitment towards society and surrounding communities. After 2000, UAB started developing important activities for knowledge transfer to the productive sector, which led to the creation of the UAB Research Park (Parc de Recerca) in 2007. The most recent decade brought new challenges for UAB in terms of significant growth combined with an economic recession which also affected public universities' finances. However, UAB has maintained its position as a leading university with the achievement of Campus of International Excellence[18] status in 2009 aiming to promote knowledge and innovation. Recently, the university became one of the first European universities offering massive open online courses (MOOCs), considered as an innovative form of teaching. Alongside celebrating the 50th anniversary, the UAB has been classified as a leading university in Spain, obtaining

---

[18] The Campus of International Excellence is a Spanish government initiative led by the Ministry of Science, Innovation and Universities, which aims at aggregating, specialising, differentiating and internationalising higher education institutions in Spain in order to promote common and transversal projects at the institution level for enhancing teaching and research quality. More information at https://www.uab.cat/web/research/itineraries/relation-with-surrounding-areas/uab-cie-campus-of-international-excellence-1345671803142.html.

a maximum score in 26 of the 33 indicators based on the European Commission's U-Multirank. Furthermore, it has been classified as ninth in the world in the QS Top 50 Under 50 Ranking.

The UAB Campus of International Excellence (CIE) project includes the UAB core (departments, research groups and scientific facilities), the research and technology facilities (research institutions and centres, new technology-based firms -NTBFs-) and other local actors (firms, local authorities and neighbouring organisations). It is not only the academic community (students, teachers, researchers and other staff) which attends daily at the UAB campus, but also many industry-related and government-related staff work within university facilities. However, UAB has a large academic community which comprises more than 3,500 professors and researchers who work within 55 academic departments, organised in 14 faculties and schools, 2,348 administrative employees and 37,077 students (including bachelor, master and doctoral levels) in the 2015-2016 academic year. In addition, UAB also attracts around 1,000 visiting researchers and professors annually. The university hosts several education and research centres and institutions, research clusters, as well as firms (spin-offs, start-ups, NTBFs and affiliated and derived companies). A key environment for this wider set of actors is the UAB Research Park, headquartered on the campus, which aims to *"promote and enhance the technology and knowledge transfer activities of its members, encourage entrepreneurship through the creation of new businesses based on research and generally facilitate interaction between research, business and society"* (Parc de Recerca, 2017). Its activities encompass several topics, especially in new technology-based disciplines such as biomedicine, climate change and communications. UAB also hosts foundations such as the Solidarity Autonomous Foundation (FAS), Association of UAB Friends and UAB Foundation, which are in charge of the projects and programmes that the university designs and implements for citizens and the community as part of its social responsibility task.

The Region

UAB's main campus is located at Bellaterra district, in Cerdanyola del Vallès city, part of Vallès Occidental (Western Valley) County, where several municipalities comprise the B30 area. The county is part of the Metropolitan Region of Barcelona in Catalonia. Catalonia is considered as the driving economic force in Spain and makes up 20% of GDP, 25.5% of industrial activity and 17.5% of trade operation (B30 Association, 2017). The Catalan Government has a special interest in engaging universities as part of a strategy to improve the competitiveness of the economy, especially demonstrated by a strategic agreement signed by the Government of Catalonia (Generalitat de Catalunya) in 2008. In this agreement, several actions related to the university sector were indicated such as promoting excellence and internationalisation in education, matching study programmes with the needs of the labour market and strengthening the relations between university and industry (OECD, 2010). Catalonia received 56% of Spain's foreign research spending between 2010 and 2014 (Manresa, 2015) and continued increasing R&D expenditures even during the economic crisis (Biocat, 2010). It strongly contrasted with the diminished budget for R&D and innovation from the national government (Maqueda & Urra, 2017), which has placed Spain as one of the EU nations with the lowest public investment in R&D.

Catalonia's orientation and strength in research and innovation are also evidenced in the existence of 12 universities, as well as 85 research and technology centres and 22 science and technology parks (Generalitat de Catalunya, 2018), some of them located at UAB campus. Nevertheless, the region has dealt with a diminished support from the national government, whose budget allocated to R&D and innovation has decreased more than 40% in the last

103

decade, causing an 'exodus' of researchers from Spain in recent years (Pain, 2012). This occurred partially because of the economic crisis, but also due to some degree of neglect shown by central government (Maqueda, 2018). This is reflected in a 2017 R&D budget, in which a significant part was meant to be used in R&D credits and loans rather than in direct investments and grants, a situation which Spanish universities and research centres were not able to handle; it led to spending not quite 38% of the available R&D budget for this year. However, the diminished and unexploited R&D national support has not impeded UAB's development.

Figure 4.1 - Maps of Barcelona and B30 Area (UAB, 2017)

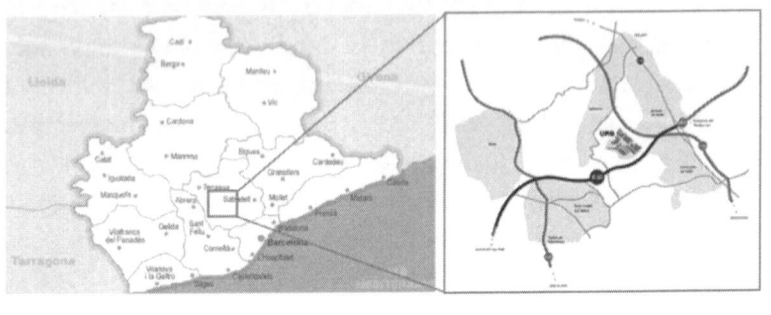

The university considers itself as a part of the B30 area (see Figure 4.1) which includes 23 local councils around the AP-7 and C-58 motorways which formed an association in October 2012. The municipalities on this stretch of route make up the leading industrial agglomeration in Catalonia particularly and in Spain generally (Solà, Sàez, & Termes, 2010). 14 out of those 23 municipalities belong to Vallès Occidental County. The B30 area covers a 50km route, a surface area of 485km^2 with a population of 1,018,166, a total of 30,173 companies and 387,478 jobs on 195 industrial estates. The B30 area is a project promoted in accordance with Catalan economic and industrial policies such as the Research and Innovation Strategy for the Smart Specialisation of Catalonia (RIS3CAT) over the 2014-

2020 period and the Industrial Policy Plan of Catalonia for the 2010-2020 period. The B30 plan aims to identify the potential of the area and to implement a joint strategy among companies, research centres, universities, local councils, business organisations, trade unions and governing organisations for the industrial and technological development of the region. The representatives of these various bodies work together to promote the B30 as the strongest area for innovation in Catalonia, and possibly one of the best areas in Southern Europe on this regard. In addition to the B30 area, due to the historical background of the university as mentioned above, Barcelona city, the capital of Barcelona province as well as of Catalonia region, is claimed as the home of UAB. In this case study, the impact of UAB in regional development is mainly explored in the context of both B30 and Barcelona city.

Current Practices in Research and Innovation

In order to understand the consistency between the university's goals towards innovation and the development of the region, one needs to examine the formally stated mission as well as the actions in practice. In alignment with the advocacy from the Association of Catalan Public Universities (ACUP), UAB has a strong focus on internationalisation with three central lines of action: 1) mobility, 2) collaboration and cooperation and 3) attraction of talent (UAB, 2017). Besides Catalan and Spanish as official institutional languages, UAB also works on the plan to make English as an additional formal language in university activities. Internationalisation is one of the means to achieve the objectives of offering high quality education, research and knowledge transfer (UAB, 2017). At the same time, UAB considers itself as an entity 'fully integrated' in the region. The university indicates its commitment in terms of regional partnerships and civic society, in which its participation in the B30 hub is a relevant example. Ultimately, UAB aims to be one of Europe's leading universities while developing the capacity for impacts on regional innovation. Between 2010 and 2017, UAB signed 315 contracts or agreements with other higher education institutions and research centres in Spain and around the world, which represent over 10% of the total number of contracts signed between UAB and other organisations. They include research and education collaborations, as well as contract research and provision of services.

Do those missions and actions appear paradoxical as indications of the significant role of a university in regional development? Not necessarily. In fact, there are two trends recognised concerning the role of universities in regional development processes. Some universities indicate their role in improving regional competitiveness through accessible and valuable education and research, while many universities purely pursue international (or global) approaches to education and research and hence possibly ignore the region in which they are located (Kolehmainen, et al., 2016). Goddard and Vallance (2013, p. 47) argued that the regional and international strategies are not necessarily contradictory. Universities with an international orientation can also have great impacts on economic development regionally since strong international collaborations serve as the basis to enhance innovation and knowledge transfer in a variety of fields, with subsequent effects on the wider economy (Goddard & Vallance, 2013, p. 47). In terms of human capital, an international orientation allows the achievement of international standards which have both international and local value. For instance, scientific production with international quality by researchers could also serve technology transfer and consultancy at regional level.

In the European context, international collaborations (in fields such as training, research and technology transfer) are usually welcomed by regions since such networks of excellence help to connect regional systems, and hence, have positive impacts on regional development (Charles, 2006, p. 128). In 2009, Barcelona City Council signed an agreement expressing its desire in collaborating with UAB and supporting the university's strategic plan for attracting researchers and entrepreneurs from different countries. This action aimed to promote the position of both UAB and Barcelona Metropolitan Area internationally (UAB, 2019). The action showed the joint approach to international competition for Barcelona and UAB. Barcelona City's international presence as a wealthy capital is considered as a *'calling card'* for UAB's international cooperation, while university campus development assists the city in attracting knowledge-intensive organisations and employees (Benneworth *et al.*, 2010). In fact, UAB has proven itself to be a university with a commitment to innovation and regional development through knowledge exchange with industry, society and public sector (government), as will be examined in the next section.

Research Activities

When examining its research activities, UAB is clearly a research-oriented university, in which the maintenance and creation of knowledge are core practices. UAB produced the second largest number of PhD theses in Catalonia (Association of Catalan Public Universities ACUP, 2016). The level of scientific production (articles, reviews, editorial materials and proceedings papers, among others) at UAB in the last 10 years has shown an increasing trend, in parallel with the university growth. Figure 4.2 shows the positive tendency of research production, especially evident after 2010, when the effects of the Research Park creation and Campus of International Excellence development started manifesting themselves, in addition to specific efforts from university and faculty directives to enhance research activities. This represented a 50% increase in scientific production between 2011 and 2012.

Figure 4.1 - Scientific Production Evolution of UAB (publications per year) 2006-2015

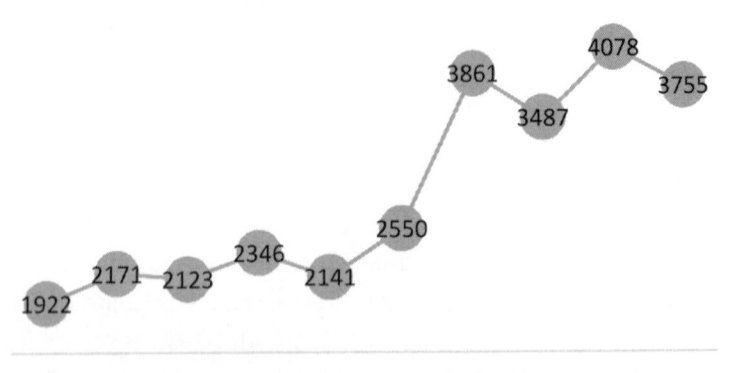

2006   2007   2008   2009   2010   2011   2012   2013   2014   2015

2014 has been the year with the greatest scientific production with 4,078 publications, doubling the number of the first years of the analysed period. From the 3,755 journal papers produced by UAB researchers in 2015, 54% were published in the first quartile and 22% in the second quartile of journal rankings, showing the high quality of research conducted at UAB, which has not only evolved in the scientific production size, but also in the research value and authors' assertiveness. The high-quality dominance in UAB scientific production has been a common factor during the last decade. UAB has been ranked among the best Spanish universities in different rankings related to research activity: second in Scimago Institution Rankings World Report 2014 for volume and impact of scientific activity, second in the Leiden Ranking 2016 for volume of papers, second in the ISSUE Rankings 2017 for research productivity, and has twelve scientific disciplines among the best 100 in the world in QS WUR by Subject 2017 (UAB, 2017).

The publication-based performance system put in practice by UAB as in many other universities can however generate tension between research activity, external collaboration and entrepreneurial

108

activities of researchers, not only due to the university policy itself, but also due to the discrepancies in terms of goals and time frameworks between academia and industry. Nevertheless, UAB has been able to develop strong relations with other organisations, as shown below.

Collaboration Practices

UAB has a wide range of formal agreements and contracts with different stakeholders. The records of the number of contracts signed between UAB and other collaborating organisations since 1983 (UAB Data Management Unit) can be observed in Figure 4.3.

Figure 4.2 - UAB Agreements Evolution 1983-2017

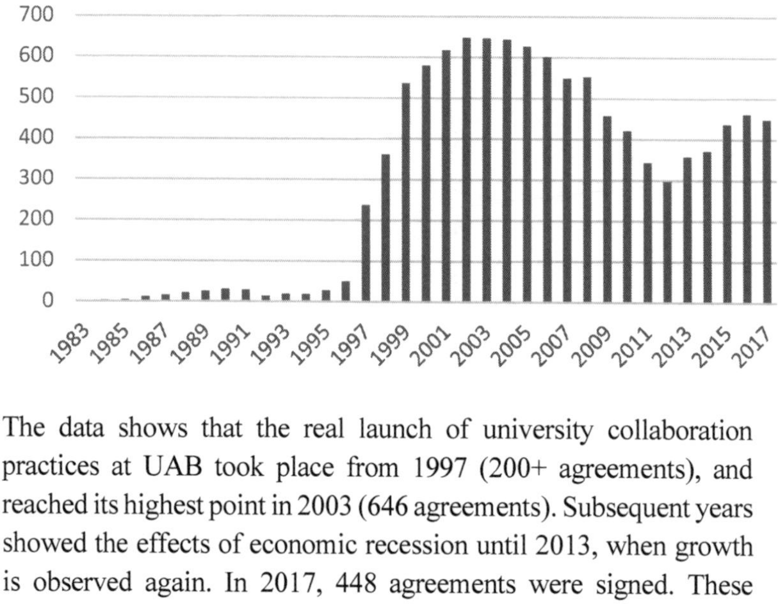

The data shows that the real launch of university collaboration practices at UAB took place from 1997 (200+ agreements), and reached its highest point in 2003 (646 agreements). Subsequent years showed the effects of economic recession until 2013, when growth is observed again. In 2017, 448 agreements were signed. These signed agreements include research and education projects, public innovation programmes, patent developments, university services provision and grants/subsidies, among others, either in the framework of university-firm collaboration (Valmaseda-Andia *et*

al., 2015), or in other collaborations taking place with other region stakeholders such as communities and public institutions.

Analysing the distribution of agreements by country during the period 2010-2017 (Figure 4.4), over 17% of UAB agreements between 2010 and 2017 took place with foreign organisations, representing UAB's internationalisation goals. The list of countries from which firms and institutions collaborate with UAB is led by the USA, followed by France and Belgium.

However, Spanish institutions and firms represent 83% of the total, as most agreements take place locally and nationally, reflecting UAB's desire to collaborate within its surrounding region. In fact, the UAB Campus of International excellence is *"known for creating highly fruitful relations between neighbouring municipalities"* (UAB, 2017). Many of these relations are seen clearly in areas in which synergies have been created among businesses, departments, institutes and research centres, through the development of training programmes, services, cultural and sports facilities, enhancing the attraction of talent and creating added value for neighbouring regions. One of the firms that UAB mostly collaborates with decided to set up an R&D facility at the UAB campus and has signed more than 20 research contracts with a budget exceeding € 6 million over the last decade. In an interview, the head of the R&D unit of this company's subsidiary in Spain (Interviewee 1) summarised their decision to locate at and collaborate with UAB in three main points: 1) tax advantages in the region, 2) openness and good will from the university to collaborate with companies, and 3) research expertise from UAB in the company's scientific field; however, this person also recognises that there are difficulties related to differences in work rhythm or speed between academia and industry. Additionally, a UAB professor who has played the role of principal investigator in the numerous research contracts with this and other companies (Interviewee 2) pointed out that collaborating with firms was neither common nor easy at UAB ten years ago, but the institution evolved towards a closer relationship with industry and became one of the pioneers in collaborative research projects in the region; this professor also recognises the importance of research and innovation projects with the participation of university for regional development, but admits that UAB's impact on regional development through research and innovation is not very clear yet.

Figure 4.3 – Top 15 Country Distribution of UAB Agreements 2010-2017 (excluding Spain)

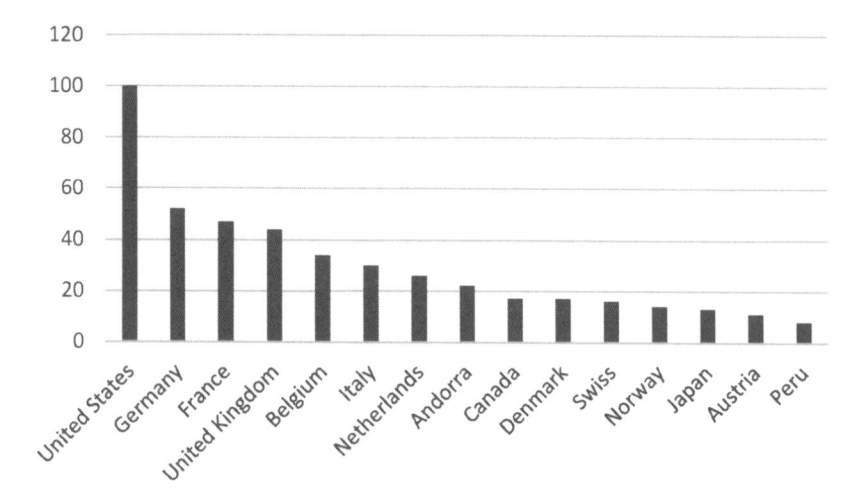

University Initiatives

UAB has developed several projects and programmes in alliance with other regional players including local governments, firms and other higher educations and research institutions. Through these initiatives, UAB has been able to generate a positive impact on the region.

Strategic Research Communities (COREs)

In response to the needs of spreading its research and innovation activities into society, since 2014 UAB has established three Strategic Research Communities (Comunitats de Recerca Estratègica - COREs) in different areas: CORE Smart and Sustainable Cities, CORE Cultural Heritage and CORE Mental Health, which are among topics encouraged by the European Union. These three research communities participate in several initiatives of innovation and regional development in collaboration with other regional players, normally led by UAB. COREs are the means by which UAB shapes research strategic activities and brings together researchers from different disciplines to work on current societal challenges. These are basically networks formed by different research centres and groups from the UAB campus (UAB, 2018).

The smart and sustainable cities network conducts research on sustainable management and urban environments with interest in a wide range of issues, including economical and sociological aspects of industrial ecological design and public urban design policies, among others. The network on cultural heritage works in research, dissemination, preservation and management activities in that field. The mental health network seeks to face a major public health challenge, including not only mental illnesses but also societal happiness and wellness, through advanced knowledge, innovative solutions and work with and for society. COREs are considered as efforts of UAB in balancing internationalisation and regional engagement, as they address societal challenges of regional interest through the application of highly talented international research teams, that is, internationally competitive research activities on fields with practical impacts on the economic growth and development of regions. COREs also help researchers in applying for international projects and funds, especially where involving different regional stakeholders is a requirement of such calls, as explained by a CORE staff member (Interviewee 3).

Creating Social Impact by Immigrants Education

The **Ítaca Campus** involves the participation of UAB, Cerdanyola del Valles' (UAB's home town) city council, the Institute of Education Sciences (ICE), Santander group and Solidarity Autonomous Foundation (Fundació Autònoma Solidaria - FAS). This social-educational programme has been promoted by UAB since September 2004, under the management of the ICE and town council with the financial support of Santander group (UAB *et al.*, 2017). Since 2015, FAS took over responsibility to organise the programme. It offers a summer school of 3-4 weeks to local 15-year-old students and primarily aims at non-EU migrants. The training activities take place under the tutorship of university lecturing and research staff from different faculties and affiliated centres appointed under a public selection process.

There has been a noticeable flow of immigrants to the region in recent years. The Ítaca Campus was established to respond to the issue of low levels of education participation among immigrants. The purposes of the programme are to provide an overview about university life and to encourage students to move into higher education. The programme also offers the opportunity for students with diverse social background to understand each other while encouraging the use of Catalan as an operational language (OECD, 2010). The pilot plan in 2004 had the involvement of 40 students, but the number of students joining the programme keeps growing. In the thirteenth call of the Ítaca Campus in 2016, there were 60 participants more than the previous year, which made a total of 388 students. Up to now, a total of 33 town councils from seven counties in Barcelona province have participated in the programme (UAB *et al.*, 2017). The typology and structure of the activities are flexibly designed and modified, based on the feedback from monitors,

113

students and staff. The universities and centres which would like to join in the tutorship need to pass the public selection process; this rule makes the programme more competitive and helps to improve its quality. However, while the programme has an increasing involvement of students, it is still rather small in scale and should be extended aiming to a greater variety of participants. Ítaca Campus project contributes to the internationalisation goals of UAB in terms of training and attraction of talent. Additionally, trained immigrants are intended to become change agents and contribute positively to the development of the region.

Training Change Agents for Sustainable Development

Digital and Green Skills Vallès (UAB, 2017), a programme initiated in early 2017, comprises part of the Smart and Sustainable Cities CORE. Undertaken by UAB, Vallès Occidental County Council and Eurecat (Technology Centre of Catalonia), this initiative combines training and employment for young people with the promotion of innovative and sustainable economies. The first phase of the programme is aimed at young professionals who are keen to participate in open innovation and co-creation projects motivated by social and economic transformation. Subsidised by the Catalonian government and the European Social Fund (ESF), this project seeks to: 1) develop and disseminate digital and green competences among academics, practitioners, citizens and firms, 2) allow citizens to access digital and sustainable transformation by mobilising social agents, 3) develop new employment opportunities in unexplored fields, 4) incorporate current and future tendencies of technology and sustainability in new professionals' profile, and 5) help these professionals become change agents for developing a new economic and social framework (UAB, Vallès Occidental County Council, & Eurecat, 2017).

This initiative is carried out and funded by the Department of Telecommunications and Systems Engineering, which shares

114

training tasks with Eurecat and other UAB research groups. The programme includes training for potential change agents in technology and green skills (e.g. digital manufacturing, big data, programming), personal and methodological competences (e.g. teamwork, communication, analysis) and entrepreneurship (e.g. leadership, innovation, business models), to be delivered through talks, workshops and visits to firms. Afterwards, participants are introduced into a network for identifying new opportunities through a platform of open innovation and co-creation. In the end, the programme expects several proposals and pilot experiences to be included in a catalogue, open to firms, which should help participants to improve their profiles and to develop new employment opportunities. This programme firstly promotes the circular economy based on open innovation as a way of economic development (Ghisellini *et al.*, 2016) in the region of Catalonia. It also creates employment opportunities and green/sustainable business ideas to be developed, and both region and university can gain competitiveness with this collaboration. The 25 selected participants (out of more than 100 eligible interested applicants), internationally competitive professionals coming from different municipalities of Vallès Occidental county, are expected to generate proposals and pilot projects in areas such as 3D printing, internet and product eco-design, among others, with a social impact on the county and a contribution to the improvement of its citizens' life quality.

Discussion on University Engagement

There is no doubt that the presence of UAB in the B30 area and Barcelona city does have impacts on innovation and the development of the region. The role of UAB may be distinguished as a passive role and active role. The passive role refers to the pure economic benefits that UAB brings as a large university in the region, while the active role reveals the university's impacts on innovation and regional development. Within the framework of this

115

chapter, the active role is focused on since it discloses more clearly the strategy that the university is pursuing. However, the passive role is briefly discussed to reinforce the importance of UAB in the region. Generally, compared with centralised university systems in some other countries in Europe, the large and decentralised structure of UAB can create a time-consuming and cumbersome decision-making process with the involvement of several stakeholders. However, the decentralised structure is increasingly connected to university´s ability to respond to societal needs (OECD, 2010). The engagement of external stakeholders in such organisational structure normally assists in establishing the links with other sectors.

Organisations with a decentralised structure tend to have a more end-user orientation (Lee *et al.*, 1995). In the case of UAB, it meets the needs of students and researchers (traditional mission), as well as firms and citizens in general (third mission), in a more effective way. However, the degree of independence given to departments and researchers in a decentralised structure might affect the institutional framework in which, for instance, university-firm interaction takes place. As evidence of this issue, the R&D head of one of UAB's collaborating companies expressed: *"here we don't have institutional level cooperation... so the administration department just takes our money and the professors who of course get some money as well they take care of the project steering..."* (Interviewee 1). It shows that a decentralised university can generate flexibility and effectiveness while diminishing the perceived institutional presence in research collaborations. Beyond that, and as conceived by Debackere and Veugelers (2005), UAB shows *"how decentralized organizational approaches and incentives that stimulate the active involvement of the research groups in the exploitation of their research findings might be combined with specialized central services offering intellectual property management and spin-off support"*. UAB does this by stimulating involvement of research groups through COREs and offering

116

intellectual property and spin-off support through its Research Park, achieving impressive results, at least in terms of 50% scientific production increase in 2 years right after the establishment of its research park.

Regardless of the existence of numerous contracts and agreements that make evident the presence of university collaboration with other stakeholders, there is no empirical evidence about the impact of this interaction on the performance of firms and on the social development of B30 area and Barcelona city, due to lack of tracking and assessment.

Passive role

UAB is an important element of the economy of the B30 area and Barcelona city, especially at a time when the region aims to become an innovation and knowledge-based economy, in alignment with the Catalonian strategy (Marinelli *et al.*, 2016). The economic impacts can be evaluated in three forms: university employment and expenditure in regional economy; the positive impacts of student and academic populations on the living and working environment of region; and the human capital effects by providing graduate workers in regional labour markets (Goddard & Vallance, 2013, p. 23).

UAB's employment and expenditure has positive impacts on the economy of the region. As mentioned previously, UAB is one of the largest employers in the region, with up to 6,000 employees. Furthermore, with a yearly budget of almost 312 million euros, the university enhances the regional economy through its spending on facilities and infrastructure. The large number of UAB students, staff and visiting researchers also has an impact the economic development of the region through the consumption of a variety of goods and services. The second impact is less tangible where many students and academic staff in the region may also have positive economic impacts by helping to create an attractive working and living environment. The presence in the region of large numbers of highly educated people contributing to local cultural and social life supports the local cultural milieu and intellectual and political debate (Bender, 1998; Burnett, 1998, Chatterton, 2000). The final role of the university noticed in this section is in providing knowledgeable and skilful human capital for the regional labour market with a large number of graduates. Studies suggest that the graduates' presence in the region positively links to levels of regional innovation (Faggian & McCann, 2006). UAB provides approximately 7,000 graduates per year which is 20% of the total graduate output in Catalonia (UAB, 2017).

Active role

UAB has strong impacts on innovation and the development of the region through its intensive knowledge spillovers and technology transfer. Although some studies have argued that the effects of knowledge spillovers and technology transfer have been overemphasised in regional development, these two elements remain as primary direct forms of engagement of universities with their regions (Goddard & Vallance, 2013, p. 35). Given the large size of UAB compared with other universities in Catalonia, and its research intensity, the university has a significant share of research projects, R&D contracts and services. In addition, UAB has also built important science/research centres (e.g. Parc de Recerca, Computer Vision Centre -CVC-), and several programmes to promote new business (e.g. spin-offs) and intellectual property (e.g. patents). UAB takes part in several innovation projects through these research centres. Since 2011, UAB has joined the Library Living Lab of Volpelleres, located at UAB's neighbour town Sant Cugat, which is coordinated by the CVC. This Library Living Lab brings a new structure for doing innovation (under the living lab concept) in a traditional institute, such as a library, and *"has been contributing on the change in the whole network of 250 libraries of Barcelona into*

118

innovation hub" (Interviewee 5). These university investments in R&D do not only provide UAB with research and economic incentives, but also assist in accomplishing its role as a significant element in regional knowledge-based economy. In respect to this area, it is worth noticing that UAB actively self-financed the development of its own centres (OECD, 2010, p. 127). UAB signed 3,133 contracts with different organisations between 2010 and 2017, with an average budget of nearly €10 million annually. More than 40% of these agreements were signed with organisations located either in Cerdanyola del Vallès (municipality where UAB is located) or in Barcelona city.

With the advantage of having a research park in the campus, the university actively assists in small and medium companies in improving their innovation. As pointed out by one of UAB's faculty Deans, the university shows good will towards collaboration with SMEs: *"Our economic environment is plenty of SMEs, small and medium enterprises, so we want to approach them ... They are very low in research, and sometimes also innovation, and from the university, we can help them"* (Interviewee 4). The university not only provides knowledge through courses with the collaboration of public sector, but also offers some activities to those companies such as energy harvesting, or product testing in the UAB campus. In the meanwhile, UAB understands that connecting strongly with industry also helps the university in recognising industry needs and orienting university research (Interviewee 4). This connection with firms is partially achieved through public-private R&D partnerships, where the public element is represented by universities and the private element is represented by firms, as is the case of collaboration between UAB and Henkel, a company from the chemicals industry (Manrique, 2018). In this sense, a principal investigator recognises that *"collaborative research provides a direct pathway from basic research to innovation"* and points out other positive effects such as researchers' training based on industrial needs and the creation of an

119

environment with a high scientific level (Interviewee 2). In the UAB-Henkel partnership, several patents have been developed, and some of them have reached commercialisation. Additionally, the company has improved its innovation capabilities in terms of human resources and research management, while UAB has got its researchers to work towards applicable and marketable research outputs.

Although the human capital effect has been mentioned as part of the passive role of UAB in innovation and regional development, there are several good active practices carried out by UAB in this area. The university succeeds in reaching outside its campus by having active contributions in solving several public concerns in the region. UAB contributes to reducing unemployment and encouraging entrepreneurship in the region by organising courses with the Catalonia entrepreneurship and public employment service (SOC). These courses provide training to citizens generally or employees of companies in both technological aspects and business planning aiming for a sustainable economy. The university also works with several big high-tech companies in talent promotion such as a hackathon with SAP where students learn about technology and design thinking, and afterwards, are required to present solutions to given problems to a wider audience. With the same purpose, different Hackathon events have been hosted by UAB School of Engineering from locally to globally, namely Wikimedia Hackathon (2018, global event) and UAB The Hacks! Blockchain? (2018, local event), among others. In addition, the university invests efforts in improving equality from a gender perspective, in research and academia generally, and in information and communications technology (ICT) specifically. Its third Equality plan (Action Plan for Equality between women and men at the UAB) emphasised that among different disciplines, women makes up only 14.9% of technology students (Observatory for Equality UAB, 2017). It is consistent with the concern from Barcelona City Council that the lack of women in ICT might lead to inequalities and gaps in any strategy that makes use of technology as an instrument of social, economic or political promotion. Only two out of six universities in Barcelona city pointed out this problem together with the proposed plan (Barcelona City Council, 2018).

In 2014, the Smart Campus initiative of UAB in Bellaterra Campus, coordinated by CORE Smart Cities officially became part of the European Network of Living Labs (ENoLL). The Smart Campus initiative considers UAB as a 'city' and combines technology relating to smart cities with some social innovations. For example, together with developing some solutions for car parking and mobility issues, UAB also encourages students and its employees in using car sharing as an action towards sustainability. UAB campus is however not inside a city which is considered as a disadvantage for the university in interacting with citizens. However, UAB has tried to address such issues through several initiatives aimed at promoting innovation projects with the engagement of different stakeholders: *"We try to make this point of contact among research, citizens, innovation, administration and enterprises. This point of contact is called the UAB Lab"* (Interviewee 3). UAB Lab pilot projects were implemented in early 2018 in collaboration with the Government of Catalonia. It aims to set up 'fab living labs'[19] in its main campus as a space for innovation and experimentation of new technologies and methodologies, opened to not only students but also citizens in the region. UAB fab living labs are expected to better connect the Quadruple Helix, different stakeholders, in the region for innovation purposes. These examples successfully illustrate the active role of UAB in integrating their education and research missions with the priorities of the region. This initiative concurs with

---

[19] More information about Fab Living Labs initiative by UAB at https://www.uab.cat/web/sala-de-prensa/detalle-noticia-1345667994339.html?noticiaid=1345742714552 and https://www.uab.cat/web/investigar/cores-uab/les-cores-uab/els-uab-labs-1345742539391.html

Charles (2006, p. 128), who points out that the university's special contribution is the "*breadth and potential in joined-up governance*" and should be observed through the ability to connect the research priorities with public concerns, and to include cultural activities.

UAB is increasingly considered as a key stakeholder in the negotiating and decision-making processes for innovation and regional development, as the B30 area consistently pursues the strategy of linking local actors for innovation and its development. UAB has actively participated in activities to exchange knowledge with firms, society and the public sector (Urbano & Guerrero, 2016).

Engagement in innovation and regional development supports UAB in earning European funding to promote its international position. Strongly collaborating with stakeholders in surrounding area is currently encouraged by European Commission when providing ERDF and some Horizon 2020 funds. In the UAB case, it concurs with Goddard and Vallance's (2013) ideas that universities with international vision can also generate great regional impacts.

Conclusion

In general, the main goals of a university can be defined as: maintaining the knowledge of mankind, generating new knowledge (research), transferring knowledge to the next generations (education) and to society (dissemination), and generating economic development (Holten-Andersen, 2015). There is no doubt about the positive role of UAB in terms of education and research both internationally and regionally. This chapter identifies notable achievements and an enormous potential of UAB for regional innovation and socioeconomic development. The university has advanced in developing its third mission and engaging with its region. UAB has also proved itself as a key stakeholder in connecting private and public sectors with several initiatives recently putting society/citizens in the centre of innovation and regional development. However, there are further improvements that could be made by UAB to reinforce its regional engagement. The design of policy in partnership with regional governance institutions, through projects and programmes, contributes necessary elements to promote and put in practice innovation and economic growth: however, the implementation and follow-up of these actions can be improved, as one can observe a set of unchained individual efforts without evidence of cohesion (coordination and coherence) among actors and practices.

Firms in the region of Catalonia in general lack the culture or ideas to collaborate with universities (Solà, Sàez, & Termes, 2010). Many firms may perceive that collaboration with other stakeholders (e.g. the university) is costly with long-term investment required while the outputs of those collaborations are not identified clearly (Segarra-Blasco & Arauzo-Carod, 2008, p. 1283). Hence, it is important to effectively manage the interface (e.g. through cluster associations), and at the same time, develop an evaluation framework based on some good practices in the region to encourage the collaborations. It is noted that university funding is partly associated with its impact on society. However, from the university's perspective, there is a challenge in developing the ability of fully engaging in such collaborations. This is due to the fact that the need for publication from the university normally does not go along with the priorities and goals of industry or the community (Miller *et al.*, 2016, p. 393). Further investigation on how to fit the university mission of regional development, including reciprocal benefits, should be carried out. Additionally, this case study is framed within the region of Catalonia and more specifically within the B30 area, without deepening on the national perspective, which however has recently experienced problems regarding R&D investments (Catanzaro, 2018).

Acknowledgements

We wish to express our gratitude to professors David Charles (Northumbria University, UK), Pilar Marquès Gou (University of Girona, Spain) and Emili Grifell-Tatjé (UAB, Spain) for their advice and guidance on this case study elaboration. Data on research and collaboration activities was provided by UAB Data Exploitation Office – Data Management Unit.

References

Arnkil, R., Järvensivu, A., Koski, P., & Piirainen, T. (2010). **Exploring the quadruple helix. Report of quadruple helix research for the CLIQ project**. Tampere: Work Research Centre, University of Tampere.

Association of Catalan Public Universities (ACUP) (2010). **Internationalisation plan of the Catalan public universities 2010-2015**. Barcelona: Nexe Impressions SL.

Association of Catalan Public Universities (ACUP) (2016). **Universities in Catalonia: The area of university excellence in Southern Europe**. Barcelona: ACUP.

B30 Association. (2017). **B30 Website**. Retrieved from http://www.b30i.cat/B30/p/B30Area_cat.asp

Barcelona City Council. (2018). **The ecosystem of ICT from the gender perspective in Barcelona**. Retrieved from https://bcnroc.ajuntament.barcelona.cat/jspui/bitstream/11703/111008/1/MAQEcosistemaTic_Barcelona_Cat.pdf

Bender, T. (1998). Scholarship, local life, and the necessity of worldliness. In Van der Wursten, H. (ed) **The urban university and its identity,** pp. 17-28. Dordrecht: Springer.

Benneworth, P., Charles, D., & Madanipour, A. (2010). Building Localized Interactions between Universities and Cities through University Spatial Development. **European Planning Studies**, 18, 1611-1629.

Biocat. (2010, January 5th). R&D investment in Catalonia up 8.8% despite economic crisis. **Biocat**. Retrieved from http://www.biocat.cat/en/news/rd-investment-catalonia-88-despite-economic-crisis

Burnett A. (1998) The University and the City Council. In: van der Wusten H. (eds) **The Urban University and its Identity**, pp 167-186. Dordrecht: Springer.

Carayannis, E. G., & Campbell, D. F. J. (2012). **Mode 3 Knowledge Production in Quadruple Helix Innovation Systems: 21st-Century Democracy, Innovation, and Entrepreneurship for Development**. Dordrecht: Springer Briefs in Business.

Catalonia Trade & Investment. (2018). **Reap the benefits of research and innovation being a strategic priority for Catalonia**. Retrieved from http://catalonia.com/innovate-in-catalonia/rd-in-catalonia/rd-in-catalonia.jsp

Catanzaro, M. (2018). Spain's biggest-ever science petition decries 'abandonment' of research. **Nature**, 556(285).

Charles, D. (2006). Universities as key knowledge infrastructures in regional innovation systems. **Innovation. The European journal of social science research**, 19, 117-130.

Chatterton, P. (2000). The cultural role of universities in the community: Revisiting the university—community debate. **Environment and planning A**, 32, 165-181.

Cooke, P., Uranga, M., & Etxebarria, G. (1997). Regional innovation systems: institutional and organizational dimensions. **Research Policy**, 26, 475-491.

Cruz-Castro, L., Holl, A., Rama, R., & Sanz-Menéndez, L. (2017). Economic crisis and company R&D in Spain: do regional and policy factors matter? **Industry and Innovation**, 25, 729-751.

Debackere, K., & Veugelers, R. (2005). The role of academic technology transfer organizations in improving industry science links. **Research Policy**, 4, 321-342.

Drucker, J., & Goldstein, H. (2007). Assessing the regional economic development impacts of universities: A review of current approaches. **International regional science review**, 30, 20-46.

Etzkowitz, H. (2003). Innovation in innovation: the triple helix of university-industry-government relations. **Social Science Information**, 42, 293-337.

European Commission (2014). **Cohesion Policy Frequently Asked Questions**. Retrieved March 2018, from http://ec.europa.eu/regional_policy/en/faq/

European Commission (2017). **What is Horizon 2020?** Retrieved March 2018, from https://ec.europa.eu/programmes/horizon2020/what-horizon-2020

Faggian, A., & McCann, P. (2006). Human capital flows and regional knowledge assets: a simultaneous equation approach. **Oxford Economic Papers**, 58, 475-500.

Freeman, C. (1987). **Technology and Economic Performance: Lessons from Japan**. London: Pinter Publishers.

Generalitat de Catalunya. (2014). RIS3CAT: **Research and Innovation Strategy for the Smart Specialisation of Catalonia**. Catalan Ministry of Economy and Knowledge, Policy Document. Retrieved from http://catalunya2020.gencat.cat/web/.content/85_catalunya_2020/docu ments/angles/arxius/07ris3cat2014_en.pdf

Generalitat de Catalunya. (2018). **Directory of R&D&I units in Catalonia**. Retrieved from Universities and Research: http://universitatsirecerca.gencat.cat/en/01_secretaria_duniversitats_ i_recerca/universitats_i_recerca_de_catalunya/recerca/directori_drdi/in dex.html

Ghisellini, P., Cialani, C., & Ulgiati, S. (2016). A review on circular economy: the expected transition to a balanced interplay of environmental and economic systems. **Journal of Cleaner Production**, 114, 11-32.

Goddard, J., & Vallance, P. (2013). **The University and the City**. New York: Routledge.

Göransson, B., & Brundenius, C. (2011). **Universities in Transition: The Changing Role and Challenges for Academic Institutions**. Ottawa, Canada: Springer. International Development Research Centre.

Holten-Andersen, P. (2015). **The Role of Universities in Modern Societies**. Copenhagen Business School Senior Management News.

Retrieved from http://www.cbs.dk/en/about-cbs/organisation/senior-management/news/the-role-of-universities-in-modern-societies

Hudson, R. (2011). From Knowledge-based Economy to … Knowledge-based Economy? Reflections on Changes in the Economy and Development Policies in the North East of England. **Regional Studies**, 45, 997-1012.

Idescat. (2017). Statistical Institute of Catalonia (Idescat) Website. Retrieved April 2017, from Official Statistics Website of Catalonia. Vallès Occidental, the municipality in figures: http://www.idescat.cat/emex/?id=40&lang=en

Izsac, K., Markianidou, P., Lukach, R., & Wastyn, A. (2013). **Impact of the Crisis on Research and Innovation Policies. Study for the European Commission DG Research and Innovation**. Technopolis Belgium and Idea Consult: Study for the European Commission DG Research and Innovation.

Jenkins, J. (2011). Accommodating (to) ELF in the international university. **Journal of Pragmatics**, 43, 926-936.

Kolehmainen, J., Irvine, J., Stewart, L., Karacsonyi, Z., Szabó, T., Alarinta, J., & Norberg, A. (2016). Quadruple Helix, Innovation and the Knowledge-Based Development: Lessons from Remote, Rural and Less-Favoured Regions. **Journal of the Knowledge Economy**, 7, 23-42.

Lee, D., Trauth, E., & Farfwell, D. (1995). Critical Skills and Knowledge Requirements of IS Professionals: A Joint Academic/Industry Investigation. **MIS Quarterly**, 19, 313-340.

Manresa, J. (2015, December 11th). Catalonia has received 56% of Spain's foreign research spending since 2010. **Ara - Explaining Catalonia**. Retrieved from https://www.ara.cat/en/Catalonia-received-Spains-research-spending_0_1484251766.html

Manrique, S. (2018). Personal Networks and Trust in Public-Private R&D Partnerships: A Case Study from Spain. Presented at the **XVI International Triple Helix Conference**, Manchester, UK, September 5th-8th 2018. doi: 10.3990/4.2535-5686.2018.12

Maqueda, A. (2018, April 2nd). El Gobierno solo gastó tres de cada 10 euros presupuestados para I+D en 2017. **El País**. Retrieved from https://elpais.com/economia/2018/04/02/actualidad/1522659336_669342.html

Maqueda, A., & Urra, S. (2017, May 1st). Spain and Portugal, EU nations with lowest public investment. **El País**. Retrieved from https://elpais.com/elpais/2017/05/01/inenglish/1493625973_290783.html

Marinelli, E., Elena-Perez, S., & Alias, J. (2016). **Universities and RIS3: the case of Catalonia and the RIS3CAT Communities. JRC Science for Policy Report**. Joint Research Centre - European Commission. Smart Specialisation Policy Brief, 18.

Miller, K., McAdam, R., Moffet, S., Alexander, A., & Puthusserry, P. (2016). Knowledge transfer in university quadruple helix ecosystems: an absorptive capacity perspective. **R&D Management**, 46, 383-399.

Molle, W. (2008). **European Cohesion Policy**. Abingdon, UK: Routledge.

Observatory for Equality UAB. (2017). **Guide for the introduction of the gender perspective in teaching: Third Action Plan for Equality between women and men at the UAB**. Retrieved from: https://www.uab.cat/doc/Guia_perspectivagenere_docencia

OECD. (2010). **Higher Education in Regional and City Development: Catalonia, Spain**. OECD Publishing.

Pain, E. (2012). Research Cuts Will Cause 'Exodus' From Spain. **Science**, 336 (6078), 139-140.

Parc de Recerca. (2017). **UAB Research Park Webpage**. Retrieved May 2017, from http://www.uab.cat/web/about-the-park/-strong-uab-research-park-/strong-1345674962855.html

Perkmann, M., & Walsh, K. (2007). University–industry relationships and open innovation: Towards a research agenda. **Journal of Management Review**, 9, 259-280.

Segarra-Blasco, A., & Arauzo-Carod, J. (2008). Sources of innovation and industry–university interaction: Evidence from Spanish firms. **Research Policy**, 37, 1283-1295.

Serra-Ramoneda, A. (2008). Dos tiempos, dos contextos: el nacimiento de una nueva Universidad (Two times, two contexts: the birth of a new University). Inaugural session of the 2008 academic year. Barcelona, Catalonia, Spain: Universitat Autònoma de Barcelona.

128

Smeby, J. C., & Trondal, J. (2005). Globalisation or europeanisation? International contact among university staff. **Higher Education**, 49, 449-446.

Solà, J., Sàez, X., & Termes, M. (2010). **Estructura industrial i tecnològica dels municipis del tram central de la AP-7/B-30** (Vol. Document d'Economia Industrial # 36). Barcelona: Centre d'Economia Industrial. Universitat Autònoma de Barcelona.

Teichler, U. (2009). Internationalisation of higher education: European experiences. **Asia Pacific Education Review**, 10, 93-106.

UAB Data Management Unit. (2018). **Historical Signed Agreements 2010-2017. Universitat Autònoma de Barcelona**. Cerdanyola del Vallès: UAB Research Management.

UAB, Vallès Occidental County Council, & Eurecat. (2017, March). Digital & Green Skills Vallès: For a sustainable economy. Retrieved October 2017, from https://digital4circular.com/

UAB. (2017). **Autonomous University of Barcelona Webpage**. Retrieved April 2017, from About the UAB: http://www.uab.cat/web/about-the-uab-1345666325480.html

UAB. (2018). **UAB Strategic Research Communities**. Retrieved March 2018, from http://www.uab.cat/web/research/cores-uab/uab-strategic-research-communities-cores-1345698259237.html

UAB. (2019). Barcelona City Council. Retrieved February 2019, from https://www.uab.cat/web/research/itineraries/relation-with-surrounding-areas/city-councils/linking-to-the-uab/barcelona-city-council-1345467954791.html?param1=1345659499521

Urbano, D., & Guerrero, M. (2016). **Autonomous University of Barcelona - HEIBusiness/External relationships for knowledge exchange**. Retrieved May 2017, from HEInnovate. An initiative of the European Commission's DG Education and Culture in partnership with the OECD Local Economic and Employment Development Programme (LEED): https://heinnovate.eu/en/resource/autonomous-university-barcelona-hei-businessexternal-relationships-knowledge-exchange

Valmaseda-Andia, O., Albizu-Gallastegi, E., Fernández-Esquinas, M., & Fernández-de-Lucio, I. (2015). La relación entre las empresas españolas y el CSIC: motivaciones, mecanismos y beneficios desde la perspectiva empresarial. **Revista Española de Documentación Científica**, 38(4), E109.

Van Damme, D. (2001). Quality issues in the internationalisation of higher education. **Higher Education**, 41, 415-441.

Vilalta, J., De-la-Rubia, M., Ortís, M., Martín, M., Berbegal, J., & Betts, A. (2011). Using the economic crisis as an opportunity for engaging universities in regional development. **Background report of the First EU-DRIVERS Annual Conference**, (pp. 1-34). Barcelona.

Chapter 5

Co-creation of localised capabilities between universities and nascent industries

The case of Aalborg University and the North Denmark region

David Fernández Guerrero and Gerwin Evers

Over the years, there has been a growing consensus about the role universities can play in stimulating the development of regional industries through the provision of graduates and the creation and transfer of knowledge (Charles, 2006; Drucker and Goldstein, 2007; Marques, 2017). We argue that universities with these activities can support the development of localised capabilities, which are regional characteristics that are difficult to replicate in other locations, supporting regional industries' sustained competitiveness (Maskell, Eskelinen, Hannibalsson, Malmberg, & Vatne, 1998). Localised capabilities result from feedback loops: this implies that an actor modifies its strategies in response to what other actors do within the same region and that the interactions between them lead to the co-creation of localised capabilities (Maskell et al., 1998). In this chapter, we contend that this line of reasoning also applies to the role of universities in stimulating regional industrial development: universities can support the

131

creation of localised capabilities in their home regions with a wide range of activities, yet this is the result of feedback loops between university actions and industry developments. The intensity of university-industry feedback loops will influence the extent to which localised capabilities are formed.

Replicating the success of cases like Stanford that played an important role in the development of Silicon Valley or the Boston area universities' involvement in the emergence of the biotech cluster in the region, has been a widely debated issue in policy circles; however, attempts at replicating such localised capabilities have been criticised for not taking sufficiently into account the importance of local actors and context in the process (Maskell et al., 1998; Palazuelos, 2005). Industrial development policies in other regions could benefit from a deeper understanding of the interplay between the processes that facilitate the formation of localised capabilities. To examine how regions can develop localised capabilities in such industries, this chapter analyses how localised capabilities are co-created between universities and nascent, science-based industries at the regional level. The focus is on the feedback loops that lead to, and result from university activities such as the creation and commercialisation of knowledge, training of students and the application of existing know-how in collaboration with external partners (Drucker & Goldstein, 2007). This enquiry is guided by the following question: How are localised capabilities co-created between universities and nascent industries at the regional level?

The chapter develops a double case study of the interaction in the North Denmark region between Aalborg University (henceforth AAU) and the ICT industry since the establishment of the university in 1974, and the interaction with the biomedical industry since the early 2000s. The North Denmark region, located in the northern tip of continental Denmark, provides an interesting setting for studying how university-industry interaction can stimulate the co-creation of localised capabilities. The focus on

132

ICT and biomedical industries represent a shift from a region which was specialised in traditional industries such as construction and shipbuilding, to a more knowledge-intensive industry structure (Nilsson, 2006; Pedersen, 2005). Also, the science-based nature of these industries suggests a greater reliance on universities' research (Pavitt, 1984), and thereby a greater likelihood that university-industry feedback loops will take place.

These industries tapped, since their early days, into the educational, research and entrepreneurial activity of AAU in order to develop innovative capabilities that could support their growth. The university, in turn, has invested increasingly in activities that could support these industries. However, the outcome of university-industry interaction has differed between the two industries: While the workforce of the ICT industry has enjoyed considerable growth until the early 2000s, the biomedical industry has expanded to a much lesser extent. Therefore, the difference in outcomes provides an excellent opportunity for investigating how localised capabilities are co-created.

We suggest that the feedback loops between a university and a nascent industry at the regional level are key to the creation of localised capabilities benefiting the competitiveness of the nascent industry. However, we also suggest that the size of the nascent industry (measured by the number of jobs and companies) during university-industry interaction will also influence the extent to which these feedback loops lead to the co-creation of localised capabilities. Industries can tap into the educational, research and entrepreneurial activities of a university in order to develop innovative capabilities. The larger the industry, the more industry actors, the greater the possibilities for university-industry interaction, resulting in the university dedicating more resources to activities that will contribute to the development of localised capabilities relevant to the industry.

The cases we analyse in this chapter take place in a specific setting. What we propose in this chapter is a contextualised explanation

(Tsang, 2013) of the processes that have facilitated the formation of localised capabilities between a specific university, AAU, and two industries (the ICT and biomedical industry) in the context of a particular region, that of North Denmark. Hence context might play a different role, in other regions, and transferability of the findings should not be presumed (Welch, Piekkari, Plakoyiannaki, & Paavilainen-Mäntymäki, 2011). Nevertheless, the findings from this chapter could be complemented with other case studies in order to identify empirical regularities, and potentially propose new theory (Tsang, 2013).

Universities and localised capabilities

The concept of localised capabilities becomes fundamental when studying how university-industry interaction can reinforce the competitiveness of nascent industries at the regional level. Maskell et al. (1998, p51) define localised capabilities as geographically located assets increasing *"the ability of firms to create, acquire, accumulate, and utilise knowledge a little faster than their cost-wise more favourably located competitors"*. Localised capabilities include the structures built in a region, formal and informal institutions regulating business behaviour, and the knowledge and skills created by the regional public or private actors. Their distinctive, (quasi)non-replicable nature offers an advantage to regional firms. Competitors in other regions might try to replicate these conditions, but this might be difficult, in particular, if these assets are tacit (such as in the case of informal institutions) or complementary.

These localised capabilities result from the feedback loops between the economic agents populating the region. That is, how each actor reacts to what other actors have done, as is happening within clusters (Maskell et al., 1998). The region where one or few businesses settle might provide no advantage to these firms at the beginning. Nevertheless, the spin-offs emerging from these pioneers might prefer to locate nearby, in order to maximise the use of the industry-specific qualifications they already possess or to benefit from a regional network of social contacts. Over time, this process might generate a varied set of unique, localised capabilities. MNCs might play a special role in this process by tapping into, and reinforcing the expansion of, the emerging localised capabilities by establishing subsidiaries (be these newly acquired firms or greenfield investments), and providing them with access to financial resources, knowledge and markets.

Nevertheless, the extent to which these processes can support a region's localised capabilities depends on whether the subsidiaries are allowed to operate autonomously. Excessive control on the part of the parent firms might mean that the subsidiaries are less able to cooperate with other regional businesses and to co-create with them localised capabilities. Moreover, the ability of local subsidiaries (and the local industry) to adapt to disruptive innovations might be curtailed by the restrictions imposed on subsidiaries' operations (Østergaard & Park, 2015; Østergaard, Reinau, & Park, 2017).

Cooperation between universities and businesses can also reinforce the development of localised capabilities. This should be especially the case for science-based industries since these are more dependent on the knowledge produced at universities, and hence on university activities (Pavitt, 1984). Drucker & Goldstein (2007) identify several different activities, including the creation and commercialisation of knowledge, training of students and the application of existing know-how in collaboration with external partners, through which universities contribute to the development of localised capabilities in industries.

The extent to which the university focuses these activities in a regional industry can be seen as part of co-evolutionary processes in which some of the educational, research and entrepreneurial activities of a university support the expansion of an emerging industry; and industrial expansion further incentivises the university to commit efforts to that industry.

The model developed in figure 5.1 shows how self-reinforcing feedback loops between university-industry interaction, the localised capabilities that are relevant to the industry, and industry growth can take place. In industries that are at an early stage of their life cycle, new producers enter an emerging market to introduce new products and services (Klepper, 1997) [20]. Some of the educational, research and entrepreneurial activities developed by a university can cater to the needs of the regional industry that is at an early stage in its life cycle, further supporting its growth. The expansion of the focal industry, in turn, stimulates further the university to commit efforts to the industry.

Figure 5.1: Conceptual model of the creation of localised capabilities through university-industry interaction

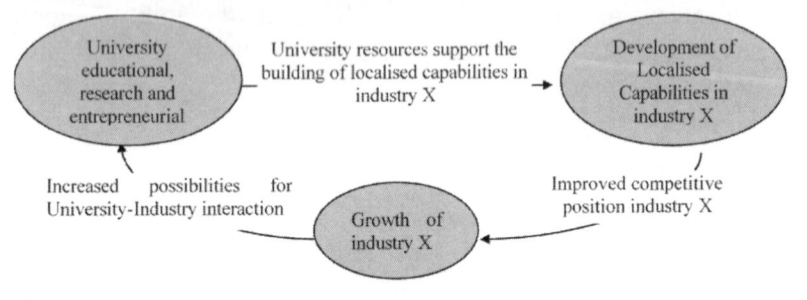

In our analysis, we aim to focus on the stages depicted in the shaded ovals in figure 5.1. We nevertheless assume the presence of the processes, depicted by the connecting lines, by which the stages indirectly affect each other. Furthermore, although we acknowledge that the region is not a closed system, and the feedback loops are also present across regional boundaries, our

---

[20] As soon as the market stabilises around a set of customer preferences and a dominant product design, the focal industry is likely to concentrate around a few producers that can tap into process innovation and economies of scale; and further industry growth is likely to be limited. Exceptions to this pattern, however, concern those industries where firms cater a diversity of markets, enabling the entry of new firms specialised in market niches, and continued industry growth[11].

interest is on university-industry interaction at the regional level. The analysis centres on the effect of the creation and commercialisation of knowledge, training of students and the application of existing know-how in collaboration with external partners by the university. We focus on these university activities because the literature suggests that they represent a key part of university-industry interaction, concerning the industries that we have chosen in this chapter (Nilsson, 2006; Stoerring, 2007; Stoerring & Dalum, 2007).

We argue that the initial size of the industry in the early stages of its life cycle (measured by the number of jobs and companies it hosts) might be key. The larger the industry, the more industry actors, the more possibilities for university-industry interaction, resulting in a stronger university reaction of dedicating more resources to activities that will contribute to the development localised capabilities relevant to the industry. The establishment of MNC subsidiaries in the region provided that they are endowed with some autonomy by the parent company can also reinforce university-industry feedback loops, by promoting the growth (and thereby the size) of the industry.

For example, the emerging industry might tap into educational programmes developed by the regional university, which support its necessities. The university graduates contribute to the development of the industry's localised capabilities, which in turn leads to stronger demand for graduates by the industry. The hiring of graduates by the growing industry might stimulate the university, in turn, to devote an increasing amount of resources to those programmes that support the needs of the industry. Hence, a series of feedback loops would take place between the university and the industry: the industry would hire more graduates, and the university would dedicate more resources to educational programmes related to the needs of the industry. These feedback loops would support the development of localised capabilities by the industry, and its expansion, resulting in further feedback loops,

137

and a larger number of workplaces at the end of the period studied in the chapter.

Note that the university is far from a passive actor in this process; the university is developing at the beginning of the process educational programmes that cater for a broad range of needs, beyond those of the regional industry. The university develops, for instance, programmes attending the needs of other industries than the focal one at the regional, national, or international level as well as public sector or broader social needs. It might furthermore develop educational programmes connected to research activities in promising new knowledge fields. The point is that some of this educational activity might fit the skills needs of a regional industry in the early stages of its life cycle; and the hiring of graduates from the focal university is more likely to incentivise the expansion of the industry, and further feedback loops, the greater the size of the industry. While students also display some autonomy in these dynamics by having a preference for what to study, which does not necessarily match with the educational offerings of universities, universities can play an influential role and attract more students in particular fields by opening new, and investing in current, programmes. Similar processes could take place concerning the creation and transfer of university knowledge, and the generation of university spin-offs.

Methodology

This chapter relies on two case studies: the interaction between AAU and the ICT industry; and the interaction between AAU and the biomedical industry. The case study method allows the tracing back in time of how the development of each industry might have stimulated actions on the part of the university, and vice versa (Yin, 2014). In both cases, the unit of analysis is the interaction that takes place between the university and the industries, in the context of the North Denmark region. The cases, therefore, are defined according to the phenomena studied (Piekkari, Welch, &

Paavilainen, 2009), which are university-industry feedback loops at the level of the North Denmark region. While taking into account that university-industry interaction often goes well beyond the regional setting, spanning to the national and international level (Drejer, Holm, & Nielsen, 2014b; Laursen, Reichstein, & Salter, 2011; Rodríguez-Pose & Fitjar, 2013), the present chapter intends to uncover how regional university-industry feedback loops can contribute to industrial development at the regional scale.

The cases are selected based on their outcome: both concern science-based industries with a strong connection to the local university (Stoerring, 2007; Stoerring & Dalum, 2007), yet their success in forming localised capabilities has differed notably. The goal, here, is to understand the processes behind the differing outcomes (Ragin, 2009). Admittedly, the choice of cases entails limitations in the transferability of findings: the regional context plays a key role in shaping the phenomena studied (Welch et al., 2011). On the other hand, this case study strategy is aimed at developing a contextualised explanation; that is it enables the uncovering of explanations that are specific to particular contexts, and that could be further extended in additional case studies aimed at identifying empirical regularities; leading in the long run to theory building (Tsang, 2013).

The case study relies on the combination of qualitative and quantitative research methods. The qualitative methods include the analysis of secondary sources such as policy reports, newspaper articles, and publications in academic journals. Also, three interviews were conducted with managers from the regional administration, the Biomed Community cluster (an organisation linked to the biomedical industry); and the BrainsBusiness cluster (an organisation related to the ICT industry). These interviews allowed the validation of parts of the data obtained from secondary sources while also providing complementary insights.

As for the quantitative methods, these include the analysis of descriptive macro-data from AAU, descriptive macro-data available online from Statistics Denmark, and micro-data of all inhabitants and companies in Denmark from the Integrated Database for Labour Market Research (abbreviated in Danish as IDA) from Statistics Denmark (Timmermans, 2010). The quantitative data is used to give insight into the growth of industries, the recruitment of university and AAU graduates by the industries over time, student numbers, and the research performance of AAU. This data complements the findings from the qualitative methods: while qualitative secondary sources allow the following of the start of educational programmes, research centres or entrepreneurial activities supporting the ICT and biomedical industry by the university, the quantitative data allows the tracking of the changes in the workforce of these industries and the employment of AAU graduates. Similarly, the interviews surfaced educational, research and entrepreneurial activities developed by AAU to support the development of the focal industries (for instance, the initiation of university-industry linkages by university graduates; or the establishment of research centres suited to industry needs), whose effects are subsequently assessed by the quantitative data. In this way, the quantitative data triangulates the findings from the qualitative analysis.

The analysis of the IDA database is limited to the North Denmark region, the individuals of interest being those that live and work in a full-time job[21] in the region between 1980 and 2010: the analysis with the IDA database ends in 2010 because of restrictions in the information available on full-time/part-time employment status. The analysis takes into account whether the individual holds a university degree and whether the latest degree has been obtained from AAU (the university is constrained to the main campus in

---

[21] This is done in order to study industry dynamics: full-time employees are more likely to develop their career within the boundaries of the industry, whilst part-time employment might respond to short-term needs (Richards & Polavieja, 1997).

140

Aalborg[22], due to the focus on North Denmark). The ICT and biomedical industries are defined using the EU NACE classification of economic activities (Eurostat, 1996). Although the firms related to these industries can be found in numerous groupings, we focused on the main ones, in order to minimise noise (see appendix 5.1 for a list of the industry groupings included).

Aalborg University: creating and being shaped by localised capabilities

Context: a regional struggle and a university initially focused on traditional industries

Assessing the specific role of AAU in our two cases requires an understanding of the regional context in which they are situated. The very origins of AAU are grounded in the needs of the surrounding region of North Jutland (the northern part of the Jutland peninsula, currently under the administration of the North Denmark region). With 587,335 inhabitants in 2017, (211,937 of them in Aalborg municipality), it is the least populated region in Denmark (Statistics Denmark, n.d.). Before the inauguration of the university in September 1974, some of the main regional actors (employers, unions and the Aalborg municipality) had been lobbying for its creation. One of the key steps in this process was the creation in 1961 of the North Jutland Committee for Higher Education, an organisation headed by a local bank manager and composed of representatives from the municipality, the Danish Parliament (an MP from North Denmark) and the business community (Nilsson, 2006; Plenge, 2014; Skaarup, 1974). The group succeeded in persuading the Ministry of Education to authorise the establishment of the Denmark Engineer Academy (DIA) in Aalborg.

---

[22] Aalborg University has also smaller campuses in Copenhagen and Esbjerg (in the southern part of Denmark).

Nevertheless, during the 1960s the Ministry was reluctant to facilitate the creation of a university in the region. Instead, a law draft submitted in March 1969 opted for the creation of a centre for higher education in Roskilde. The government perceived that it was necessary to cover the growing need for higher education institutions in the country, yet preferred to prioritise the regions surrounding Copenhagen (Plenge, 2014).

The resistance on the part of the Ministry of Education to satisfy the demands of North Jutland led to the creation, by the Committee, of the North Jutland University Association in June 1969. This position gained further support in the same year when 1,000 youngsters from the region demonstrated in front of the Christiansborg Palace, the site of the legislative, executive and judicial powers. Inside the parliament, a majority supported the association plans (Folketings-redaktion, 1969; Plenge, 2014; Pyndt, 1969; Statsministeret, n.d.). Shortly afterwards, a new university law draft included the promise of establishing a higher education institution in Aalborg between 1974 and 1975 (Koldbæk, 1974). The DIA and other higher education institutions present in the region would be integrated into the new Aalborg University Centre, founded in 1974 and re-named as Aalborg University in 1994 (Aalborg University, n.d.a; Nilsson, 2006; Plenge, 2014).

The resulting university combined a strong technical character with a large share of social science degrees. Although the technical specialisation was reduced over time by the expansion of social sciences, it still reflected the needs of the regional industries at that time, such as shipbuilding and construction (see for further context box 5.1). The student intake of Aalborg University was 1,635 students in 1974, 765 of them in the Faculty of Engineering and Science, 681 in the Faculty of Social Sciences and 189 in the Faculty of Humanities. At that time, the Aalborg University Centre trained graduates in construction for the building industry; while mechanical engineering graduates were employed by

142

Box 5.1 The regional setting and characteristics of Aalborg University

North Jutland has been historically a region specialised in traditional industries: branches related to construction (quarrying, non-metallic mineral products) or shipbuilding (fabricated metal products) industries have been overrepresented when compared to the Danish average; and this is also the case for industries such as food and agriculture, or the manufacturing of tobacco (Nilsson, 2006; Pedersen, 2005).Within this context, AAU started as a university combining a technical imprint with a large share of degrees in social sciences. This mixed character is still visible: in 2017, 40% of the students were enrolled in one of the degrees of the technical and natural science faculties, 48% if the Faculty of Medicine is included in the calculation. Together with Medicine, the university is based on four other faculties (Humanities, Social Sciences, Engineering and Science, the Technical Faculty of IT and Design) from which the Faculty of Social Sciences is the largest, with 6,287 students (30%). The university has campuses in three cities of which the Aalborg campus hosts most of students (82%).

Compared to other universities, a large share of the graduates move to other regions: only 54% of Aalborg University graduates (with a bachelor, master or PhD degree) who entered the labour market between 2000 and 2010 did so in North Denmark, a significantly lower proportion than that of the other Danish universities. Moreover, 65% of AAU graduates who established their first firm between 2001 and 2010 did so in the same region, the lowest percentage compared to the rest of higher education institutions. This trend is related to the small size of the local labour market in relation to the number of students trained at the university, resulting from a high share of students coming from other regions to study at AAU, who are more likely to move after graduation back to their home region or another region. In fact, 49% of the AAU students who graduated between 2000 and 2010 came from regions other than North Denmark, the largest proportion among Danish universities (Drejer, Holm, & Nielsen, 2014a; Drejer et al., 2014b). Thus, Aalborg also plays an important role as an educational institution at the national level.

companies such as the Aalborg Shipyard (Nilsson, 2006). Over time the university experienced rapid growth, and with 20,654 students in 2017, it is the fifth-largest higher education institution in Denmark (Aalborg University, n.d.b).

In parallel, AAU pioneered together with Roskilde University the Problem-Based Learning (PBL) method in Denmark. This approach to learning entails that students work in project teams on self-defined, interdisciplinary problems, many of them related to challenges faced by local firms. In this respect, PBL offers various advantages for businesses: firms can host students while they develop their projects. Through these projects, students can help firms in solving specific problems; and businesses can screen suitable candidates for their workforce. Moreover, PBL projects have increased the interest of SMEs in hiring AAU graduates (Gregersen, Linde, & Rasmussen, 2009). The number of projects grew to the point that in recent years AAU continuously hosts between 2,000 and 3,000, and in 2016 53.1% of the master theses were undertaken in collaboration with businesses or other external partners (Aalborg University, 2017; Kendrup, 2006). Industries such as construction and shipbuilding continued to exist into the 1980s, and during that decade their weight in North Denmark employment was above average compared to the overall Danish labour market. In other regional strongholds, such as the food, beverage and tobacco industries, North Denmark employment was also higher than the average share in Denmark (Pedersen, 2005). Nevertheless, employment in agriculture, fishing and forestry was halved between 1983 and 1999; and shipbuilding experienced a major crisis, together with the rest of the industry in the other parts of Denmark, leading to the closure of shipyards like Aalborg Værft and Danyard Frederikshavn. These closures led to the establishment of spin-offs (Holm, Østergaard, & Olesen, 2017, pp. 249–250) and a growing specialisation in the provision of services such as ship maintenance and repair (Hermann, 2015). Within this context, the transformative role of the university was quickly put into practice, as will be shown in the first case.

Case 1: AAU adapts (and supports) activities related to the ICT industry

The 1980s and 1990s saw the expansion of the ICT industry in North Denmark. According to the IDA database, the industry workforce increased from 2,203 to 3,786 jobs between 1980 and 1990 and reached a peak of 9,022 employed persons by 2001[23] (see figure 5.2). These developments reflected the rapid expansion of the businesses specialised in wireless communications in North Denmark and the growth of their number to 40 in 2000 (Dalum, Østergaard, & Villumsen, 2005). The origins of this transformation can be found in the entry in the 1960s of SP Radio, a radio and TV manufacturer, in the market of radio communications for maritime vessels. The emergence of spin-offs followed the success of this company. One of these companies would move in the early 1980s into the emerging mobile phone market, whose expansion was propelled by the introduction of the Nordic standard for Mobile Telephony (NMT) in 1981. The success of the NMT standard and the boom of the market favoured a new round of spin-offs from these firms (Dahl, Østergaard, & Dalum, 2010; Dalum et al., 2005). At that point, the state of the ICT industry can be aligned to that of an industry at the initial stages of its life-cycle (Klepper, 1997), with new rounds of spin-offs trying to cater an emerging demand for mobile phones.

The nascent ICT industry tapped into already existing educational and research activities at AAU, that could support the human capital and research needs of its firms. ICT businesses could approach the 200 academic members that AAU employed from its very start in two electrical engineering departments (Dalum et al.,

---

[23] The trend displayed here is similar to the findings of (Pedersen, 2005), however there are some slight differences in the definition of the ICT industry.

2005; Stoerring, 2007; Stoerring & Dalum, 2007). Shortly after its foundation, AAU established the Department of Electronic Systems in 1979. Over time, the university acquired a prominent position in international rankings in areas related to ICT research, such as mathematics and computer science (CWTS Leiden University, 2017). The firms in the ICT industry tapped into AAU's educational and research activities to acquire human capital and increase their innovation capacity.

Figure 5.2 Number of employees in North Denmark's ICT industry

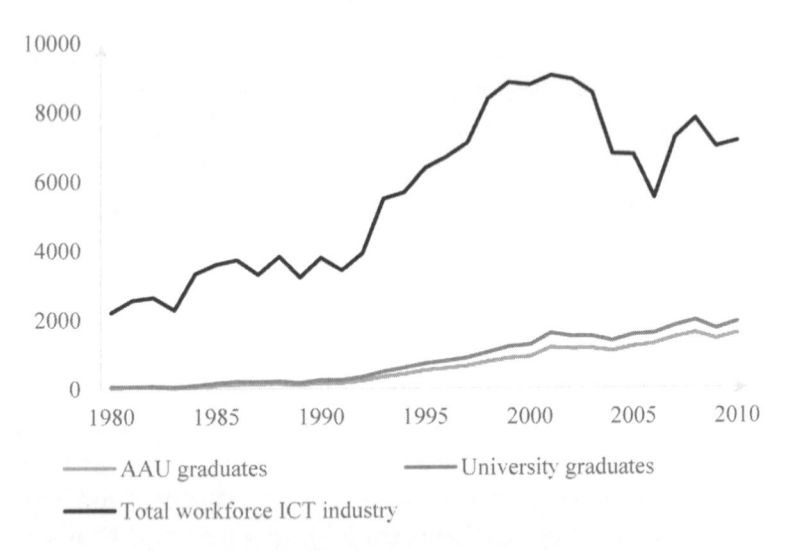

Source: Own elaboration with data from Statistics Denmark

The importance of the AAU's educational activities for the ICT industry is best visible when using the IDA database to look at the share of the university graduates in the industry. The solid grey-line in figure 2 indicates a growing number of university graduates employed in the ICT industry, while the dashed grey-line in figure 5.3 shows that AAU increased its importance as a supplier of graduates. By 2000, 73% of university graduates in the local ICT industry had been trained by the AAU. Like in the previous figure, most of the increase is concentrated in the 1980-2000 period: the share of AAU graduates in ICT graduate employment grew from 40% to 63% between 1980 and 1990, and to 73% in 2000. This suggests that AAU played an important role, by enabling and keeping pace with the growth of the ICT industry, which otherwise would have been limited in the development of localised capabilities due to high-skilled labour shortages at an early stage of its industry life cycle. In addition, the data also points towards an increasingly intense relationship between AAU and the ICT industry, owing to the growing predominance of AAU graduates in the industry's graduate workforce.

The jump from 1G to the 2G cellular telephony standard during the second half of the 1980s represented another feedback loop between university and industry. Staff members of the Department of Electronic Systems contributed together with the city council and a local bank to the establishment of the NOVI science park at the university campus between 1987 and 1989. The park aimed at promoting the development of wireless communications start-ups, but it eventually provided a site where two of the major companies in the cluster, Dancall and Cetelco, could work together in the development of the technology for a 2G terminal. Their joint venture, DC Development, succeeded in the task in 1992, although the parent firms were acquired by Amstrad and Hagenuk, due to financial problems derived from the technological jump (Hedin, 2009; Østergaard et al., 2017; Stoerring, 2007; Stoerring & Dalum, 2007).

Figure 5.3: Share of AAU graduates in North Denmark's ICT industry

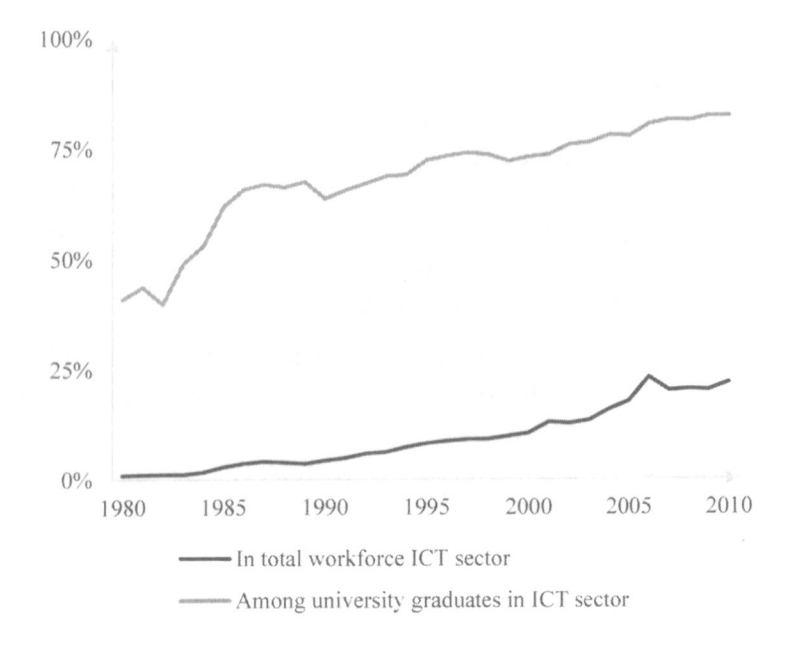

In total workforce ICT sector

Among university graduates in ICT sector

Source: Own elaboration with data from Statistics Denmark

The establishment of the NOVI science park can be seen as an additional research effort of AAU in support of an emerging ICT industry, in particular of those businesses interested in the leap towards GSM phones. AAU staff was also actively involved in the establishment of the ICT cluster organisation, NorCOM, that settled in the NOVI premises in 1997 (Nilsson, 2006; Stoerring, 2007; Stoerring & Dalum, 2007). Currently, the science park hosts 100 companies and 1,000 employees from which the majority are active in the ICT industry (NOVI, n.d.).

In 1993, shortly before the start of NorCOM, the university committed additional research efforts in areas related to the ICT industry, with the opening of the Centre for Personal Communication (CPK). The start of CPK suggests another

148

feedback loop, in which the research efforts of the university further supported the growth of the ICT industry. The main goal of this centre was to develop basic research on radio communications technology and speech recognition, with the involvement of university researchers and employees from businesses specialised in wireless communications (Dalum et al., 2005; Østergaard & Park, 2015). In 2004 its successor, the Center for TeleInFrastruktur (CTIF), was established (Dalum et al., 2005; Hedin, 2009).

The co-creation of localised capabilities between ICT firms and AAU in the 1990s, nevertheless, cannot be fully understood without taking into account the role played by MNCs. Through newly established subsidiaries, these firms provided the emerging industry with access to finance, knowledge and markets, thereby stimulating its growth (Østergaard & Park, 2015; Østergaard et al., 2017). Indeed, the involvement of foreign firms in the industry helped overcome the financial constraints that local firms faced, which could have prevented the expansion of the industry: one example of this is the acquisition of Dancall and Cetelco by Amstrad and Hagenuk, after these firms had been drained by the financial effort involved in supporting DC development. Many other foreign firms entered into the industry through greenfield investments or local acquisitions in the 1990s and 2000s[24], and the regional subsidiaries of these multinationals focused on developing their R&D activities with the goal of exploiting the local knowledge base of the ICT industry. Moreover, these firms tapped into the AAU's research and graduates, further fuelling the development of localised capabilities in the field of ICT (Østergaard et al., 2017). The CTIF, for example, received funding from some of the largest MNCs in the industry in the 2000s, such

---

[24] In the 1990s firms such as Analog Devices, Lucent, Bosch Telecom, Maxon, Texas Instruments, L.M. Ericsson, and Nokia established subsidiaries in the region. The same can be said in the 2000s of multinational corporations such as Flextronics, Siemens, Infineon, Motorola, and Intel (Østergaard et al., 2017).

as Samsung, Siemens and Nokia, as well as funds from local firms and foundations, and the EU (Dalum et al., 2005; Hedin, 2009).

Previous research also suggests, however, that the way in which MNCs managed their subsidiaries also hindered the development of localised capabilities in the 2000s (Østergaard & Park, 2015; Østergaard et al., 2017): after the burst of the dot-com bubble at the beginning of the decade, some of the MNCs present in the region moved R&D activities to their home countries. Because of the restrictions set by their parent companies, the remaining subsidiaries had limited margin of manoeuvre and autonomy in developing their R&D strategies and in cooperating with competitors, and they focused on narrow R&D in specific technologies, rather than on multiple parts of the value chain or a wider variety of technologies. As a result, their ability to respond to disruptive innovations was curtailed. This was the case of the shift from the 2G to the 3G cellular telephony standard (some of the parent firms preferred to continue exploiting the 2G standard until it became non-competitive); or the entry in the market of Apple and Google with the iOS and Android systems, between 2007 and 2008. The economic recession that affected Denmark between 2008 and 2010 deepened the effect of this technological disruption.

These shocks led to a wave of closures. Through the decade, many of the foreign MNCs decided to reduce their activities in the region or leave altogether (Østergaard & Park, 2015; Østergaard et al., 2017), and this is visible in the IDA database: between 2001 and 2007, the number of jobs dropped from 9,022 to 7,233 (see figure 2). Although changes in the NACE classification between 2007 and 2008 prevent a full comparison, the data points to the effect of the recession that hit Denmark at the end of the decade. Total employment decreased from 7,780 to 6,972 jobs between 2008 and 2009, although the latest record (2010) suggests a slight recovery, to 7,133 jobs. In the aftermath of these developments, NorCOM was integrated into the BrainsBusiness cluster

150

organisation, a public-private partnership in which AAU, Aalborg and the region take part (Østergaard & Park, 2015). Contrary to NorCOM, the focus of BrainsBusiness goes beyond wireless communications, covering other parts of the ICT industry (Lindqvist, Olsen, Arbo, Lehto, & Hintsala, 2012).

Despite the shocks suffered by the ICT industry, the data does not suggest a substantial decrease in the interactions between this industry and AAU. BrainsBusiness organises, according to one of its managers, networking activities between ICT firms and AAU researchers to promote research collaboration, and tries to promote firm involvement in PBL projects, which can be seen as a combination of research and educational involvement on the part of the university. However, connections between businesses and researchers tend to rely on pre-existing networks set by employees trained at AAU (interview BrainsBusiness). Hence, there appears to be a continuity in the research links between AAU and the ICT industry, supported by employee links. The fact that Drejer & Østergaard (Drejer & Østergaard, 2017) observe that having employees trained by the AAU positively correlates with the likelihood of firms collaborating for innovation with AAU, also suggests that research collaborations are supported by the links that these employees provide between their companies, and the university.

The data from the IDA database, in addition, suggests that the AAU's importance as a provider of graduates to the ICT industry has increased along the 2000s. Figures 2 and 3 show that the proportion of AAU-trained professionals over graduates has grown from 73% to 81% between 2000 and 2008, and to 82% in 2010; although the absolute numbers have shifted with the turbulences experienced by the industry: The number of AAU graduates in the industry dropped from a peak of 1,165 in 2001 to 1,064 in 2004, but by 2007 it had already recovered to 1,452; and 1,559 AAU graduates worked in the industry in 2010.

In sum, it can be said that AAU has contributed, while developing its educational and research activity, to the development of the localised capabilities which have made North Denmark an attractive region for ICT firms, which is visible in the growth in the number of industry jobs. At the same time, the growth of these businesses ensured that more resources were dedicated to promoting education and research activities connected to the ICT industry. Indeed, much of the current interactions can be seen as a consequence of the feedback loops between AAU and the ICT industry: even when the BrainsBusiness staff try to build networks between SMEs and university researchers, many of these businesses already employ AAU graduates with existing acquaintances in academia. This organisation also promotes the participation of businesses in hosting students, as part of their PBL projects (interview BrainsBusiness). In addition, AAU has been able to achieve scientific excellence in areas related to the ICT industry, such as those of mathematics and computer science (CWTS Leiden University, 2017), and the staff numbers at the faculty of Engineering and Science have grown faster than those of the other faculties at AAU (Aalborg University, n.d.c). These feedback loops were reinforced by the arrival of foreign multinationals in the region, during the 1990s: by converting local firms into their subsidiaries, they provided the regional industry with access to finance, knowledge and markets, strengthening the expansion of the industry and the co-creation of localised capabilities with AAU. The industry seems to have a reached a stage of maturity in its life cycle, in which some of its players left the region in the 2000s; however, this does not seem to have weakened the intensity of the educational and research efforts developed by the university. The maintenance of the links between AAU and the ICT industry suggests that the vigour of the university-industry feedback loops depends on the extent to which the industry is able to take-off, and grow towards a state of maturity. In order to assess further the relevance of industry growth for university-industry feedback loops, the next section provides a comparison assessing the role that the university played in the development of the biomedical industry.

Case 2: Attempts to support activities related to the biomedical industry

When the activities of AAU in support of the biomedical industry started in the early 2000s, this industry was at an earlier stage of development compared to the ICT industry and had not reached a critical mass similar to that of ICT. These differences appear to explain why the support activities developed by AAU have not triggered an expansion process like that of ICT: When these educational and research activities started, they encountered an industry whose critical size was insufficient to tap into them and grow. The university has continued supporting the industry, but the slow growth of the biomedical businesses does not suggest that AAU can trigger feedback loops like those observed in ICT. Until now, the life cycle of the biomedical industry in North Denmark has not led to a rapid expansion in the number of its businesses and its size. The developments of the biomedical industry find resonance with those of the rest of the biomedical industry, globally. Despite the success of cluster initiatives like the Medicon Valley in the regions of Copenhagen and Malmö (Pålsson & Gregersen, 2011), the limited pervasiveness of the biomedical industry has limited its growth. So far, it is unclear whether it will be able to produce a technological revolution like that of ICT (Archibugi, 2017; Hopkins, Martin, Nightingale, Kraft, & Mahdi, 2007; Wydra & Nusser, 2011).

The activities of AAU related to the biomedical industry have been focused around a cluster initiative, which started in 2000 and was formalised in 2003 under the name of Biomed Community. The university had already developed biomedical research, but in that year started collaborating actively with Aalborg Hospital and Aarhus University, under the umbrella of the HEALTHnTECH Research Centre, supporting the development of new products by the industry. The actors involved in the cluster initiative also facilitated the establishment of the Research House facility, next to the Aalborg Hospital. The Research House provides educational and research services, spaces for testing new products and a business incubator. The university also invested resources in the training of graduates, by providing two medical specialisations within Electrical Engineering and starting a degree in Health Technology in 2000 (Aalborg Universitetshospital, 2015; Stoerring, 2007; Stoerring & Dalum, 2007). Hence, the actions developed by the university could have benefited the industry through the creation and commercialisation of knowledge, provision of human capital and the application of existing know-how to support innovation in the industry (Drucker & Goldstein, 2007).

The Biomed Community included 35 firms at its start, but many of these worked in the distribution of health care equipment or were small university spin-offs. Others were subsidiaries of large Danish businesses with headquarters in the Capital Region of Denmark, such as Oticon, Novo Nordisk or Coloplast (Stoerring & Dalum, 2007). The analysis of the IDA database (figure 5.4) suggests that these businesses provided only a small company base and that the industry's capacity to absorb university graduates was somewhat limited, providing little ground for the start of a series of feedback loops between university actions and industry demand. As a result, many graduates from degrees with a medical specialisation opted for moving either to other regions in Denmark or to the ICT industry (Stoerring, 2007; Stoerring & Dalum, 2007). This has been the case despite a further analysis with the IDA database (see figure 5.5) suggests an increasing involvement of AAU graduates, approaching the levels of the ICT firms.

In addition, the university failed to develop general scientific excellence in the biomedical field, scoring last in Denmark and below average among the universities included in the CWTS Leiden Ranking (CWTS Leiden University, 2017). However, there are some niches in which the university has acquired a prominent position. This is particularly the case for the Centre for Neuroplasticity and Pain, and the Centre for Sensory-Motor Interaction who have prominent positions in their respective fields at the national and international level. This specialisation is also visible in the AAU publication output: most of the AAU's medical publications between 2000 and 2018 are within fields related to these centres such as neurosciences and neurology (1,280 publications, 20.43% of the total, a considerably higher share than other Danish universities) (Danish National Research Foundation, n.d.; Pubmed, 2018; Thomson Reuters, n.d.).

Figure 5.4: Number of employees in North Denmark's biomedical industry (excluding hospital)

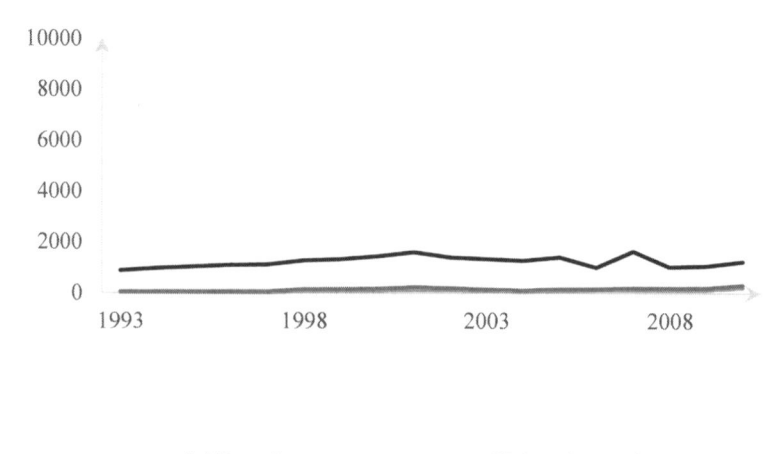

Source: Own elaboration with data from Statistics Denmark

Supporting the view that the biomedical industry in North Denmark has a relatively limited potential for the development of feedback loops with the activities developed by the university, Stoerring (Stoerring, 2007; Stoerring & Dalum, 2007) argued that the growth dynamics that could lead to an expansion in the number of biomedical firms in North Denmark might take more time than the period she covered (mid-2000s). Stoerring also argued that the activities developed by AAU; and the acquisition of a university start-up (Neurodan) by a German firm (Otto Bock) might trigger the expansion of the industry in the region[25]. However, the analysis of the IDA database up to 2010 (figures 5.4 and 5.5) suggests that the feedback loops between AAU and the biomedical industry have not stimulated an expansion of the latter, measured as the number of jobs at the end of the period. In fact, most of the graduates already came from AAU by the start of the cluster initiative. If anything, their importance has continued increasing until 2010, yet this trend did not seem to accelerate after 2000. Moreover, with 38 businesses the number of firms in the Biomed Community cluster has not increased substantially (Biomed Community, n.d.).

Figure 5.5: Share of AAU graduates in North Denmark's biomedical industry (excluding hospital)

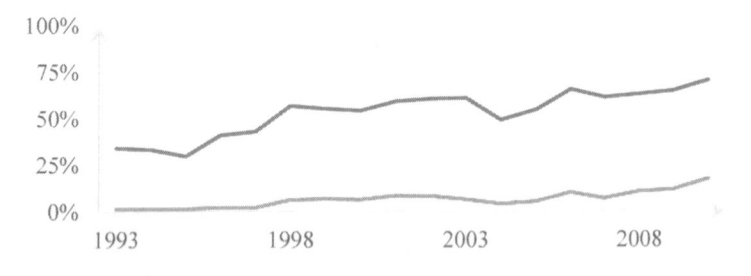

In total workforce biomedical sector (excl. Hospital)

Source: Own elaboration with data from Statistics Denmark

[25] Stoerring(Stoerring, 2007; Stoerring & Dalum, 2007) focused on processes of cluster growth, and hence her research differed from industry studies. Clusters, in fact, can include firms from different industries (Porter, 2000). However, the insights from Stoerring are still useful, given the similarity between the clusters she studied, and the industries compared in this chapter.

Despite the lack of feedback from the biomedical industry, AAU has taken part in further efforts to stimulate the growth of these businesses. This is the case of the Empowering Industry & Research Initiative (EIR) in which the university has participated since 2011 (Aalborg University, n.d.). A number of public actors such as the university, the Aalborg municipality, the regional administration and the Aalborg hospital have been involved in the initiative, investing more resources in the formation of the industry, with various goals in mind[26] (Hopkins et al., 2007; Østergaard & Park, 2015; Østergaard et al., 2017; Welch et al., 2011). The opening of the Faculty of Medicine in 2010, which led to a substantial increase in the medical publication output, might also be seen as another development that could support the biomedical industry (Aalborg University, n.d.a; Thomson Reuters, n.d.).

Discussion and conclusion

This chapter has given insight in the feedback loops between a university and two industries of its region; and how these processes affect the creation of localised capabilities, reinforcing the competitiveness of these industries and their growth. A conceptual model has been devised, which is applied to the case of the ICT and biomedical industry in the North Denmark region. The data suggest that the industries included in these cases have evolved differently: the ICT industry grew considerably, while the workforce of the biomedical industry remained more or less stable. The conceptual model sheds some light on the role played by university-industry feedback loops in shaping the localised capabilities of the ICT and biomedical industries.

---

[26] University professionals, for example, are interested in being able to train medical doctors in order to stimulate health professionals' involvement in the development of research (Stoerring, 2007; Stoerring & Dalum, 2007). Another reason is to ensure that the region retains a university hospital (interview regional expert)

One fundamental aspect here seems to be the employment size and the life cycle of the regional industry during university-industry interaction. The workforce of the ICT industry was larger than that of the biomedical industry at the start of university engagement, and the gap in the size of these industries grew over time. The establishment of foreign MNCs' subsidiaries in the region also seems to have reinforced the feedback loops between ICT firms and AAU: by acquiring local firms, foreign businesses provided access to funding, knowledge and markets to the industry; whilst tapping into AAU's research and education activity to the point of financing research centres such as CTIF. As expected in the conceptual model, the difference in the size of the industry seems to have influenced the extent to which the industries could tap into the education, research and entrepreneurship activities already developed by the university; and thus the start of university-industry feedback loops. The employment size of the ICT industry facilitated the start of a series of feedback loops and the creation of localised capabilities strengthening the position of the businesses and their expansion until the industry faced a series of crises at the beginning of the 2000s. The effect of these crises, in turn, seems to have been increased by the lack of flexibility that foreign MNCs imposed on their subsidiaries when exploring different technologies or cooperating with other businesses in the region. These restrictions might have curtailed the ability of the subsidiaries to co-create localised capabilities between them, and with the university (Østergaard & Park, 2015; Østergaard et al., 2017).

Meanwhile, the smaller size of the biomedical industry seems to have prevented the co-creation of localised capabilities through university-industry interaction, despite the presence of multinational subsidiaries in the region. So far, the life cycle of the biomedical industry has not led, in the region to a critical mass of businesses that can tap into AAU activities to grow. University actions are unlikely to generate the localised capabilities that will guarantee the competitiveness of the industry and its growth. The creation of localised capabilities depends on the extent to which a university and an industry can influence each other via feedback loops. In this sense, this chapter complements the research conducted by Stoerring (Stoerring, 2007; Stoerring & Dalum, 2007), who observed weaker growth dynamics in the biomedical firms of North Denmark than in their ICT counterparts, until the mid-2000s. Our research covers later years in the development of the biomedical industry (until 2010), observing that this industry has not experienced the growth dynamics observed in the ICT industry.

Here, another important factor might have been the presence of inter-industrial competition for labour, similar to the Dutch disease; in the early days of the ICT industry competition for labour was limited and the growing ICT industry could absorb workers that were laid off by the declining traditional industries. However, the biomedical industry faces a much stronger competition for labour due to the presence of the ICT industry, in which people with a medical degree, or a degree with a medical specialisation, can also find employment. In this respect, the findings from previous research suggest that this could be the case: in the early years of the Biomed Community cluster initiative, health technology professionals experienced difficulties in finding jobs in the biomedical industry, common alternatives being emigration to other regions of Denmark or employment in the ICT industry (Stoerring, 2007). Moreover, our research with the IDA database indicates that the ICT industry was at its employment peak by 2001, shortly after the start of the biomedical cluster initiative, and its employment size has not diminished substantially afterwards, despite shocks such as the burst of the dot-com bubble or the shift from the 2G to the 3G cellular standards. This is especially the case of the number of university graduates, which has proved to be particularly robust.

The insights delivered in this chapter contribute to the university-industry interaction literature by offering a contextualised explanation of how university-industry feedback loops stimulated the development of specific industries. The findings suggest that, in North Denmark the extent to which universities and nascent industries co-create regional localised capabilities depends on the size of these industries during industry-university collaboration, as measured by industries' number of employees and companies. Because this is an explanation in principle applicable to a context like the one reviewed in the chapter; the findings are, for now, transferable to similar cases. Further research, providing insights on cases whose context differs from that of the present chapter, could extend the reach of our findings, identifying empirical regularities and proposing new theory on how university-industry interactions relate to the formation of localised capabilities in different types of regions.

With all these words of caution, the findings also suggest implications for regional innovation policies. The lack of strong bottom-up dynamics at the industry side (that is, the absence of industries that experience strong growth as part of their life cycle) might pose a challenge to policies relying on universities as main drivers of regional development. Both parts, university and industry, seem to be necessary for the development of localised capabilities. In a way, these suggestions are similar to the smart specialisation strategy approach (Asheim, 2014), basing innovation policies on the existing strengths of the regions: policymakers might be interested in developing new industries, but if these developments do not build from already existing developments, they are less likely to thrive. The same might go for the role of the university as a trigger for regional development.

Acknowledgements

The authors wish to thank Ina Drejer and Christian Østergaard (Aalborg University) and David Charles (Northumbria University) for their comments on this chapter. Thanks are also due to the members of the IKE Research Group and the participants in the RUNIN special session at the 12th Regional

Innovation Policies Conference in Santiago de Compostela. The usual disclaimer applies.

References

Aalborg Universitetshospital. (2015). **Forskningens Hus**. Retrieved September 19, 2017, from http://www.aalborguh.rn.dk/forskning/forskningens-hus

Aalborg University. (n.d.a). **Aalborg Universitets Historie**. Retrieved December 28, 2018, from http://www.aau.dk/om-aau/historie-priser/historie/

Aalborg University. (n.d.b). **Aalborg University in figures and facts**. Retrieved September 4, 2017, from http://www.en.aau.dk/about-aau/figures-facts

Aalborg University. (n.d.c). **AAU in figures 1974-2012**. Retrieved December 28, 2018, from http://www.en.aau.dk/about-aau/figures-facts/1974-2012/

Aalborg University. (n.d.d). **Empowering Industry & Research**. Retrieved June 7, 2017, from http://www.hst.aau.dk/innovation-co-operation/empowering-industry-research/

Aalborg University. (2017). **Årsrapport 2016**. Retrieved August 22, 2017, from http://www.e-pages.dk/aalborguniversitet/518/html5/

Archibugi, D. (2017). Blade Runner economics: Will innovation lead the economic recovery? **Research Policy**, 46, 535–543.

Asheim, B. T. (2014). **North Denmark Region RIS3 Expert Assessment**. An expert assessment of behalf of DG Regional and Urban Policy.

Biomed Community. (n.d.). **Biomed Community**. Retrieved June 7, 2017, from http://www.hst.aau.dk/innovation-co-operation/empowering-industry-research/

Charles, D. (2006). Universities as key knowledge infrastructures in regional innovation systems. **Innovation: The European Journal of Social Science Research**, 19(1), 117–130.

CWTS Leiden University. (2017). **CWTS Leiden Ranking 2017**. Retrieved May 19, 2017, from http://www.leidenranking. com/ranking/2017/list

Dahl, M. S., Østergaard, C. R., & Dalum, B. (2010). Emergence of regional clusters: the role of spinoffs in the early growth process. In Boschma, R. And Martin R. (eds) **The Handbook of Evolutionary Economic Geography** (pp. 205–221) Cheltenham, UK: Edward Elgar.

Dalum, B., Østergaard, C. R., & Villumsen, G. (2005). Technological life cycles: lessons from a cluster facing disruption. **European Urban and Regional Studies**, 12, 229–246.

Danish National Research Foundation. (n.d.). **Liste over alle fondens Centers of Excellence**. Retrieved February 6, 2018, from http://dg.dk/centers-of-excellence/liste-over-alle-fondens-centers-of-excellence/

Drejer, I., Holm, J. R., & Nielsen, K. (2014a). **Aalborg Universitets bidrag til udvikling i Region Nordjylland**. Retrieved from http://www.rn.dk/~/media/Rn_dk/Regional Udvikling/Regional Udvikling sektion/Analyser og rapporter/AAU_bidrag_til_udvikling _i_Nordjylland_analyserapport.ashx

Drejer, I., Holm, J. R., & Nielsen, K. (2014b). **To what extent is a "regional university" regional? The case of Aalborg University**.

Drejer, I., & Østergaard, C. R. (2017). Exploring determinants of firms' collaboration with specific universities: employee-driven relations and geographical proximity. **Regional Studies**, 51, 1192–1205.

Drucker, J., & Goldstein, H. (2007). Assessing the regional economic development impacts of universities: a review of current approaches. **International Regional Science Review**, 30, 20–46.

Eurostat. (1996). **NACE Rev. 1 Statistical classification of economic activities in the European Community. 1–196**. Retrieved from https://publications.europa.eu/en/publication-detail/-/publication/ 212c93fc-53ca-437f-827d-b91a61908145

Folketings-redaktion. (1969). Universitetsdebatten i folketinget viste, at det skal være alvor i Aalborg i 1975. **Søndags Stiftstidende Aalborg Nordjysk Amtstidende**, December, p. 4.

Gregersen, B., Linde, L. T., & Rasmussen, J. G. (2009). Linking between Danish universities and society. **Science and Public Policy**, 36, 151–156.

Hedin, S. (2009). Higher education institutions as drivers of regional development. **Nordregio Working Paper 2009:3** Retrieved from https://archive.nordregio.se/en/Publications/Publications-2009/Higher-education-institutions-as-drivers-of-regional-development/index.html

Hermann, R. R. (2015). **Greening of the maritime industry: Delivering product and service eco-innovations.** Aalborg: Aalborg Universitetsforlag. (Ph.d.-serien for Det Teknisk-Naturvidenskabelige Fakultet, Aalborg Universitet). https://doi.org/10.5278/vbn.phd. engsci.00015

Holm, J. R., Østergaard, C. R., & Olesen, T. R. (2017). Destruction and Reallocation of Skills Following Large Company Closures. **Journal of Regional Science**, 57(2), 245–265.

Hopkins, M. M., Martin, P. A., Nightingale, P., Kraft, A., & Mahdi, S. (2007). The myth of the biotech revolution: An assessment of technological, clinical and organisational change. **Research Policy**, 36, 566–589.

Kendrup, Sø. (2006). OECD / IMHE project Supporting the Contribution of Higher Education Institutions to Regional Development. Subreport: Aalborg University Jutland-Funen, Denmark. OECD / IMHE, (January).

Klepper, S. (1997). Industry Life Cycles. **Industrial and Corporate Change**, 6, 145–182.

Koldbæk, J. (1974). Det begyndte i sol - og endte i regn (not available online). **Søndags Stiftstidende Aalborg Nordjysk Amtstidende**, September pp. 2–3.

Laursen, K., Reichstein, T. & Salter, A. (2011). Exploring the effect of geographical proximity and university quality on university–industry collaboration in the United Kingdom. **Regional Studies**, 45, 507–523.

Lindqvist, M., Olsen, L. S., Arbo, P., Lehto, V., & Hintsala, H. (2012). Strategies for Interaction and the Role of Higher Education Institutions in Regional Development in the Nordic Countries – Case Studies. Nordregio Working Paper 2012:3.

163

Marques, P. (2017). Human capital and university – business interactions : an example from the wine industry. **Regional Studies, Regional Science**, 4, 154–160.

Maskell, P., Eskelinen, H., Hannibalsson, I., Malmberg, A., & Vatne, E. (1998). **Competitiveness, Localised Learning and Regional Development. Specialization and Prosperity in Small Open Economies**. London: Routledge.

Nilsson, J. (2006). Regions with comprehensive technical universities. In J. Nilsson (Ed.), **The Role of Universities in Regional Innovation Systems: A Nordic Perspective** (pp. 115–142). Frederiksberg: Copenhagen Business School Press.

NOVI. (n.d.). **About Novi**. Retrieved June 7, 2017, from http://novi.dk/en/about-novi

Østergaard, C. R., & Park, E. K. (2015). What Makes Clusters Decline? A Study on Disruption and Evolution of a High-Tech Cluster in Denmark. **Regional Studies**, 49, 834–849.

Østergaard, C. R., Reinau, K. H., & Park, E. K. (2017). The Dual Role of Multinational Corporations in Cluster Evolution: When You Dance with the Devil, You Wait for the Song to Stop. In F. Belussi & J.-L. Hervás-Oliver (Eds.), **Unfolding Cluster Evolution** (pp. 39–55). Routledge.

Palazuelos, M. (2005). Clusters: Myth or realistic ambition for policy-makers? **Local Economy**, 20, 131–140.

Pålsson, C. M., & Gregersen, B. (2011). Biotechnology in Denmark and Sweden. In B. Göransson & C. M. Pålsson (Eds.), **Biotechnology and Innovation Systems: The Role of Public Policy** (pp. 245–276). Cheltenham: Edward Elgar.

Pavitt, K. (1984). Sectoral patterns of innovation; Towards a taxonomy and a theory. **Research Policy**, 13, 343–374.

Pedersen, C. Ø. R. (2005). **The Development Perspectives for the ICT Sector in North Jutland.** PhD thesis submitted to Aalborg University. Retrieved from http://vbn.aau.dk/files/197132182/CRP_PhD_Thesis.pdf

Piekkari, R., Welch, C., & Paavilainen, E. (2009). The Case Study as Disciplinary Convention. **Organizational Research Methods**, 12, 567–589.

Plenge, P. (2014). **Ledelse af AAU: syv fortællinger fra AAU's ledelseshistorie**. Aalborg: Aalborg Universitet, AAU Kommunikation.

Porter, M. E. (2000). Economic Development : Local Clusters in a Global Economy. **Economic Development Quarterly**, 14, 15–34.

Pubmed. (2018). Pubmed search results. Retrieved February 6, 2018, from https://www.ncbi.nlm.nih.gov/pubmed/?term=alborg+Universit*%5BAffiliation%5D+OR+aalborg+Universit*%5BAffiliation%5D

Pyndt, J. (1969). Protestrejsen til København blev en værdig bevighend. **Søndags Stiftstidende Aalborg Nordjysk Amtstidende**, December, 2.

Ragin, C. C. (2009). Reflections on casing and case-oriented research. In C. C. Ragin & D. Bryne (Eds.), **The Sage handbook of case-based methods** (pp. 522–534). Sage publications.

Richards, A., & Polavieja, J. G. de. (1997). Trade unions, unemployment and working class fragmentation in Spain (No. 112). Centro de Estudios Avanzados en Ciencias Sociales, Madrid.

Rodríguez-Pose, A., & Fitjar, R. D. (2013). Buzz, Archipelago Economies and the Future of Intermediate and Peripheral Areas in a Spiky World. **European Planning Studies**, 21, 355–372.

Skaarup, J. P. (1974). AUC vil gøre landsdelen mere attraktiv. **Søndags Stiftstidende Aalborg Nordjysk Amtstidende**, 9.

Statistics Denmark. (n.d.). **Statbank Denmark**. Retrieved April 5, 2020, from http://statbank.dk/

Statsministeret. (n.d.). **Statsministre siden 1848**. Retrieved June 7, 2017, from http://www.stm.dk/_a_1596.html

Stoerring, D. (2007). **Emergence and growth of high technology clusters**. Doctoral Dissertation. Retrieved from http://www.business.aau.dk/~ds/publications/EmergenceAndGrowthOf HighTechnologyClusters_PhD_Stoerring.pdf

Stoerring, D., & Dalum, B. (2007). Cluster emergence: a comparative study of two cases in North Jutland, Denmark. In Cooke, P. & Schwartz, D. (eds.), **Creative Regions: Technology, Culture and Knowledge Entrepreneurship** (pp. 127–147). London: Routledge.

Thomson Reuters. (n.d.). **Web of Science database**. Retrieved February 16, 2018, from webofknowledge.com

Timmermans, B. (2010). **The Danish Integrated Database for Labor Market Research: Towards Demystification for the English Speaking Audience**. Draft, (10). Retrieved from http://webdoc.sub.gwdg.de/ebook/serien/lm/DRUIDwp/10-16.pdf

Tsang, E. W. K. (2013). Case study methodology: Causal explanation, contextualization, and theorizing. **Journal of International Management**, 19, 195–202.

Welch, C., Piekkari, R., Plakoyiannaki, E., & Paavilainen-Mäntymäki, E. (2011). Theorising from case studies: Towards a pluralist future for international business research. **Journal of International Business Studies**, 42, 740–762.

Wydra, S., & Nusser, M. (2011). Diffusion and economic impacts of biotechnology - A case study for Germany. **International Journal of Biotechnology**, 12, 87–103.

Yin, R. K. (2014). **Case study research: Design and methods** - fifth edition. Sage publications.

Appendix 5.1: Variables used in quantitative analyses

List of the variables included in the quantitative analysis, as they are available in the Danish Integrated database for Labour Market Research (IDA, in Danish). The data for these variables could be merged into a common dataset, using personal identification numbers. The variables for the industry in which the individual is employed (PDB932, PDB03) are only available for some of the years covered in the analysis, as indicated below. More information about the IDA database is provided by Timmermans (2010).

Variable	Variable Name	Specification
Institution of highest completed education	HFINSTNR	Aalborg University: 280776, 851416, 851446 Universities (including PhD schools): 101441, 101455, 101530, 101535, 101560, 101582, 147406, 151413, 173405, 265407, 265415,

		280776, 280777, 280778, 280779, 280780, 280781, 280782, 280783, 280784, 280785, 280786, 280787, 280788, 280789, 280790, 280791, 280833, 280834, 280835, 280836, 280837, 280838, 280839, 280840, 280841, 280843, 280844, 280845, 280846, 280847, 280848, 280849, 280850, 280857, 280858, 280859, 280860, 280861, 280904, 280907, 313402, 330401, 461416, 461437, 461450, 537406, 561408, 561411, 621406, 657410, 751418, 751431, 751453, 751465, 851416, 851446
Industry where the individual is employed	PDB932 (1980-2003)	**NACE1(.1) 1980-2007** *ICT industry:* Manufacture of office machinery and computers (30), Manufacture of radio, television and communication equipment and apparatus (32), Computer and related activities (72), Telecommunications (642), Research and experimental development on natural sciences and Engineering (731), Reproduction of computer media (2233), Manufacture of insulated wire and cable (3130), Manufacture of instruments and appliances for measuring, checking, testing, navigating and other purposes, except industrial process control equipment (3320), Wholesale of electrical household appliances and radio and television Goods (5143), Wholesale of office machinery and equipment (5164), Wholesale of other machinery for use in industry, trade and navigation (5165), Wholesale of computers, computer peripheral equipment and software (5184), Wholesale of other office machinery and equipment

		(5185), Renting of office machinery and equipment, including computers (7133) *Biomedical industry (without hospital and related activities):* Manufacture of pharmaceuticals, medicinal chemicals and botanical products (244), Manufacture of medical and surgical equipment and orthopaedic appliances (331), Research and experimental development on natural sciences and Engineering (731), Wholesale of pharmaceutical goods (5146)
	PDB03 (2004-2010)	**NACE2 2008-2010** *ICT industry:* Telecommunications (61), Computer programming, consultancy and related activities (62), Manufacture of electronic components and boards (261), Manufacture of computers and peripheral equipment (262), Manufacture of communication equipment (263), Manufacture of irradiation, electromedical and electrotherapeutic equipment (266), Manufacture of optical instruments and photographic equipment (267), Manufacture of wiring and wiring devices (273), Software publishing (582), Data processing, hosting and related activities; web portals (631), Repair of computers and communication equipment (951), Manufacture of instruments and appliances for measuring, testing and navigation (2651), Manufacture of office machinery and equipment (except computers and peripheral equipment) (2823), Repair of electronic and optical equipment (3313), Construction of utility

		projects for electricity and telecommunications (4222), Wholesale of computers, computer peripheral equipment and software (4651), Wholesale of electronic and telecommunications equipment and parts (4652), Other research and experimental development on natural sciences and engineering (7219), Renting and leasing of office machinery and equipment (including computers) (7733) *Biomedical industry (without hospital and related activities):* Manufacture of basic pharmaceutical products and pharmaceutical preparations (21), Manufacture of medical and dental instruments and supplies (325), Wholesale of pharmaceutical goods (4646), Research and experimental development on biotechnology (7211), Other research and experimental development on natural sciences and engineering (7219)
Location of employment	ARBKOM	Municipality codes are used to determine the region, in which the individual`s workplace is located (according to the most recent geographical map of Denmark)
Type of employment (full-time/part-time)	PJOB	Full-time employment if PJOB=1

Chapter 6

From Transplantation to Diversification?

The University of Stavanger's Role in the Economic Development of Rogaland

Utku Ali Rıza Alpaydın, Kwadwo Atta-Owusu and Saeed Moghadam-Saman

Located in Western Norway, Stavanger is at the centre of Rogaland region, in what had predominantly been a rural community until the end of the 1960s, when the offshore oil reserves were discovered. Since then, its economy has expanded rapidly, and the region has become one of the most significant centres of the Norwegian economy. The University of Stavanger (UiS), whose emergence also dates back to the end of the 1960s, plays a complementary role in the regional development and innovation system of Rogaland through its impacts on teaching, research and 'third mission' activities. Despite being oriented towards meeting the need for qualified human resources and conducting research activities for the oil and gas sector since its inception, the UiS has managed to transform into a multidisciplinary character over time.

This transition is also reflected in the regional engagement endeavours of the UiS, which are further strengthened by closely cooperating with public and private sector institutions in various ways, such as joint projects and common interfaces for R&D, innovation and commercialisation. Although the UiS has become more engaged in regional economic and social issues, the level of regional engagement seems to differ between faculties and departments, and the oil and gas sector related fields continue to dominate the regional engagement of the university. Moreover, the roles that the UiS has played in the innovation systems of prevalent industrial sectors of Rogaland have also seen several shifts corresponding with the evolution of those sectors.

This chapter, therefore, examines the role of the UiS in innovation and the development of Rogaland region. The next section examines the economic structure of Rogaland mainly through statistical data. Then, theoretical approaches dealing with the role of universities in innovation-led regional development will be examined briefly in order to provide the conceptual framework for the subsequent discussion. This is followed by an explanation of the formation and structure of the UiS with a focus on its education and research activities, and the trajectory of the regional engagement of the UiS. The chapter concludes with a discussion about the role of the UiS in Rogaland and policy recommendations drawn from the case.

Regional economic structure of Rogaland

The economic history of Rogaland

Fisheries and related industries dominated the economy of Rogaland until the 1970s. In the mid-1800s, herring fishing and its trade constituted the source of wealth in the region (Fitjar, 2010). When the region started to industrialise in the early 1900s, the sardine canning and shipbuilding industries became the pillars of the economy (Oftedal and Iakovleva, 2015). However, the bright days of the canning industry lasted only until the early 1960s. The shipbuilding industry also started to face severe international competition in the 1970s. The discovery of petroleum in the North Sea in late 1960s, when the two leading industries went into decline, was an auspicious development that marked the beginning of the economic transformation of Rogaland region. Since then, the regional economy of Rogaland has mainly expanded around the oil and gas industry. Now, the region hosts a fully-fledged supply chain in the oil and gas industry, with a varied range of companies operating in the sector (Kyllingstad and Hauge, 2016).

The start of the transformation dates back to late 1962, when the American oil company Phillips sought permission to explore the Norwegian continental shelf with the possibility of finding oil reserves. During the following years, the foundations of the Norwegian oil and gas sector were institutionalised by the politicians in Oslo. However, it was Stavanger, the capital city of Rogaland region, which attracted the attention of international oil and gas companies to locate their operations mainly because of the geographical proximity to the planned exploration sites in the North Sea (Nerheim, 2014). Yet, it was not until the autumn of 1969, when the Ekofisk oil field was discovered, that the prospects for the economic transformation of the region could be realised. Within a couple of years, the endeavours of international firms were intensified and the institutionalisation of the sector continued. The establishment of the Norwegian Petroleum Directorate and Statoil[27], a wholly owned state company, in 1972 in Stavanger strengthened further the position of the city as the hub of the oil and gas sector in Norway. From then on, the fate of the regional economy was shaped by the developments in the

---

[27] Statoil changed its name to "Equinor" in 2018.

international oil and gas sector, rather than indigenous regional dynamics (Nerheim, 2014).

Effects of international oil sector developments in Rogaland's economic structure

The existing economic structure of Rogaland and the competences in terms of shipbuilding and construction created a supportive foundation for the oil and gas sector in the region (Ryggvik, 2015). However, in the early years, the large multinational corporations operating in the North Sea conducted their engineering and planning works from their original headquarters or offices outside Norway. Even for the actual implementation phase, they relied on expatriates rather than the Norwegian workforce.

Until the mid-1980s, the oil and gas industry in Norway grew exponentially. The share of the sector in GDP increased from nothing in 1971 to 17% in 1984. In the same year, the sector constituted a quarter of investments, almost half of exports and a fifth of revenues in the country (see Figure 7.A1 in the appendix). However, the plummeting oil prices in 1986 hit the Norwegian economy severely and Rogaland felt the effects two years later. The registered unemployment rose by 67.5% in 1988 as compared to the previous year and by 74.5% in 1989 (Statistics Norway). The number of establishments also declined by 12.5% between 1987 and 1989. The economic turbulence lasted until 1993 from when the regional economy began to recover.

The Rogaland economy again suffered adversely following the 1998 Asian financial crisis. As a result, oil investments declined for four years. Consequently, the unemployment situation in Rogaland worsened, exceeding the national average in November 1999 and remained higher until June 2002. The year 2003 marked the return of high growth for Rogaland that lasted until 2008, when another financial crisis began. The number of registered

174

unemployed persons declined by 70% during this period (from 7,926 in 2003 to 2,362 in 2008). However, 2009 witnessed a sharp increase of 93.5% in registered unemployment.

Recently, the oil price crisis of 2014 negatively influenced Rogaland, whose effects are still being felt in the regional economy despite symptoms of revival. While the share of the oil and gas sector in Norwegian GDP fell by 20% for two consecutive years (it came down to 11.8% in 2016 from 18.4% in 2014) (See Figure 7.A1 in the Appendix), the regional unemployment rate in Rogaland doubled and reached 4.5% in 2016.

Sectoral composition of the regional economy in Rogaland

When the composition of the Rogaland economy is examined through employment figures and value added for two periods 1997-2007 and 2008-2015 (Statistics Norway), a number of significant changes can be discerned (see Tables 7.A3 and 7.A4 in the Appendix).

The first point is related to the skyrocketing share of "oil and gas extraction including services". In terms of employment, its share almost doubled (from 5.04% to 9.73%), while its share in regional value added increased by 60% (from 11.44% to 18.36%) when compared to 1997-2007. Another sector that continued to expand during these two periods is construction. It came to account for 7.41% of regional employment and 7.34% of regional value added on average for the period 2008-2015. Health and social work constitute the third sector where the increasing shares are witnessed, but not as high as the previous ones. Its employment share rose to 17.16%, while its value-added share increased to 9.71%.

The second striking point is the decreasing share of the manufacturing sector from 16.80% to 11.55% in employment and

175

from 17.00% to 10.39% in value added. The biggest decline in manufacturing is seen in "the building of ships, oil platforms and modules and other transport equipment". Its share in employment reduced from 5.55% to 2.48%. A similar decline is also seen in terms of value added of the sector (by 3.35 points). Agriculture and forestry also faced diminishing shares both in terms of employment (from 4.19% to 2.41%) and value added (from 1.46% to 0.92%).

The statistics indicate that Rogaland region has been economically dependent on the oil and gas sector and the recent increasing shares of the sector in the composition of Rogaland's economy seem to show a deepening of the dependence. As the oil price crisis of the mid-2010s has shown, the dependence on such a volatile sector results in the vulnerability of the regional economy to external shocks. The ongoing economic problems caused by the recent crisis have led to calls for a more diversified regional economy, which entails serious repercussions for Rogaland as being the centre of gravity of the Norwegian economy. Several actors from the public and private sector have embraced the calls for diversification and introduced some initiatives either by themselves or in collaboration with other actors. In the face of these developments, the University of Stavanger, being a significant player that connects many other stakeholders, faces a challenging environment to (re-)position itself and (re-)define its role as an actor that can help shape the future regional economy in Rogaland.

Literature review and analytical approach

The literature highlights the different roles universities perform in their regions. These are broadly delineated as knowledge production, entrepreneurial and developmental roles (Charles, 2006; Gunasekara, 2006; Uyarra, 2010). The presence of universities produces enormous economic impact on local economies. Because teaching and learning –to a significant extent– take place in a localised setting, local firms tend to benefit from the activities of universities. Their utilisation of new knowledge and hiring of skilled graduates enhances their innovative capacities and competiveness (Feldman, 2003; Goddard and Vallance, 2011).

While the knowledge production role of universities remains crucial, this alone does not engender the needed stimulus. However, their adoption of an entrepreneurial mission is assumed to provide the right impetus to stimulate economic growth (Clark, 1998; Etzkowitz, 2004), the argument being that encouraging universities to exploit commercially their research results in regional economic benefits. Such benefits include the creation of new firms, renewal of existing firms, evolution of clusters, job creation, and the attraction of creative talent and capital (Power and Malmberg, 2008; Trippl *et al.*, 2015). Consequently, the commercialisation of university research in the form of licensing, patents and spin-offs has become a core mission of most universities (Grimaldi *et al.*, 2011).

However, doubts have been raised about the potential of universities' entrepreneurial activities to catalyse regional growth (e.g. Philpott *et al.*, 2011). Some have argued that universities without a strong science research base may be unable to achieve a meaningful economic impact on their regions. Even among those with strong research base, few are able to profit from their intellectual property rights (IPRs) with the majority failing to reap significant returns from their technology transfer activities (Abreu *et al.*, 2016; Huggins *et al.*, 2008).

The weaknesses inherent in the narrow entrepreneurial roles have prompted calls for universities to consider broader developmental roles with social as well as economic impacts (Abreu and

177

Grinevich, 2013; Arbo and Benneworth, 2007). Under this developmental approach, universities adapt their teaching and research to meet both the industrial as well as the societal needs of their localities. Universities' staff, faculty and students adopt a proactive stance by setting the agenda for community development and working with other stakeholders or network of actors to solve community challenges (Chatterton and Goddard, 2000; Gunasekara, 2006). The extent to which the developmental roles of universities affect their host regions is contingent on numerous factors. These include age and type of university, regionalisation of the higher education system, nature of the region, regional identity and networks (Benneworth, 2013; Boucher *et al.*, 2003; Trippl *et al.*, 2015).

Although this developmental role has gained currency among policy makers, the utility of this approach in helping solve regional development challenges has been questioned (Uyarra, 2010). While universities are located in regions, they equally remain part of a vast scientific community from which they gather resources (Benneworth and Hospers, 2007). Therefore, adapting teaching and research to fulfil a region's developmental needs might be detrimental to the long run success and relevance of universities (Uyarra, 2010).

In sum, there seems to be a blur in the boundaries between these roles. Universities perform a combination of these functions in their engagement with regions or localities (Uyarra, 2010). This suggests that universities' contribution to regional development can be analysed through different conceptual approaches (Goldstein, 2010). We turn to discuss briefly the approach and conceptual frameworks we have used to analyse our case.

Conceptual frameworks

The objective of this chapter is to assess the role UiS has played in the development of the energy, healthcare, and manufacturing sectors in Rogaland. Specifically, we focus on the petroleum, renewable energy, healthcare, maritime, and food production industries. Since these are different sectors, they are obviously characterised by unique innovation systems. Therefore, we draw on Lester's (2005) industrial transformation model, and Tödtling and Trippl's (2005) RIS failures typology to help capture the intricate details in our analysis. We apply these frameworks side-by-side to enable us discover various deficiencies prevailing in these sectors and the type of innovation-led growth pathway applicable in each context. Moreover, it aids in assessing the way UiS has confronted the demands of the regional innovation system in each priority sector of the region. The details of the analysis are presented later. However, we briefly discuss each of these frameworks in the following.

Industrial transformation model

Lester (2005) highlights the roles universities play during periods of local industrial transitions. The framework identifies four possible transformations namely, indigenous creation, industrial transplantation, diversification into related industries, and upgrading of existing industries. Indigenous creation involves the establishment of an entirely new industry without any link to existing technology in the region's economy. Under this transition, typical university activities include facilitating new business formation through incubator programs, developing favourable licensing regimes, and linking academics with local entrepreneurs.

The introduction of an existing industry from one region to another constitutes an industrial transplantation. In this context, the industry may be longstanding in the locality of origin. However, it

179

represents a new development in the destination region. Key university functions entail developing new study programmes, upgrading of existing curricula, and introducing flexible learning programmes to meet the human capital needs of the new industry. Another transformation relates to diversification into technologically related industries. This happens when technological assets of a struggling or collapsed industry are harnessed to develop a similar but new industry in its place. Universities' key roles in this process include connecting previously separate local actors or technological activity, and promoting the legitimacy of the new industry locally.

Lastly, industrial upgrading denotes enhancing the technological base of an existing industry through improvements in production technologies or the introduction of new products and services. Introducing novel technologies helps to sustain the competitiveness of an existing or mature industry. Local universities support this transition by increasing problem-solving interactions with industry, and helping industry leaders search and adopt global best practices.

RIS failures typology

Tödtling and Trippl (2005) distinguish between three primary types of RIS failures (or RIS deficiencies): organisational thinness, lock in, and fragmentation. Organisationally thin innovation systems are characterised by weakly developed or non-existing clusters primarily comprising SMEs. Furthermore, emphasis is more on incremental and process innovation. There are inadequate levels of knowledge transfer among actors and little networking in the innovation system because of weak clustering.

Conversely, lock-in innovation systems are often dominated by large firms operating in declining industries. In addition, innovation activities follow mature technological trajectories, and there is weak coordination between specialised knowledge transfer organisations. There are closely-knit inter-firm networks and strong relationships between key private and public actors.

RISs with fragmentation failures have many industries or services but lack knowledge-based clusters. Research and development activities are mostly concentrated at the headquarters of firms, often outside the region. More so, there is a lack of interaction and knowledge exchange among public research organisations and firms, resulting in low levels of product innovation and new firm formation.

The founding, educational and research impact of the University of Stavanger

Brief history

The University of Stavanger (UiS) has experienced a period of accelerated development in the last few years, resulting from a series of actions rooted in the support given by regional elites and industry (Fitjar, 2006). The idea of establishing a regional university was proposed by local politicians and industrialists in the early 1960s. Following the decline of the region's key industrial activities, regional leaders and captains of industry reasoned that academic research could provide the impetus for economic development. However, they could not obtain the support of the government at that time because a new university had then just been established in Tromsø. This notwithstanding, the need to establish a higher academic institution in Stavanger became pertinent, following the discovery of oil in the early 1970s. In order to train a skilled workforce for the oil exploration, a regional college and a technical college merged to start a three-year oil technology education (Oftedal and Iakovleva, 2015; Westnes *et al.*, 2009).

In 1989, the vision of establishing a university in Stavanger received a major boost when parliament adopted the Hernes Committee's recommendation of reducing the number of state colleges. Consequently, in 1994 six public colleges and one private college joined to form the University College of Stavanger (HiS). The university college had to wait for another 10 years to receive a charter as an autonomous public university. The king of Norway, his Majesty King Harald, officially commissioned the young university in 2005. Figure 7.A2 in the appendix traces the chronological events leading up to the establishment of UiS.

Education impact

From its inception, the university recognised its role as providing education to meet the human resource needs of the local industry. The growth of the oil and gas industry profoundly influenced the development of its academic programmes. At the initial stage of its founding, UiS focused on providing engineering and technology education with particular emphasis on oil technology and petroleum engineering programs (Westnes *et al.*, 2009). Although UiS carved a niche for itself as a technical university, over the years, it has diversified its study programmes. Consistent with the rising trends in Norway towards interdisciplinary study programmes (Vabø and Aamodt, 2008), it now provides career-oriented courses and professional qualifications ranging from arts to technology studies. Recent reorganisation of the academic structure of the university mirrors this change in strategy. For instance, three new faculties namely, Health Sciences, UiS Business School and Performing Arts have been created in addition to the three existing ones (faculties of Science and Technology, Social Sciences and Arts and Education).

The expansion of faculties and the addition of new programmes indicates the growth of the university. The student population has followed a consistent increase since 2007, growing from 7,441 in

2007 to 8,788 in 2012, and by the 2017 academic year, the number stood at 10,368. Although its growth rate surpassed the national average, its enrolment was lower than similar sized national universities. For instance, the student population of University of Agder (UiA) was around 7,500 but this increased to 9,497 and 11,421 in 2012 and 2016 respectively (Tilstandsrapport-hovedrapport, 2017). Nevertheless, two disciplines –health and education– have recorded impressive growth. For instance, 364 students graduated from these programmes in 2012 while 589 students completed in 2016, exceeding the target of the Ministry of Education by 15%. By this result, UiS performed better than the established universities (University of Oslo, University of Bergen and University of Tromsø) which failed to achieve their targets.

The employability of graduates from the university benefits from the industry-focused and multidisciplinary educational model designed to meet the needs of the labour market. A study by NIFU in 2015 shows that a high share of Master's graduates from the university are able to find jobs a year after graduation compared with their peers from the traditional universities. For instance, in 2013, 88% of UiS graduates secured relevant jobs compared with 85%, 77% and 76% of graduates from the Norwegian University for Science and Technology (NTNU), University of Bergen (UiB) and University of Oslo (UiO) respectively. Even at the height of Norway's economic crisis in 2015, seventy-six percent of the university's graduates found employment as against an average of 73% from the other three universities (NIFU, 2016, p.17).

Research and technology transfer impact

Research represents another key area of the university's functions that was influenced by the oil industry. The commercial exploration of oil in 1973 prompted the need for research institutions to conduct testing and other applied research for the industry. The local authorities realised the regional college possessed barely any capacity in this area. Therefore, they established Rogaland Research (RF) as the research arm of the then regional college. RF became an independent research institute not long after its founding. In 2006, it underwent restructuring and became the International Research Institute of Stavanger (IRIS)[28] which is jointly owned by UiS and the Rogaland Research Foundation (Westnes *et al.*, 2009).

While UiS's initial research activities were shaped by the oil and gas industry, it has redirected its focus on achieving excellence in academic research. Research centres linked to various faculties spearhead the university's research efforts. Most of the centres' projects are multidisciplinary involving researchers from diverse scientific fields. These research centres also maintain research cooperation with regional, national and international research partners. The regional collaborators include the University Hospital, Business School BI Stavanger, the Norwegian School of Veterinary Science and the Diakonhjemmet College Rogaland (Oftedal and Iakovleva, 2015). The research interaction of the centres outside the region is diverse. While some are active in national research projects, others are involved in international projects.

The university has made some strides in achieving research excellence as well. There has been steady growth in its publication outputs, even though it lags behind the traditional universities on some indicators. A study by NordForsk in 2017 reveals that UiS's publication volume has been increasing at an average rate of twelve percent annually from 1999 to 2014. Similarly, there was a rise in its publication points from 739.1 in 2015 to 805 in 2016 placing it ninth in the leading Norwegian higher education institutions (Tilstandsrapport-hovedrapport, 2017). Relatedly, the

---

[28] IRIS became part of NORCE Norwegian Research Centre A.S. from the beginning of 2018.

184

quality of the publications has also improved. Its publications in the top ranked journals (level 2) rose from 17.6% to 20.5% in 2014 and 2016 respectively.

Internationally, UiS has achieved modest gains in its research collaborations. The proportion of its outputs that were international co-publications shot up from 30% in 2010 to 46% in 2016. These gains notwithstanding, it still fell behind the more prestigious Norwegian universities. However, in contrast, on citation rates UiS performs better than its established counterparts. Although it produces a few hundreds of publications, these publications command high citations. A sizeable share of this comes from research in mathematics, natural sciences and technology subjects. This depicts a fascinating picture of the university's research orientation. Even though it has made sustained efforts at broadening its research scope, its technology and engineering antecedents are still dominant.

It is instructive to note that the university also prioritises research commercialisation and technology transfer to industry. From its initial years, UiS has maintained an active partnership with the Innovation Park of Stavanger (Ipark) and Prekubator to bring its breakthrough scientific and technological ideas to the market. Ipark, which is Norway's first science park, is situated close to the university. It houses knowledge-based start-ups and other companies that provide support services to these nascent firms. One such service provider was Prekubator. It was set up in 2002 to provide technology transfer services to the then University College and other partner institutions in the region. Its function was to ensure the commercialisation of ideas or discoveries of researchers and students through patenting, licensing or spin-off ventures. To ensure the efficient provision of these services, Ipark and Prekubator merged in 2016 to form Validé. This current entity manages the intellectual property and venture portfolios of UiS. In

2012, the university's total commercialisation (i.e. business ideas, patent applications, licences and new enterprises created) was 39. This figure increased to 60 and 78 in 2015 and 2016 respectively[29].

Trajectory of UiS's regional engagement

Focussing on regional engagement through university-industry relations, based on Lester's (2005) categorisation of the university roles in regional innovation-led growth, there has been an evolution in the roles that UiS has played so far in the development of industries in the Rogaland region. Before examining this though, the development of university-industry relations in the broader Norwegian context is examined. This relationship is particularly important at the policy level, where the national innovation system exerts huge influence over the regional innovation system (cf. Korres, 2013). This is even more so for the Rogaland region, where the (currently) most crucial industrial sector for the Norwegian national economy, the oil and gas industry, is concentrated.

Layers of Norwegian industry

Wicken (2007) has argued that the Norwegian innovation system has developed three layers of industries. These include:

- Small-scale decentralised industries (the first layer) which developed during the early 1900s.
- Large-scale centralised industries (the second layer) which became an important element of the Norwegian economy during the first two decades of the 20th century.
- R&D intensive network-based industries (the third layer) which emerged during the last part of the 20th century.

---

[29] See: UiS Annual Report, 2016-2017 (in Norwegian). Available online at: http://www.nsd.uib.no/polsys/data/filer/aarsmeldinger/AN_2016_25618.pdf

As noted by Sejerstedt (1993) and Wicken (2007), the first public sector R&D labs in Norway were instituted at the end of the 19th century to support the first layer of the Norwegian innovation system, i.e. the small-scale decentralised industries, and more specifically, the agriculture and fisheries sector. However, the establishment of the technical university NTH in Trondheim in 1910 is actually considered as the start of public research support targeted at industry in Norway (Gulbrandsen and Nerdrum, 2009). This makes Norway a late comer in public research effort with an industrial purpose in the European context. Moreover, the reorganisation of NTH which strengthened its ability to support Norwegian industrialisation happened only after WWII.

Firms in the second layer, i.e. the large-scale centralised industries such as metals, chemicals and wood pulp, have mainly appeared during the 20th century - based on the exploitation of the vast hydropower resources across the country - and have had some internal R&D capacities but have also cooperated with universities and colleges. Nevertheless, Wicken (*ibid*) explains that until the mid-20th century, the small-scale decentralised industries were still dominant in the Norwegian economy, and that political support for the large-scale centralised industries in Norway increased particularly after WWII. He also mentions university departments as the main partner for the industrial labs of the firms in the 2nd layer.

Commercialisation-oriented research institutes in the 3rd layer, emerged during the last decades of the 20th century, and due to the vast influence and importance of the oil industry, many of them have focused their activities on serving the needs of the firms in the 2nd layer, and mainly those in the oil and gas industry . In other words, the firms in the 3rd layer have largely formed an *enabling sector* for the firms in the 2nd layer (Wicken, *ibid*).

The dawn of university-industry relations in Norway

Gulbrandsen and Nerdrum (2007) explain that in Norway, a considerable increase in the share of industry funding of university R&D took place in the 1980s. The authors relate this increase specifically to the technological challenges of the companies that are active in the North Sea, and also the development of large firms within the electronics and computer industry. Accordingly, they provide data indicating that in 2003 (just one year before UiS applied for university status), the share of external funding for the University College of Stavanger (HiS) was 47%, which was higher than that of any Norwegian university at the time[30]. This was partly due to the oil industry's role in the Stavanger region and its need for external R&D. At the same time, in 2003, Norway removed the so-called "professors' privilege", and the higher education institutions gained the rights over intellectual property related to inventions from research carried out at the higher education institutions. Previously IP rights were held by the inventor. Furthermore, at the turn of the century, several research policies were passed in Norway, which had implications for higher education and research organisations, giving them a statutory duty to interact with external users (Thune, 2006).

UiS's engagement through second and third mission activities

When the system of regional colleges was instituted in the 1970s in Norway, they were primarily established as a tool for regional development, rather than for improving the national system of higher education (Sæther et al, 2000). However, their involvement in R&D was lower than that of the fully-fledged "universities". Gulbrandsen and Nerdrum (2007) imply that the engineering

---

[30] However, the fact that HiS had lower total expenditure compared to the Norwegian full-fledged universities shall be taken into account here.

college in Stavanger was an exceptional case among its peers in Norway in conducting substantial R&D. This was mainly done through the institute Rogaland Research (Rogalandforskning or RF) which was established in 1973 jointly by Rogaland Regional College (itself being established in 1969) and Rogaland County Council, and contributed largely to the newly-established oil industry in the country and the region.

The main focus of the constituting colleges of the HiS before (and also to a large extent, after) their consolidation in 1994-1995 was limited to education, except for the department of petroleum engineering which, using RF as its applied research arm, conducted some research activities. In particular, the Centre for Oil Recovery (COREC) was established in 2002 as a joint initiative of HiS, RF, and a number of leading Norwegian and international firms in the oil and gas industry. COREC itself contributed to the establishment of UiS in 2005, and is hosted now by the NORCE, and UiS is still a partner. Additionally, the Collaborative Competence Cluster for Industrial Asset Management (CIAM) was established in 2002 following a public-private partnership effort which began in 1998. Since its inception, the partner companies from the oil industry have remained the key members with its activities mostly related to offshore construction.

When the oil industry in Stavanger set up a fund to transform the state college in the city (i.e. the HiS) into a university, part of the requirement for this was to have four PhD specialisations established. This requirement was fulfilled by starting PhD programmes in petroleum technology and offshore technology in 1999 and risk management and educational sciences in 2003. In fact, three out of the four PhD programmes by HiS (i.e. petroleum engineering, offshore engineering, and risk management) were directly related to the activities of the oil and gas industry in the region. With gaining university status in 2005, three other PhD

189

programmes were also established in the same year, in the areas of *information technology, chemistry and biological sciences*, and *management, economics and tourism*. Indeed, with the acquiring of university status, the establishment of research centres became a priority for the UiS. But these were also initially formed mainly around the research needs of the petroleum industry in the region as well as the long-established relations with the healthcare sector. The reorganisation of RF to IRIS in 2006 is one of these efforts. The Centre for Organelle Research (CORE), focused on cell biology, was also founded in 2006, again as a joint initiative of UiS and IRIS, but also in cooperation with the Stavanger University Hospital (SUS). In fact, a considerable proportion of all PhD candidates or graduates are being trained (or were trained) in petroleum technology and natural sciences related programmes. (See Table 6.1 for details.) This further confirms the pivotal role of the relation with the aforementioned two sectors in the university's science and technology-related research activities.

The new research centres emerging in the later years have shown an "interdisciplinarity" focus, which might be considered only as signs of preparation for a future transition to a Mode 2 university[31] (Gibbons *et al.*, 1994), and can eventually transform the social and economic engagement model of the UiS. In particular, the Centre for Risk Management and Societal Safety (SEROS) was established by UiS and IRIS in 2009, which today consists of research groups from three and two departments at UiS and IRIS respectively. One of the growing areas of engagement for SEROS is its participation in the Norwegian Tunnel Safety Cluster (NTSC). This is in line with the growing share of the construction industry in the region's economy, which has mainly taken place due to the recently intensifying tunnel construction activities in the

---

[31] *Transdisciplinarity* is considered a characteristic of Mode 2 universities, which goes beyond interdisciplinarity, in the sense that the interaction of scientific disciplines is much more dynamic.

region. In 2012, the Centre for IP-based Service Innovation (CIPSI) started its activities, which is hosted by the department of Electrical Engineering and Computer Science, but has internal collaborations with most of the other research centres at the UiS. Its goal is to strengthen the applied ICT research at UiS and IRIS, including the use of Big Data analysis in 'smart cities'.

In parallel with organising the research centres and programmes, the debate around the role of UiS in *innovation* led to the establishment of Prekubator TTO in 2002. Expressed in terms of technology readiness levels (TRLs), the focus of this technology transfer office's activities is on technology optimisation as well as proof-of-concept stages, and does not cover the operationalisation and commercialisation of the ideas (Annual Report of Prekubator, 2015). The number of commercialisation activities based on ideas coming from UiS has so far been very low, however. Indeed, innovation activities in the departments other than the petroleum engineering and health sciences are not very focused yet, and are of anecdotal nature (P. Ramvi[32], personal communication, September 7, 2017). Therefore, it can be said that the interdisciplinary research activities which have emerged in the last ten years in the UiS have not systemically delivered innovation outputs yet. Furthermore, there has been efforts to upgrade the traditional sectors of agriculture and fishing into a food cluster through new initiatives like NCE[33] Culinology programme, which was established in 2007 in the Ipark, and was considered Norway's largest industrial gastronomy research group, but was closed down after the end of its funding period in 2017.

---

[32] Special Advisor at UiS on Research and Innovation
[33] NCEs: National Centres of Expertise in Norway

Table 6.1. The number of PhD candidates in UiS's PhD education specialisations.

PhD programmes	Established	Candidates Dec. 2016	Doctoral defences 2008-2016
Offshore Technology	1999	19	36
Petroleum Technology	1999	48	40
Risk Management and Societal Safety- social sciences	2003	9	19
Risk Management and Societal Safety- science and technology	2003	28	36
Educational Sciences	2003	43	36
Information Technology, Mathematics and Physics	2005	31	22
Management, Economics, Tourism	2005	46	37
Chemistry and Biological Sciences	2005	34	27
Literacy	2007	22	11
Health and Medicine	2011	60	4
Sociology, Social Work, Culture and Society	2011	18	5

Role of supra-regional research networks

Supra-regional networks are an important part of the knowledge architecture in understanding the relations between academic research and industry in Rogaland. Strand *et al.* (2017) point out that the industrial county of Rogaland bypasses national knowledge institutions by making direct contact with international knowledge institutions and customers (see also Strand and Leydesdorff, 2013). Strand *et al.* (*ibid*) point to the high rate of co-invention between Rogaland and the Houston area in the U.S., indicating the strong link between the Norwegian and U.S. oil and gas industries. This has been reflected in the research and development activities of the UiS as well. In December 2015, the *Norway Pumps and Pipes (NP&P)* initiative was introduced following the example of Houston. It is an interdisciplinary research and development programme, which aims at using the knowledge and competencies gained in the oil and gas industry within the healthcare sector. Areas of interdisciplinary research fall within cardiology, stroke treatment technology, simulation and modelling, signal and image processing, and risk modelling. The cooperative partners behind the initiative are Stavanger University Hospital (SUS), NORCE Norwegian Research Centre AS, University of Stavanger (UiS) and Greater Stavanger. NP&P aims to reach academic and research communities across the European continent and become a European hub for the programme. Thus, it is expected that this already supra-regional (and supra-national) network, which has learned tremendously from its counterpart in the U.S., continue growing in its outreach across Europe.

Furthermore, the knowledge networks of the other Norwegian regions have also been serving some part of the knowledge demand in the Rogaland region. Fitjar and Rodriguez-Pose (2011) point to the division of labour between Stavanger as the petroleum

193

capital of the country and Trondheim as the main centre of research in the natural sciences in Norway. A similar supra-regional relation has been formed for research on offshore wind energy, where Christian Michelsen Research AS, located in Bergen (Hordaland region), hosted the Norwegian Centre for Offshore Wind Energy (NORCOWE) from 2009 till 2017, with UiS's CIAM as an associated partner. When it comes to the agriculture, fisheries and food industry, the research and higher education centres in other regions, such as Hordaland (UiB), Akershus (Norwegian University of Life Sciences-NMBU) and Troms (Nofima) have served the knowledge demands of the sector in Rogaland more than regional institutions.

Latest changes in UiS research directions with potential for regional engagement

When it comes to engagement with industry, the science and technology departments are more inclined to get involved. The Faculty of Science and Technology had initially targeted petroleum and offshore technology, risk management and social security as priority areas in its 2014-2020 strategy. However, this was revised in 2017 focusing on the following thematic areas:

- Oil and energy
- Oceanic science and technology
- Healthcare technology
- ICT and infrastructure

Indeed, the priority areas of the faculty had previously been related to the disciplinary areas. Nevertheless, such focus is changing to prioritise cross-sectoral themes in a way that enables the faculty to deal with societal challenges more directly (Ø. L. Bø[34], personal communication, September 21, 2017).

---

[34] Dean of the Faculty of Science and Technology at the University of Stavanger

Furthermore, the faculty has ventured into research and education in Big Data. For instance, it recently introduced a Master's degree programme in Applied Data Science. Considering this renewed focus on ICT and infrastructure, there is the potential for faculty to increase engagement activities especially in smart city projects.

Overall, the university has prioritised regional engagement in its 2017-2020 strategy document. For instance, the strategy targets an increase in the share of externally funded research projects as a proportion of its total income from 20.1% (in 2016) to 25% in 2020. In fact, engagement with society is a big focus of the university now (T. G. Jacobsen[35], personal communication, May 29, 2017). Hence, it appears that UiS is consciously following a policy of deepening engagement with its regional environment. At the heart of this societal engagement strategy with the goal of societal development and innovation lies a newly created forum by the UiS. We elaborate on this in the following section.

Intensification of triple helix practice in the region

Strand *et al.* (2017) use the county-level data in Norway, and decompose the Triple Helix synergy (i.e. synergy in University-Industry-Government relations) in the counties into three components of *geographical*, *technology*, and *organisational synergy*. They conclude that the county of Rogaland has shown the highest level of regional Triple Helix synergy in Norway, but that this synergy is more specifically *technological*.

Inspired by the success of Linköping city-region in Sweden with the formation of a Triple Helix (and later, Quadruple Helix) organisation for interaction, the UiS board has recently (in 2016) formed a *value creation forum* (verdiskapingsforum), which is led by the rector. Industry executives, public-sector leaders and policy

---

[35] Research and Innovation Director of the University of Stavanger

makers from the region also participate in this forum. The primary goal is to discuss key issues of economic value creation. It has four *coordinated action groups*, including:

- *Innovation and commercialisation*: the purpose of this group is to strengthen the link between research, industry and entrepreneurial activities, including student entrepreneurs. The secretariat is located in Validé, the official technology transfer company for the UiS.

- *Big projects and cluster development*: the purpose of this group is to contribute to large-scale research and innovation projects receiving regional support. The secretariat is located at the Research and Innovation Department of the University of Stavanger.

- *Innovation initiative*: the purpose of this group is to provide connection between innovation initiatives and conferences and arenas. The secretariat is at the Greater Stavanger authority.

- *Ullandhaug*: the purpose of this group is to become the meeting place of board directors and daily managers of the institutions located in Ullandhaug competence area. The secretariat is situated at the University Fund (Universitetsfondet).

The Forum is to advise the management of UiS with regard to its new regional and national engagement directions and areas.

It is evident the latest strategy adopted by the university is geared not only at diversification of its priority areas for research but also broadening of regional engagement activities. Signs of the transformation from being a reactive actor to a more proactive engaging university is gradually emerging. Nevertheless, the success of this most recent approach remains to be seen in the coming years.

Sectoral impact

In the preceding sections, we have highlighted the economic and academic developments of Rogaland in the last half century. In this section we synthesise the extent to which these developments have evolved together and propose policy options for enhancing their growth into the future. We use Lester's (2005) framework to analyse the role of UiS in an innovation-led growth path of the industries in the Rogaland region. Previous use of this framework in analysing the role of UiS was primarily informed by the dominance of university-industry relations in the region around the petroleum industry. Comparing the roles that the Universities of Stavanger and Tromsø have played in the development of their respective regions, Gjelsvik and Arbo (2014, p.14) conclude, "...the universities' role in local innovation processes depends on which transition pathway the region is experiencing." The authors argue that the initial role of the higher education sector in Stavanger was to consolidate the industrial transplantation (Type 2 path). However, the oil and gas cluster in the region has experienced maturation thus forcing UiS to transform its role in helping the upgrading of existing industries (Type 4 path). They further assert that the long-term collaboration underlying this path evolution is based on trust and tacit knowledge.

As indicated earlier, a return to good years for the petroleum industry in Norway (in 1969, 1993, 2003) has taken place on one or two years prior to historic milestones of the university (which were in 1969, 1994, 2005). These seemingly fortuitous happenings prevented the university from departing from its historical focus on petroleum related education and research.

197

However, we argue that the role of UiS in the industrial development of Rogaland region is not homogeneous across all the departments and faculties, as the RIS deficiency with which the industries in Rogaland are faced, are not all the same, and do not necessarily call for a similar role from the knowledge generation institution. Lester (*ibid*, p.28) points to this when writing about the university's contribution to local economic development: "it will likely be different in different parts of the same university to the degree that different industries are present in the region."

Accordingly, we aim to take a broader perspective in covering industries crucial for Rogaland. As previously stated, the most important economic sectors in the Rogaland region in terms of value added include:
- Oil and gas extraction including services
- Health and social work
- Manufacturing

The contribution of manufacturing industries to the regional economy has dropped compared to a decade ago. However, this is not a new occurrence for the region. In fact, shipbuilding –which was the primary manufacturing activity in the region – has stagnated to date following the advent of the petroleum industry. The other two important sectors, however, have retained and even increased their share in the regional economy.

Referring to the VRI programme[36] in Rogaland (2007-2016), Jakobsen et al. (2012) suggest the county's industrial structure

---

[36] VRI is an abbreviation of *Virkemidler for Regional FoU og Innovasjon*. The English title of the programme is Programme for Regional R&D and Innovation. VRI is a public innovation programme operated by the Research Council of Norway and was introduced in 2007 to stimulate research and innovation at a regional level through cooperation between research and development (R&D) institutions and industry.

(excluding the petroleum sector) is organised in three priority areas. These represent (renewable) energy, maritime industries[37], and food industries[38]. The healthcare industry later emerged as the fourth priority area, with special emphasis on welfare technology.

Based on this delineation, we have chosen to focus our assessment on the role UiS has played in the development of energy (petroleum and renewable), healthcare, and manufacturing (with focus on maritime and food production) sectors. In order to analyse the role of UiS in the development of these industries we need to firstly understand the specifics of the regional innovation system related to each of these industries. So, our analytical approach is based on putting the RIS deficiencies of each sector based on Tödtling and Trippl's (2005) typology, vis-à-vis Lester's categorisation of university roles in regional innovation-led growth pathways.

Energy sector

When it comes to the energy sector, the risk of (sectoral) RIS failure in the form of R&D lock-in is high in the region[39], due to the fact that applied research in the region has been heavily dominated by the prioritisation of the petroleum industry. The history of UiS and IRIS's R&D activities, which have been heavily dominated by petroleum engineering, itself is a clear testimony to this risk.

---

[37] In the Rogaland region, special weight lies within the petro-maritime industry.
[38] Rogaland has the highest employment numbers in the agriculture sector among the Norwegian regions, and follows Oslo very closely in terms of employment in the food industry.

[39] Narula (2002) argues about the problem of systemic R&D lock-in in Norway. Further evidence comes from the industry specialisation of the country; according to OECD (2011), between 1998 and 2008, Norway had the greatest increase in sectoral specialisation among OECD countries (the Hannah-Kay index for Norway decreased by 40%), making it the third most specialised OECD economy.

Using Lester's (*ibid*) categorisation of university roles in the alternative regional innovation-led growth pathways, we witness the addition of new roles along the time vector. The UiS's role started with the transplantation of the petroleum industry into the region. It assisted with this process through the training of requisite human resource and providing responsive curricula since its establishment. Later, the upgrading of that maturing industry has been added to the first role since the establishment of IRIS and also the establishment of PhD programmes in petroleum and offshore engineering. Recently, the diversification of this old industry into (technically) related new one(s) has been added to those previous layers. Specifically, research on environmentally friendly and renewable energy, is benefiting from the already existing competencies in the academic and business[40] sectors in the region. The establishment of forums like the Science Meets Industry Stavanger (with focus on offshore wind energy), Nordic Edge Expo (with focus on smart cities), and also the university's recent research focus on the geothermal and offshore wind energies can be considered as the early signs of UiS's new role in this diversification path.

Referring to Lester's four categories, Isaksen and Karlsen (2010) explain that the last two roles (i.e. diversification and upgrading) may have become more important as a result of the introduction of the open innovation model, i.e. that firms rely more on external sources of knowledge and technology in their innovation activity. Accordingly, the emergence of an era of the region's economic diversification could provide a bigger role for UiS as an innovation partner, as the actors involved in the diversification or upgrading of the established energy sector would open up for cooperation with knowledge generating bodies in the region.

---

[40] The largest onshore wind farm in Norway (Tellenes wind farm) was inaugurated in 2017 in Rogaland.

Healthcare sector

Concerning the healthcare sector, the current policies in the region have apparently targeted a perceived fragmentation in the sector. The plans around establishing the new university hospital at the university campus area (according to which the hospital will be ready for use in 2023) is a clear indication of this. Furthermore, potential plans on establishing a Medical School in the university target the knowledge flow aspect. The UiS (and its predecessor institutions) have developed relevant educational curricula (specifically nursing education) in the higher education sector of the region, and have long been supplying the sector with the necessary human resources. In response to the fragmentation in the RIS of the healthcare sector in the region, as of 2011, PhD programmes in health and social work have constituted the latest two PhD programmes established at the university. Some of the PhD research works within the biological sciences (established in 2005) have also served the healthcare sector research needs. Furthermore, CORE, SAFER (Stavanger Acute Medicine Foundation for Education and Research), Norway Pumps and Pipes, and Smart Care Cluster of Norway are some of the research and innovation initiatives which have been developed by, or in collaboration with UiS. As noted, a new university hospital will be established in the Ullandhaug competence area, which would intensify the relation between UiS and healthcare sector in the region. Furthermore, IRIS has medical technology as a new priority in its research portfolio, specifically in connection with its involvement in the Norway Pumps and Pipes initiative. Therefore, using Lester's model, we can see an evolving of UiS's role in the healthcare sector from supporting the transplantation of the sector in the region in the last century through supplying the sector with human resource and responsive curricula, to the upgrading of the sector in the region through contract research and global best practice scanning and replicating. In other words, UiS's role has evolved to upgrading of the healthcare sector in the region.

Maritime sector

Concerning the maritime industry, the declining shipbuilding industry in the region[41] has left the main activities of the industry in the Rogaland region around oil platform construction. While UiS's CIAM and its PhD programme on offshore technology have established some connections to the sector, supra-regional research networks seem to play a more significant role for the R&D needs of the sector. Benito *et al.*'s (2003) survey showed that the level of contact between companies in the Norwegian maritime sector and R&D institutions is generally quite low. The Global Maritime Knowledge Hub initiative was launched by the Norwegian Shipowners' Association and Maritime Industry Forum of Norway in 2008. 21 professorships and research centres were defined within the initiative to be sponsored by the Norwegian companies in the sector. Almost half of the positions were defined within NTNU, Norway's main technical university. None of the Knowledge Hub positions were allocated to the UiS. Hence, organisational thinness appears to be the RIS deficiency of the maritime sector in Rogaland, as there is no academic research and innovation capacities developed in the UiS to contribute to the functioning of the sector's RIS in the region. As an exception, the research activities at the UiS around the offshore technology can be mentioned, as it partly contributes to the maritime industries in Norway through knowledge spill-over from the shared technologies.

---

[41] In fact nowadays the large shipyards are concentrated on the North-Western coast of Norway and Ålesund area, while shipping cluster is mainly formed in Bergen.

Food production

Similar to the shipbuilding industry, fish canning, which was one of the first industries established in Rogaland, experienced decline during the last three decades on the 20th century (Fløysand and Jakobsen, 1999). Also, a situation similar to Rogaland's maritime sector can be noticed for the wider food production sector in the region, where there is no dedicated academic department for the R&D activities of the sector, and supra-regional research and training institutions (e.g. NMBU, UiB, NTNU, Nofima) play a more significant role in this respect. This is despite the fact that the agriculture and food industry in the Rogaland region is the largest among Norwegian regions. An exception is CORE's research relations with Nofima, as well as the Centre for Innovation Research's role in research on food waste and fisheries economics in Norway. However, these do not seem to fill the structural hole in the RIS of the food production sector in the region. Therefore, it can be said that organisational thinness is the RIS deficiency of food industry too in Rogaland, and UiS has not striven to contribute to the innovation-led growth of these industries in the region. For instance, NCE Culinology which was dubbed as Norway's largest research group within industrial gastronomy was closed down in 2017. UiS was one of the R&D members in this only NCE of Stavanger. An evaluation report stated that NCE Culinology had still a way to go to achieve a nationally recognised gravity for the food sector (Oxford Research, 2013). The Faculty of Science and Technology's new strategy on including the oceanic science and technology in its research portfolio includes fisheries and aquaculture as a potential area of new research focus, so its implementation remains to be observed. Table 6.2 summarises our conclusion regarding the role UiS has played in corresponding to the RIS deficiencies of the priority sectors for the Rogaland region.

Table 6.2. Summary of UiS's role in addressing the RIS needs of priority industries in Rogaland

Priority industry	RIS deficiency	UiS role	Assessment
Energy	Lock-in	Transplantation, upgrading, and recently, diversification into related new industries.	Diversification into new related industries is a suitable response to the lock-in risk. But it is a new direction in the university's research, hence premature for assessing its success.
Healthcare	Fragmentation	Transplantation and upgrading.	Upgrading is a fitting response to the fragmentation problem. The continuously increasing relation between the university, hospital and other healthcare actors in the region indicates a successful role.
Maritime	Organisational thinness	No significant role	-

Food production	Organisational thinness	No significant role	-

Conclusion and policy implications

Based upon our findings from studying the role that the University of Stavanger has played in the innovation-led growth of priority industries in the Rogaland region, we can outline four main policy implications of the paper. First, the fact that academic research policies and the extent of their thematic concentration in regions are vastly influenced by the national higher education policies implies that there is a need for closer dialogue between regional and national innovation system actors in order to harmonise the long-term development of strategic sectors in the regions with the knowledge production capacities. The case of petroleum engineering education and research in Rogaland is a success story in this respect, even though it has not followed a smooth path. Second, in order to provide the regions with a potential for securing regional resilience through adopting path renewal and path creation strategies (cf. Coenen *et al.*, 2016), higher education policies should embed a diversification vision within the curricula concentration map across the regions. The case of UiS shows us that overemphasising the educational and research requirement of one industry may impede the sectoral RISs related to other important industries in the region from achieving their innovation aspirations. Third, the transition towards the Mode 2 university model, and closer engagement with the societal challenges through transdisciplinary research and innovation, requires a long-term tradition in the 'disciplinary' research areas in the first place. The fact that the oil industry and healthcare sector in Rogaland have managed to replicate a global best practice interdisciplinary research collaboration (Houston Pumps and Pipes) for the region, while these two sectors in Rogaland enjoy the best and longest relationships with the higher education sector, can indicate such a conditionality. Finally, higher education policies at the university level need to have a deep understanding of regional (as well as national) innovation system deficiencies in each specific sector, and tailor their industry engagement strategies accordingly. The case of the food sector in Rogaland implies that R&D collaboration by universities needs to be adapted to the realities of value chain as well as innovation cycle that is active and influential at each point in time and space, so that it delivers results in correspondence with the sectoral RIS and NIS needs.

Appendix 6.1

Table 6.3. Sectoral Employment Averages in Rogaland

1997-2007 Average		2008-2015 Average		Change
Total industry	%	Total industry	%	
Agriculture, hunting and forestry	4.19	Agriculture and forestry	2.41	-1.77
Fishing and fish farming	0.41	Fishing and aquaculture	0.32	-0.08
Oil and gas extraction incl. services	**5.04**	Mining and quarrying	0.33	0.03
Oil and gas extraction	2.07	**Oil and gas extraction including services**	**9.73**	**4.70**
Service activities incidental to oil and gas	2.96	¬ Oil and gas extraction	NA	
Mining and quarrying	0.30	¬ Service activities incidental to oil and gas	NA	
Manufacturing	**16.80**	**Manufacturing**	**11.55**	**-5.25**
Food products, beverages and tobacco	2.55	¬ Food products, beverages and tobacco	2.15	-0.40
Textiles, wearing apparel, leather	0.36	¬ Textiles, wearing apparel, leather	0.17	-0.19
Wood and wood products	0.72	¬ Wood, wood products and paper products	0.58	-0.14
Pulp, paper and paper products	0.07	¬ Printing and reproduction of recorded media	0.23	-1.17
Publishing, printing, reproduction	1.40	¬ Refined petroleum, chemical and pharmaceutical products	0.08	-0.56
Refined petroleum, chemical and mineral products	0.63	¬ Rubber, plastic and mineral products	0.66	
Basic chemicals	0.11	¬ Basic metals	0.59	
Basic metals	1.20	¬ Machinery and other equipment n.e.c	3.15	-0.79
Machinery and other equipment n.e.c.	3.94	¬ **Building of ships, oil platforms and moduls and other transport equipment**	**2.48**	**-3.07**
Building of ships, oil platforms and moduls	**5.55**	¬ Furniture and other manufacturing n.e.c	0.32	0.04
Furniture and other manufacturing n.e.c.	0.28	¬ Repair and installation of machinery and equipment	1.15	
Electricity and gas supply	0.50	Electricity, gas and steam	0.35	-0.15

207

Water supply	0.05	Water supply, sewerage, waste	0.44	0.39
Construction	**6.28**	**Construction**	**7.41**	**1.13**
Wholesale and retail trade, rep. of mot. veh. etc.	12.81	Wholesale and retail trade, repair of motor vehicles	12.08	-0.73
Hotels and restaurants	3.17	Transport via pipelines	0.00	0.00
Transport via pipelines	0.00	Ocean transport	2.32	-0.52
Ocean transport	2.85	Transport activities excl. ocean transport	4.46	0.13
Other transport industries	4.33	Postal and courier activities	0.55	0.00
Post and telecommunications	1.25	Accommodation and food service activities	3.14	-0.03
Financial intermediation	1.26	Information and communication	2.41	
Dwellings (households)	0.04	Financial and insurance activities	1.13	
Business services	9.39	Real estate activities	0.70	
Public administration and defence	4.78	Imputed rents of owner-occupied dwellings	NA	
Education	6.97	Professional, scientific and technical activities	4.72	
Health and social work	**16.14**	Administrative and support service activities	5.14	
Other social and personal services	3.45	Public administration and defence	4.55	-0,23
General government	25.01	Education	6.40	-0,57
CENTRAL GOVERNMENT	5.53	**Health and social work**	**17.16**	**1.03**
Civilian central government	4.87	Arts, entertainment and other service activities	2.65	
Defence	0.67	Mainland Norway	0.00	
LOCAL GOVERNMENT	19.48	¬ General government	23.68	
Market producers	72.71	¬¬ Central government	6.66	
Non-market producers	27.30	¬¬ Local government	17.03	

Source: Statistics Norway, Regional Accounts. Authors' own calculation. (Retrieved from http://www.ssb.no/en/nasjonalregnskap-og-konjunkturer/statistikker/fnr)

Table 6.4. Sectoral Value Added Averages in Rogaland

1997-2007 Average	%	2008-2015 Average	%	Change
Total industry	%	Total industry	%	Change
Agriculture, hunting and forestry	1.46	Agriculture and forestry	0.92	-0.54
Fishing and fish farming	0.92	Fishing and aquaculture	0.57	-0.35
Oil and gas extraction incl. services	**11.44**	Mining and quarrying	0.48	-0.07
Oil and gas extraction	6.44	**Oil and gas extraction including services**	**18.36**	**6.92**
Service activities incidental to oil and gas	5.00	¬ Oil and gas extraction	NA	
Mining and quarrying	0.54	¬ Service activities incidental to oil and gas	NA	
Manufacturing	**17.00**	**Manufacturing**	**10.39**	**-6.60**
Food products, beverages and tobacco	2.25	¬ Food products, beverages and tobacco	1.70	-0.54
Textiles, wearing apparel, leather	0.25	¬ Textiles, wearing apparel, leather	0.13	-0.12
Wood and wood products	0.51	¬ Wood, wood products and paper products	0.36	-0.15
Pulp, paper and paper products	0.06	¬ Printing and reproduction of recorded media	0.18	-0.84
Publishing, printing, reproduction	1.01	¬ Refined petroleum, chemical and pharmaceutical products	0.16	-0.63
Refined petroleum, chemical and mineral products	0.78	¬ Rubber, plastic and mineral products	0.51	
Basic chemicals	0.22	¬ Basic metals	0.74	-1.46
Basic metals	2.20	¬ Machinery and other equipment n.e.c	3.07	-1.01
Machinery and other equipment n.e.c.	4.08	¬ **Building of ships, oil platforms and moduls and other transport equipment**	**2.05**	**-3.35**
Building of ships, oil platforms and moduls	**5.40**	¬ Furniture and other manufacturing n.e.c	0.28	0.05
Furniture and other manufacturing n.e.c.	0.23	¬ Repair and installation of machinery and equipment	1.23	
Electricity and gas supply	2.54	Electricity, gas and steam	1.95	-0.59
Water supply	0.17	Water supply, sewerage, waste	0.57	0.40

209

Construction	5.78	Construction	7.34	1.56
Wholesale and retail trade, rep. of mot. veh. etc.	8.92	Wholesale and retail trade, repair of motor vehicles	7.10	-1.82
Hotels and restaurants	1.86	Transport via pipelines	0.00	
Transport via pipelines	0.00	Ocean transport	1.84	-1.89
Ocean transport	3.73	Transport activities excl. ocean transport	4.59	0.68
Other transport industries	3.90	Postal and courier activities	0.35	
Post and telecommunications	1.39	Accommodation and food service activities	1.60	-0.26
Financial intermediation	2.60	Information and communication	3.59	
Dwellings (households)	4.94	Financial and insurance activities	2.92	0.32
Business services	11.64	Real estate activities	2.75	
Public administration and defence	4.15	Imputed rents of owner-occupied dwellings	3.81	
Education	4.91	Professional, scientific and technical activities	6.13	
Health and social work	9.14	Administrative and support service activities	4.42	
Other social and personal services	2.95	Public administration and defence	4.27	0.13
General government	16.78	Education	4.69	-0.23
CENTRAL GOVERNMENT	4.86	Health and social work	9.71	0.57
Civilian central government	4.30	Arts, entertainment and other service activities	1.65	
Defence	0.56	Mainland Norway	0.00	
LOCAL GOVERNMENT	11.92	¬ General government	16.36	
Market producers	77.80	¬¬ Central government	5.83	
Non-market producers	22.20	¬¬ Local government	10.53	

Source: Statistics Norway, Regional Accounts. Authors' own calculation. (Retrieved from http://www.ssb.no/en/nasjonalregnskap-og-konjunkturer/statistikker/fnr)

Figure 6.1. Macroeconomic indicators for the petroleum sector, 1971-2017.

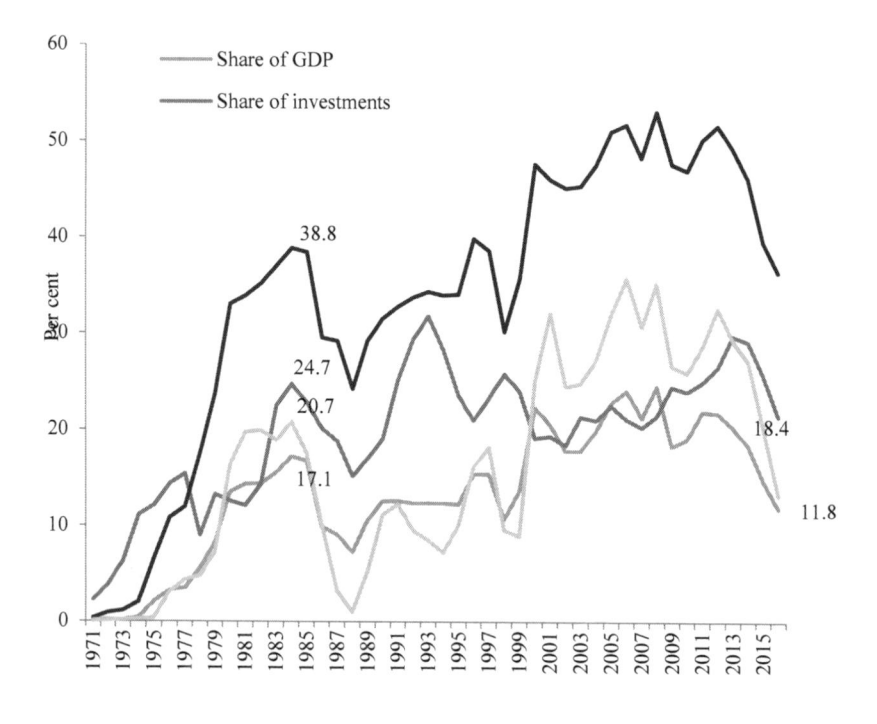

Source: Norwegian Petroleum Directorate. (Retrieved from
http://www.norskpetroleum.no/en/economy/governments-revenues/)

Figure 6.2. The chronology of events leading to the founding of UiS

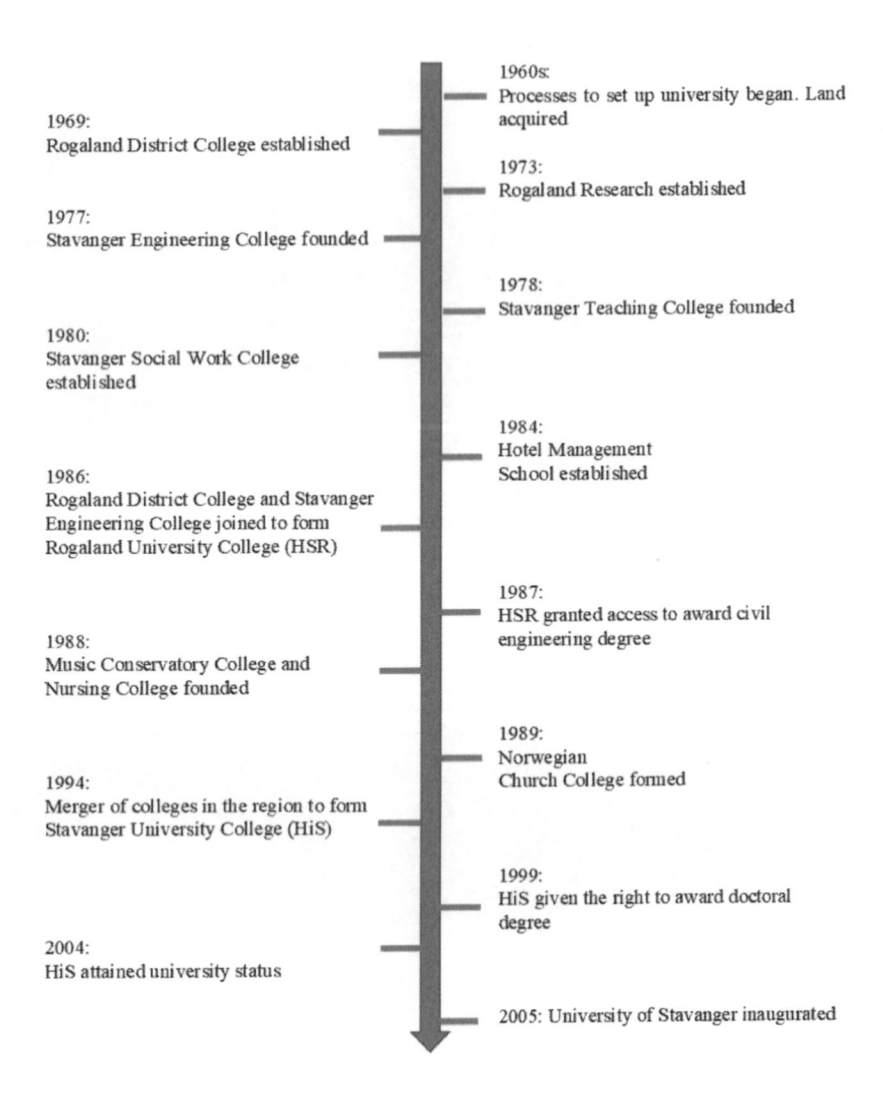

1960s:
Processes to set up university began. Land acquired

1969:
Rogaland District College established

1973:
Rogaland Research established

1977:
Stavanger Engineering College founded

1978:
Stavanger Teaching College founded

1980:
Stavanger Social Work College established

1984:
Hotel Management School established

1986:
Rogaland District College and Stavanger Engineering College joined to form Rogaland University College (HSR)

1987:
HSR granted access to award civil engineering degree

1988:
Music Conservatory College and Nursing College founded

1989:
Norwegian Church College formed

1994:
Merger of colleges in the region to form Stavanger University College (HiS)

1999:
HiS given the right to award doctoral degree

2004:
HiS attained university status

2005: University of Stavanger inaugurated

References

Abreu, M., Demirel, P., Grinevich, V., & Karataş-Özkan, M. (2016). Entrepreneurial practices in research-intensive and teaching-led universities. **Small Business Economics**, 47, 695-717.

Abreu, M., & Grinevich, V. (2013). The nature of academic entrepreneurship in the UK: Widening the focus on entrepreneurial activities. **Research Policy**, 42, 408-422.

Arbo, P., & Benneworth, P. (2007). Understanding the regional contribution of higher education institutions: A literature review. **OECD Education Working Papers**, (9), 1.

Benito, G. R. G., Berger, E., Forest M., & Shum, J. (2003). A cluster analysis of the maritime sector in Norway. **International Journal of Transport Management**, 1, 203-215.

Benneworth, P. (2013). University engagement with socially excluded communities. In P, Benneworth (Ed.), **University engagement with socially excluded communities** (pp. 3-31). Netherlands: Springer.

Benneworth, P., & Hospers, G. J. (2007). The new economic geography of old industrial regions: universities as global—local pipelines. **Environment and Planning C: Government and Policy**, 25, 779-802.

Boucher, G., Conway, C., & Van Der Meer, E. (2003). Tiers of engagement by universities in their region's development. **Regional Studies**, 37(9), 887-897.

Charles, D. (2006). Universities as key knowledge infrastructures in regional innovation systems. **Innovation: the European journal of social science research**, 19, 117-130.

Chatterton, P., & Goddard, J. (2000). The response of higher education institutions to regional needs. **European Journal of Education**, 35, 475-496.

Clark, B. R. (1998). The entrepreneurial university: Demand and response **Tertiary Education & Management**, 4, 5-16.

Coenen, L., Asheim, B., Bugge M. M. & Herstad, S. J. (2016). Advancing regional innovation systems: What does evolutionary economic geography bring to the policy table? **Environment and Planning C: Government and Policy**, 35, 600-620.

213

Etzkowitz, H. (2004). The evolution of the entrepreneurial university. **International Journal of Technology and Globalisation**, 1, 64-77.

Feldman, M. (2003). The locational dynamics of the US biotech industry: knowledge externalities and the anchor hypothesis. **Industry and Innovation**, 10, 311-329.

Fitjar, R. D. (2006). Building regions on economic success: Prosperity and regionalism in Rogaland. **Scandinavian Political Studies**, 29, 333-355.

Fitjar, R. D. (2010). **The rise of regionalism: causes of regional mobilization in Western Europe**. Routledge, London.

Fitjar, R. D. & Rodríguez-Pose, A. (2011). Innovating in the Periphery: Firms, Values, and Innovation in Southwest Norway. **European Planning Studies**, 19, 555- 574.

Fløysand, A. & Jakobsen, S. E. (1999). **The Norwegian fish processing industry. Regional adaptation and national policy implications**, Geografi i Bergen: Meddelelser fra Institutt for geografi Nr.233. 15s.

Gibbons, M., Limoges, C., Nowotny, H., Schwartzman, S., Scott, P., & Trow, M. (1994). **The new production of knowledge: The dynamics of science and research in contemporary societies**. London: Sage.

Gjelsvik M., & Arbo P. (2014). The Differentiated Role of Universities in Regional Development Paths. Paper presented at **RIP 2014 - 9th Regional Innovation Policies Conference**. Available online from: http://www.uis.no/getfile.php/Conferences/RIP2014/Publish_RIP2014 %20ID1368%20Gjelsvik% 20and%20Arbo.pdf

Goddard, J., & Vallance, P. (2011). Universities and regional development. In: A. Pike, A. Rodriguez-Pose & J. Tomaney (Eds.), **Handbook of local and regional development** (pp. 425-437). London: Routledge.

Goldstein, H. A. (2010). The 'entrepreneurial turn' and regional economic development mission of universities. **The Annals of Regional Science**, 44, 83-109.

Grimaldi, R., Kenney, M., Siegel, D. S., & Wright, M. (2011). 30 years after Bayh–Dole: Reassessing academic entrepreneurship. **Research Policy**, 40, 1045-1057.

214

Gulbrandsen, M., & Nerdrum, L. (2007). University-Industry relations in Norway, **TIK Working Paper on Innovation Studies No. 20070613**

Gulbrandsen, M., & Nerdrum, L. (2009). Public sector research and industrial innovation in Norway: A historical perspective. In J. Fagerberg, D. C. Mowery, & B. Verspagen (Eds.), **Innovation, path-dependency, and policy: The Norwegian case** (pp. 61–88). Oxford: Oxford University Press.

Gunasekara, C. (2006). Reframing the role of universities in the development of regional innovation systems. **The Journal of Technology Transfer**, 31, 101-113.

Huggins, R., Johnston, A., & Steffenson, R. (2008). Universities, knowledge networks and regional policy. **Cambridge Journal of Regions, Economy and Society**, 1, 321-340.

Isaksen, A. & Karlsen, J. (2010). Different Modes of Innovation and the Challenge of Connecting Universities and Industry: Case Studies of Two Regional Industries in Norway, **European Planning Studies**, 18, 1993-2008.

Jakobsen, S., Byrkjeland, M., Båtevik, F. O., Pettersen, I. B., Skogseid, I. & Yttredal, E. R. (2012). Continuity and change in path-dependent regional policy development: The regional implementation of the Norwegian VRI programme, **Norsk Geografisk Tidsskrift - Norwegian Journal of Geography**, 66, 133-143.

Korres, G. M. (2013). The European national and regional systems of innovation. In E. G. Carayannis and G. M. Korres (Eds.), **The Innovation Union in Europe: A Socio-Economic Perspective on EU Integration** (pp. 85–98). Edward Elgar Publishing Limited.

Kyllingstad, N., & Hauge, E. S. (2016). Knowledge transfer in different regional contexts. In Johnsen, H. C. G., Hauge, E. S., Magnussen, M. L., & Ennals, R. (2016). **Applied Social Science Research in a Regional Knowledge System: Balancing validity, meaning and convenience**, Routledge, pp. 61-74.

Lester, R. (2005). **Universities, innovation, and the competitiveness of local economies. A summary Report from the Local Innovation Systems Project: Phase I**. Massachusetts Institute of Technology, Industrial Performance Center, Working Paper Series.

Narula, R. (2002). Innovation systems and 'intertia' in R&D location: Norwegian firms and the role of systemic lock-in. **Research Policy**, 31, 795-816.

Nerheim, G. (2014). Oil Shocks in an Oil City: The View from Stavanger, Norway, 1973-2008. In Pratt, J.A., Melosi, M.V., & Brosnan, K.A. (eds.). **Energy Capitals: Local Impact, Global Influence**, Pittsburgh: University of Pittsburgh Press, pp. 127-142.

NIFU (2016). Kandidatundersøkelsen 2015: I hvor stor grad er nyutdannede mastere berørt av nedgangskonjunkturen? **NIFU-rapport 17/2016**. Available at: //brage.bibsys.no/xmlui/bitstream/ handle/11250/2393490/NIFUrapport2016-17.pdf?sequence=1 Accessed on: 11/10/2017

NordForsk (2017). Comparing research at Nordic higher education institutions using bibliometric indicators covering the years 1999-2014. Policy Paper 4/2017

Oftedal, E. M. & Iakovleva, T., & (2015). Stavanger: from petroleum focus to diversified competence through crisis and consensus. In Foss, L., & Gibson, D. V. (eds.). **The Entrepreneurial university; context and institutional change**, London: Routledge, pp. 221-248.

Oxford Research AS (2013) Evaluering av NCE Culinology, Kristiansand.

Philpott, K., Dooley, L., O'Reilly, C., & Lupton, G. (2011). The entrepreneurial university: Examining the underlying academic tensions. **Technovation**, 31, 161-170.

Power, D., & Malmberg, A. (2008). The contribution of universities to innovation and economic development: in what sense a regional problem? **Cambridge Journal of Regions, Economy and Society**, 1, 233-245.

Prekubator TTO AS (2016) **2015 Annual Report**, Stavanger: Author.

Ryggvik, H. (2015). A Short History of the Norwegian Oil Industry: From Protected National Champions to Internationally Competitive Multinationals. **Business History Review**, 89, 3-41.

Sejersted, F. (1993). **Demokratisk kapitalisme**, Scandinavian University Press, Oslo.

Statistic Norway. **Labour Market Statistics 1990**. Retrieved from https://www.ssb.no/a/histstat/nos/nos_b965.pdf

Strand, Ø. & Leydesdorff, L. (2013). Where is synergy indicated in the Norwegian innovation system? Triple-Helix relations among technology, organization and geography. **Technol. Forecast. Soc. Change** 80, 471–484.

Strand, Ø., Ivanova, I. & Leydesdorff, L. (2017): Decomposing the Triple-Helix synergy into the regional innovation systems of Norway: firm data and patent networks. **Quality and Quantity**, 51, 963-988.

Sæther, B., Mønnesland, J., Onsager, K., Sørlie, K, and Arbo, P. (2000). **Høgskolenes regionale betydning**. Oslo: Norsk institutt for by- og regionforskning. ISBN: 82-7071215-9

Thune, T. (2006). **Formation of research collaborations between universities and firms**. Oslo: BI, PhD Thesis 8/2006.

Tilstandsrapport-hovedrapport (2017). **Tilstandsrapport for høyere utdanning 2017**. Available at: https://www.regjeringen.no/no/dokumenter/tilstandsrapport-for-hoyere-utdanning-2017/id2552473/. Accessed: 03/10/2017.

Trippl. M., Sinozic T., & Lawton Smith, H. (2015). The role of universities in regional development: conceptual models and policy institutions in the UK, Sweden and Austria. **European Planning Studies**, 23, 1722-1740.

Tödtling, F. & Trippl. M. (2005). One size fits all? Towards a differentiated regional innovation policy approach. **Research Policy**, 34, 1203-1219

The University of Stavanger (2017) **Strategy for the University of Stavanger 2017 – 2020**, Stavanger.

Uyarra, E. (2010). What is evolutionary about 'regional systems of innovation'? Implications for regional policy. **Journal of evolutionary economics**, 20, 115-137.

Vabø, A., & Aamodt, P.O. (2008). Nordic higher education in transition. In T. Tapper & D. Palfreyman (Eds.), **Structuring mass higher education. The role of elite institutions** (pp.57-72). New York & London: Routledge.)

Westnes, P., Hatakenaka, S., Gjelsvik, M., & Lester, R. K. (2009). The role of universities in strengthening local capabilities for innovation—A comparative case study. **Higher Education Policy**, 22, 483-503.

Wicken, O. (2007). The Layers of National Innovation Systems: The Historical Evolution of a National Innovation System in Norway. **TIK Working Papers on Innovation Studies**, Centre for Technology, Innovation and Culture, Oslo.

Chapter 7
Evolutionary Analysis of a University's Engagement in a Less-Developed Region:
The case of the University of Aveiro

Liliana Fonseca, Rıdvan Çınar, Artur da Rosa Pires, Carlos Rodrigues

The growing emphasis on the knowledge economy, particularly since the turn of the millennium, has raised the perceived importance of universities in society. In addition to teaching and research, the concept of a third mission for universities involving engagement with external actors has become more prominent, effectively institutionalising their role in economic development. In one response to help leverage knowledge flows and manage these new-found linkages, universities around the world have established intermediate offices, such as incubators and technology transfer offices, assuring their place in innovation networks. Despite the fulfillment of this role across various territorial levels, the region has become particularly important as universities' most immediate concern. This is given as it is often a socio-political and economic context which directly determines the opportunities of a higher education institution (HEI) to assert itself in other, broader geographical scales. The presence of an HEI can greatly boost regional innovation dynamics given the increased knowledge exchange that can occur between multiple stakeholders in the region. So the establishment of a university in a region may unlock dormant innovative potential, promoting the development of not just more interactive region-university relations, but also enabling the formation of links across other institutional boundaries (Chatterton & Goddard, 2003).

Studies focused on place-based approaches in regional development have put substantial emphasis on the geographical context, namely territory, culture, people and institutions (Barca, 2009). Research on economically successful regions indicates the importance of *institutional thickness* (Amin & Thrift, 1995; Rodríguez-Pose, 2013). HEIs, as significant regional actors, contribute to the development of regional institutions that affect the development trajectory of their respective regions. So, there has been a growing pressure on universities to play a part in their regions, to contribute to regional development and increase competitiveness and innovation capacity, with mutual benefits emerging from this interaction (Pinheiro et al., 2012).

In the literature, Less Developed Regions (LDRs) are characterised by a lack of structural resources and support services overall, as well as organisational and institutional thinness (Huggins & Johnston, 2009a; Tödtling & Trippl, 2005), low growth trajectories and a lack of innovative capacity. Universities located in LDRs offer the opportunity to nurture the innovative and competitive potential of their regions, partly because they are inextricably linked to the development of their surroundings (Goddard & Chatterton, 1999), and because in these contexts they can emerge as *animateurs* of the region's innovative and institutional fabric (Rodrigues et al., 2001).

This case-study of the University of Aveiro (UA) examines the experience of an HEI in a less-developed region. Well-positioned in national and international rankings and self-identifying as an entrepreneurial and innovative university, it faces typical regional problems: a weak institutional landscape, lack of financial

220

resources, a regional economic fabric dominated by SMEs operating in traditional sectors, and competition for investment and students with surrounding urban poles and universities. Located between the oldest Portuguese university – Coimbra – and the second largest city in the country, with its own university and renowned institutes – Porto – UA has sought, since its origins, to distinguish itself by encouraging a special connection to its region coupled with international research and teaching excellence. Nonetheless, these developments were not always linear, underlining the importance of analysing this link in an evolutionary manner and through a long-term perspective.

This study seeks to understand the particularities of building a university's regional engagement mechanisms and channels when located in an LDR. It aims at unraveling the role of UA in the region's development trajectory, especially relevant in managing the tensions in framing UA's efforts regionally without jeopardising its international position. Accordingly, this chapter briefly reviews universities' challenges in stimulating endogenous innovation in LDRs and how they are particularly equipped to circumvent them. It then elaborates on the role of UA in its region and reflects on the most prominent initiatives. It is suggested that UA has contributed towards innovation dynamics in Aveiro region in supplying both R&D needs as facilitating networked collaboration between regional actors. Yet, it faces internal organisational challenges which may hinder a potentially more fruitful and higher level of collaboration.

Universities and the nature of the development challenges in less developed regions

Characterising the less-developed region

The European Union (EU) developed its Cohesion Policy to reduce the persistent socio-economic disparities between and within its increasing roll of member-states. These disparities have become more emphasised in an increasingly globalised, capitalist economy, generating a growing divide between more and less-developed regions (Scott & Storper, 2003). To counterbalance them, the economic development and improvement of regions' well-being gradually came into focus within EU's discourse, as territory and economic geography also rose in importance. Faludi (2007, p. 568) placed value on the incorporation of this territorial aspect in the cohesion debate, referring to it as a way to "*unlock dormant potential*" in fields such as regional innovation.

The importance placed on the closing of regional economic gaps is reflected in the EU's budget, where one third is assigned to cohesion policy to restructure and revitalise deteriorating industrial areas and diversify rural impoverished regions, although cohesion policy also provides some support to even the wealthier regions now. While all regions are encompassed in this cohesion framework, they fall within different economic, goal-oriented categories. In the present 2014-2020 agenda, funding is allocated according to gross domestic product (GDP) measures between regions considered 'more developed' (with over 90% of the EU average of GDP per capita), those in 'transition' (75%-90%), and 'less developed' (less than 75%) (figure 8.1). Additional funds are also allocated for those member-states with a gross national income (GNI) per capita under 90% of the EU average. Following this logic, the largest amount of funding is allocated to those considered less developed, which include most of the newest member-states and Southern European countries, such as Greece, Portugal, southern Italy, along with a few Spanish and UK regions. Most of these regions can be included in what Rodríguez-Pose & Fratesi (2007) categorise as 'sheltered economies' in Southern Europe, i.e., isolated regions, with low employment absorption and high unemployment, that depend on

222

the central government for their economic survival (Fonseca, 2017).

Figure 7.4 - 2014-2020 EU's Regional Policy classification of regions. Source: European Commission, 2011.

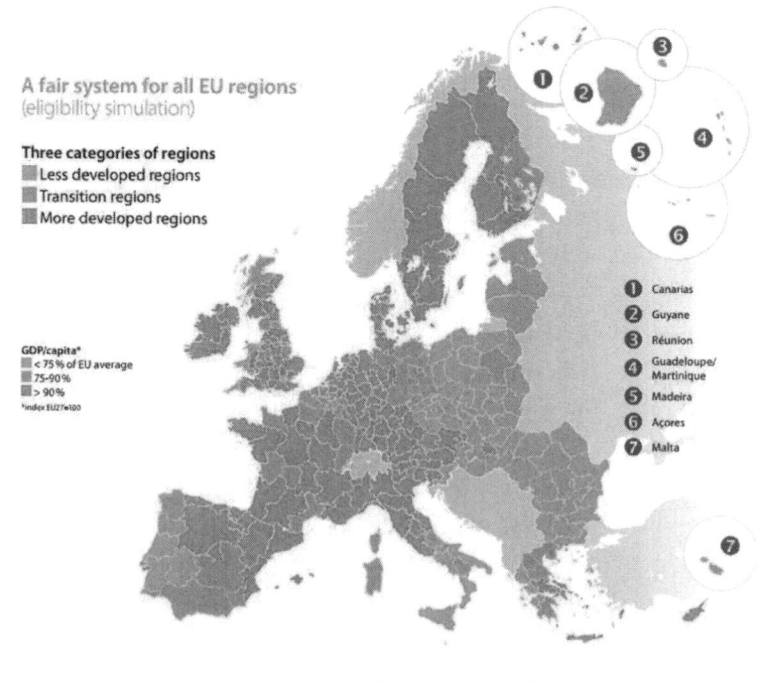

© EuroGeographics Association for the administrative boundaries

It is possible to associate the LDR categorisation to Tödtling & Trippl's (2005) description of a peripheral region. As with LDRs, these are characterised as having a low level of R&D, lack of qualified human capital, an SME-prevalent economy, a lack of clustering efforts, lack of specialised services and organisational and institutional fragmentation overall. Similarly, Huggins & Johnston (2009) indicate these regions tend to lag behind in competitiveness and knowledge indicators, such as economic output per capita, employment levels, innovation, patenting, and knowledge-intensive firms; they exhibit low growth trajectories and fragmented links to external knowledge sources. This implies LDRs have a need for building not just structural factors, but institutional and organisational factors as well to develop their innovation capacity and development levels.

Stimulating innovation in LDRs

Innovation has become inextricably linked to the future development of LDRs. This is especially tied to the shifting of gears of EU's Structural Funds from 'heavy' (roads, buildings, basic training) to 'soft' infrastructure (innovation support services, digitalisation, environment and social inclusion). This change was sought for cohesion policy to address both the symptoms of peripherality (e.g., low GDP per capita, high unemployment) and the causes (weak innovation capacity) (Morgan & Nauwelaers, 2003). The present consensus views innovation as the triggering factor for socio-economic development (Rodrigues et al., 2001; Rodríguez-Pose, 2013), involving complex feedback and learning mechanisms enriched by a high degree of interactivity between science, technology, production, policy and demand (Guile & Fosstenløkken, 2018). It is also argued that innovation is a geographical process, with the effectiveness of interactive learning being greatly influenced by a variety of spatial features, such as urbanisation, localisation and diversity, and more generally agglomeration and interconnectivity (Feldman & Kogler, 2010). Concomitantly, as a process based on social relations among several actors, e.g. government, universities and industry, innovation is shaped by a region's institutional and cultural context (Cooke et al., 1997; Guile & Fosstenløkken, 2018; Morgan, 1996).

The requirements of fostering innovation mean a panoply of barriers for peripheral, less-favoured economies to overcome. There is a regional innovation paradox (Oughton et al., 2002), in that although lagging regions would need to receive and spend more public funds on innovation, they lack the capacity to effectively absorb them. According to Rodrigues et al. (2001), two challenges are usually more prevalent when attempting to promote innovation-based development in an LDR: (1) promoting a high-level of interaction between economic and institutional agents; (2) nurturing locally-based R&D activities. For the first challenge, the characteristic institutional fragmentation and weak ties of these regions hinder the spreading and reinforcement of learning dynamics, key to developing competitive capacity (Guile & Fosstenløkken, 2018; Morgan, 1996; Rodríguez-Pose, 2013). Structural factors related with the region's demand for innovation, such as the nature of the productive sector and the institutional framework, can also help explain the technology gap in LDRs (Landabaso, 1997). These can include: the lack of ability within traditional industries to identify and effectively assess opportunities and needs for innovation; the inadequacy of the financial system to adapt to inherent risks of innovation; low levels of interactivity and cooperation between the public and private sectors; lack of business support services; insufficient technological intermediaries; and detachment of the academic system from the productive sector (Jongbloed et al., 2008; Landabaso, 1997; Rodrigues et al., 2001).

Imbuing LDRs with the capacity to craft prosperous and sustainable interactive networks able to promote endogenous learning, innovation and development is therefore deemed of paramount importance (Huggins & Johnston, 2009b; Morgan & Henderson, 2002). The inability to engage in effective collaborative, collective action and networking characterises LDRs, suggesting institutional innovation and interinstitutional cooperation as crucial abilities to develop in this context. However, for a dialogue to develop, some level of mutual understanding needs to be reached. According to Morgan & Nauwelaers (1999, p. 3) "[…] *the most significant innovation* [in

LDRs] *might be to develop voice-based mechanisms through which firms and public agencies can begin to interact locally so as to explore joint solutions to common problems*". By building "local cultural cohesion", a region is more likely to develop the core competency of inter-institutional learning (Lawton Smith et al., 2001; Niosi & Bas, 2001). This echoes Hirschman's (1958, p. 25) argument of human agency in development, in that "[…] *the fundamental problem of development consists in generating and energising human action in a certain direction*". Aside from a scarcity of physical capital, education or entrepreneurship, alongside other conventional factors, the great obstacle in balancing development lies in "*the basic deficiency in organisation*" (Hirschman, 1958, p. 25). Hirschman (1958, p. 5) also posits economic development depends on activating "*hidden, scattered or badly utilised*" resources, which Morgan & Henderson (2002) agree as a way to unlock institutional inertia in LDRs.

The second challenge of developing effective R&D expenditure is key, as it is positively correlated with GDP levels (Rodrigues et al., 2001). More developed regions in the EU generally demonstrate a higher concentration of R&D investment, and other technological innovation outputs such as patenting activities (CEC, 2004). However, there is a rather weak correlation between regional growth and R&D expenditure and higher education levels (Sterlacchini, 2008). While the capacity to absorb highly educated people into the productive sector has seemingly improved in both developed and lagging regions, in the latter the effects can only be seen in the medium to long-term. Furthermore, in LDRs in Southern European countries such as Portugal, the above-average presence of a critical mass and R&D activities does not translate directly into GDP growth. Sterlacchini (2008) suggests this may be partly explained by a weakness in the regional innovation system of the LDRs, with characteristic weak linkages between the actors that compose it, namely industries and business enterprises, government, universities and research centres. Thus, higher education could assume a major role in the socio-economic development of LDRs, producing the main resource to fuel innovation – scientific and technological knowledge.

The pervasive role of universities

Universities are increasingly recognised as essential and legitimate strategic actors as nnovation is brought to the centre of regional economic strategies (Arbo & Benneworth, 2007; Uyarra, 2010; Pinheiro et al, 2012). As complex organisations they assume various activities with socio-economic impact, being employers and purchasers of services; knowledge and human capital creation and transfer; research-led technological innovation; capital investment; and impacting on the regional entrepreneurial, institutional and knowledge infrastructure (Drucker & Goldstein, 2007). This interactive character of relations between universities and other institutions within a region has been widely conceptualised under engagement models such as: the entrepreneurial university (Clark, 1998), enabling, through an enhanced development of linkages with external actors (namely businesses), to diversify universities' funding base; the triple helix model of university-industry-government relationships (Etzkowitz et al., 2000), with these nodes interfacing supported by intermediates (e.g. technology transfer offices); and the civic university model (Goddard et al., 2016), which emphasises community engagement and purposeful, institution-wide application of knowledge for the betterment of society. Aside from certain key differences, in all these conceptualisations the university emerges as a pivotal institution within a regional ecosystem, providing a key asset for competitive economic dynamics – scientific and technological knowledge. By generating an essential component of regional growth, universities become central interfaces, finding themselves at the nexus of innovation dynamics between policy, markets and other regional stakeholders (Edquist, 1997; Guile & Fosstenløkken, 2018; Rodríguez-Pose, 2013). This grants them the privileged position to build innovation capacity within a region, as by working closely with multiple actors they are improving feedback mechanisms and learning dynamics that will improve their individual competitiveness and strengthen trust and network ties overall.

In lagging regions, universities are thus seen as vital players in their regeneration, not just having a 'stake' in their development trajectory, but potentially assuming a leading role in a fragmented institutional structure and landscape. Indeed, universities, especially in LDRs, may have a pervasive role through their regular missions of teaching and research, but also actively engaging with other institutional actors and mobilising innovation capacity through the incorporation of the third academic mission. A regionally engaged university holds a position of influence in interactive and collaborative innovation networks, identifying key agents in the system, exploring development resources, creating linkages and enabling collective action, all particularly relevant for LDRs. In this sense, universities are capable of tackling the two major challenges of LDRs pointed out by Rodrigues et al. (2001). They are uniquely positioned to animate inter-institutional relations, namely between the public and private sector, and they provide and capture the R&D knowledge with the potential of building regional innovation capacity.

Not all are optimistic about the regional role of universities however, with scepticism regarding their 'boundary-spanning' capacity to act as institutional intermediaries (Krücken, 2003), and a disenchantment regarding their ability to successfully respond to local needs, particularly in less-developed or peripheral regions (Bonaccorsi, 2016). In the first instance, Krücken (2003) considers universities' organisational structure might not yet be adequately prepared to face the challenges and demands of the third mission, exhibiting a certain inertia in its arrangement and in its response to external needs. For Bonaccorsi (2016), a university's strategic vision is inevitably linked to the international recognition of research excellence, a focus that might diverge it from regional problematics. The commitment of a university to its local economy will increase with the degree of growth and development of its surroundings (Goddard & Chatterton, 1999). However, as stated by Arbo & Benneworth (2007), the absorptive capacity of university's local partners, i.e., their ability to successfully integrate and utilise investment or knowledge, is relatively smaller in LDRs, representing a limiting factor on the possible impacts of university's engagement.

The integration of a third mission of regional engagement presupposes organisational and managerial challenges for the university itself. This is particularly the case in a global higher education landscape, in which the quest for world-class universities raises competitive dynamics and shapes academic behaviour accordingly (Deem et al., 2008). Within LDRs, the low demand for advanced technical and scientific knowledge and the low financial dividends obtainable from regional engagement activities, diminishes the likelihood of the region being under focus, particularly by technology-related fields (Arbo & Benneworth, 2007). As a characteristically 'loosely-coupled' institution, the high autonomy of its academics leads to significant disparities between and even within fields – to fragmentation – hindering the application of a unified, coherent strategy for engagement (Gunasekara, 2006). Academics' motivation to engage is necessarily influenced by the time they have available to do so, with greater pressure given to perform in teaching and research activities for career progression. External engagement does not often yield satisfactory rewards, such as career progression, for individual academics, and the third mission inevitably tends to come in third place after research and teaching (D'Este & Perkmann, 2011; Rose et al., 2013).

Thus, albeit institutionalised, the third mission is not seamlessly introduced in the organisational framework and cultural setting of a university – *"the interaction between academia and society does not occur spontaneously"* (Rodrigues et al., 2001, p. 253), with certain prejudices needing to be overcome for it to work, both from the side of the university and from other regional actors. While a common issue in all regions, the lack of a supportive policy framework in LDRs for the development of such cooperative activities means there will be a greater difficulty in establishing this link. Universities can thus emerge as *animateurs* in the region (Pugh et al., 2016), as the task of devising an adequate strategy to foster links in an innovation network is mostly left to them. Universities in many LDRs are taking on this leading role, developing policies and strategies to promote engagement with their communities (Rodrigues et al., 2001). However, one must acknowledge the *"complexities and challenges facing contemporary HEIs in their attempt to address the multiple and often conflicting demands from a variety of external stakeholders"* (Kohoutek et al., 2017, p. 401). These range from the global and supranational to the national, regional and local levels, including the tensions and contradictions between different policy strands, namely education, science, innovation and development policies. Under these circumstances, whether the required changes at the organisational and behavioural level are enforced and become effective, is a matter of further analysis.

Considering the Challenges

In a less-developed region, where building competitive capacity and stimulating innovation and creative dynamics are imperative objectives, regionally embedding the university and promoting a more active dialogue between it and multiple agents, are core capacities to develop. Nonetheless, a *lack of relevant interaction between institutional agents* and a *low propensity of endogenous R&D activities* can be identified as potential obstacles to overcome. In these contexts, the existence of R&D resources does not immediately signify a boost in innovation-related activities, with a *lack of absorptive capacity* figuring characteristically in LDRs. This means the regional economy might not be able to effectively capture the scientific and technological knowledge available, implying that centres of research excellence may be less connected to the regional context than would be desired.

On the university side, the last point directly relates to the commonly discussed tension between international recognition of research excellence and regional embeddedness. Academics might be more focused on the former given the particularities of career progression. Likewise, since teaching and research are more easily quantifiable, evaluated and recognised, *academics' motivation* to engage with external partners, especially in a regional setting, is significantly inhibited. While regional engagement is now formally a part of the institutional mission of many universities, *organisational and managerial challenges* stemming from a fragmented system remain a key factor in inertia in the response to external demands. Consequently, the lack of a unified approach towards the region can hamper universities' ability to interact with other institutions.

Finally, also characteristic of LDRs, the *lack of an overall supportive policy framework* for the promotion of inter-institutional collaboration and for building meaningful

231

connections between university and society results in more isolated rather than regionally comprehensive endeavours. Capacity-building efforts are essential in such a context, and here universities can emerge as *animateurs*.

Considering these challenges, the next section presents the case of the University of Aveiro, based on content analysis of documents and in-depth interviews with academics, top-managers, intermediate offices and other regional agents. Emerging trends and tensions are identified to illustrate the evolving link between the university and the region.

The Aveiro region and the university: a historical overview

The territory in which UA operates can be divided into three administrative levels, namely Centro Region (provincial NUTS II), the District of Aveiro and the Intermunicipal Community of Aveiro Region (CIRA) (figure 7.2). The region of Centro consists of 8 sub-regions and 100 municipalities with a population of approximately 2.3 million. Focusing in on Aveiro, its district includes 19 municipalities with a population of around 713.000. The equivalent to the NUTS III level is CIRA, formed by 11 of these municipalities with around 370.000 inhabitants, with Aveiro, Ovar and Águeda being the most populated.

In the 1970s, the region had already a well-established industrial sector, though dominated by SMES in predominantly traditional sectors, namely in the municipalities of Águeda, Santa Maria da Feira, S. João da Madeira and Oliveira de Azeméis. However, this was relatively spread out throughout the territory with no salient urban area to anchor it. While growing in importance, this industry still coexisted with significant activities in the primary sector, such as agriculture, forestry, clay extraction, fisheries and animal farming. Presently, non-metallic minerals, automobile, chemical, food and metallurgy constitute more than 60% of the industry and productive sector (Rodrigues & Teles, 2017). Albeit still categorised as an LDR under the European Commission's categorisation, Aveiro region's industrial sector has undergone considerable changes in the last four decades, and it now appears to be sophisticatedly varied.

Figure 7.2 - Map of Portugal divided into NUTS II regions, showing Aveiro region inset. Regions in dark shading are categorised as less-developed by the European Commission. Source: InfoRegio (2017)

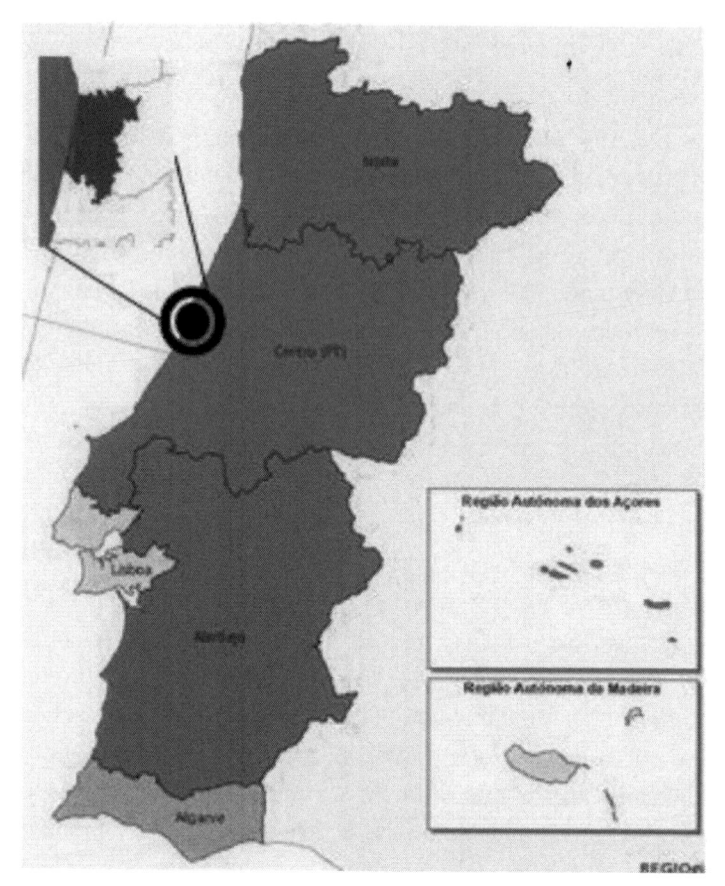

Two major actions have contributed to this evolution in the region's economic trajectory: the establishment of the Innovation Centre of Portugal Telecom and the consequent creation of the University of Aveiro (UA). Since then, the economy and industrial sectors have diversified with new activities such as ICT, petroleum derivatives, advanced forestry, ceramics, chemical, cork products, and finally, tourism. Mostly SME-dominated, the region can be characterised as industrially-diffused, both sectoral and geographically, with no significant urban growth accompanying its industrialisation process and with a diversity of activities, including a continuing importance of agriculture and growing industrial activities (Rodrigues & Melo, 2012; Rosa Pires, 1986).

During the 1970s and 1980s, several challenges affecting the region's development prompted more networked and concerted institutional action. The most pressing challenge was the environmental crisis related with the ria, the lagoon area and estuary river that encompasses 10 of the 11 CIRA municipalities. As a growing industrial region, and with few environmental regulations at the time, the ria was becoming heavily contaminated with a potentially serious threat to the population's health coming from mercury pollution (Pereira et al., 2009). With the objective of resolving this situation and improve environmental quality and living conditions, the Association of Municipalities of the Ria of Aveiro (AMRIA) was created in 1989 as a collaborative attempt at tackling a shared problem. With the scientific expertise of UA, namely its environmental sciences department, AMRIA carried out several projects to clean the ria and valorise the natural territory. This networked solution worked as the seed for future intermunicipal cooperation in the region. Another challenge at this time was a relative stagnation of the sectors of ceramics and materials, which despite a very gradual transformation still lacked significant knowledge resources and

234

research capacity to compete on a growing global stage. Overall, the industries in the region needed to diversify and be updated to incorporate more modern means of production and inter-sectoral innovation. A new sector was also emerging, namely telecommunications, or ICT. The Innovation Centre of Portugal Telecom (PT), the largest telecommunications provider in the country, was established in the city of Aveiro, and in need of specialised people and training in this area.

According to Rodrigues & Teles (2017), aside from the creation of PT's Innovation Centre, the implantation of a higher education institution – the University of Aveiro – demarked the emergence of an innovative and entrepreneurial ecosystem within the region. The University of Aveiro was created in1973, in a time of expansion and revitalisation of the higher education system in Portugal. more sensitive and attuned with regional needs and development potential, leading to the establishment and the progressively greater involvement of the university in the region. UA commenced its journey in the premises of the Innovation Centre of Portugal Telecom, an act which later had substantial impact in framing its identity and mission as a science and technology-based innovative university. The predominant industrial sectors in the region, the partnership with the Innovation Centre and the regional environmental challenges shaped the initial strategic direction of UA, enabling a facilitated university-industry connection that developed UA scientifically and technologically. In the context of its creation, UA was thus aimed at being regionally-embedded, but nonetheless possessed a specialised knowledge frame that enabled it to develop its international research excellence strategy. Therefore, it can be argued that the regional focus attributed to UA in its conception was mutually beneficial, both for itself and the region.

Growing in or with the region?

To understand UA's regional dimension, an overview of the national context is also needed. At the time of its creation, the economic structure of Portugal was shifting alongside the socio-political and educational system. The 60s and 70s were characterised by budget constraints and stagnation, first resulting from the colonial wars, but later due to the inflation of oil prices and a global crisis of capitalism. Globally, nonetheless, higher education was moving to a mass system, and particularly after the 1974 revolution Portugal needed to invest more in its knowledge infrastructures, to expand its higher education sector and renew it from a classicist focus to one that incorporated more technological and industry-related disciplines (Amaral et al., 2002). From the 70s onward, several universities were built throughout the country, with UA being one of them.

Because of the financial restrictions of the time, the new universities grew slowly at first. In the mid-80s, UA's physical expansion was limited as was, consequently, the development of its research and curricula (Amaral et al., 2002). At first, as proposed by regional commissions and considering the local context, its programme focused primarily on specificities and needs of Aveiro and Centro region, namely telecommunications and electronic engineering, glass and ceramics engineering, environmental sciences and pedagogic training – the latter especially relevant considering the need for professors in a growing higher education system. This was essential to differentiate UA from the established university centres of Porto and Coimbra, more classicist in nature . Anchoring itself in the region enabled the creation of UA's institutional identity, and its specialised curricula to give it a greater influence with both prospective students and local firms (Amaral et al., 2002). Concomitantly, UA sought to achieve competitive advantage through high quality teaching and research measured against international standards. This orientation towards the region and its actors, paired with a more global outlook has been identified in the UA discourse as its 'dual strategy', and can be summarised as a purposeful contribution towards the development of society.

From the late 80s onward, the access to more substantial financial resources permitted the expansion of UA's physical structure and curricula (namely to the social sciences and humanities), granting it a more competitive foothold on a regional, national and international level. To strengthen university-business and society links, UA created an executive structure called GrupUnave, in 1998, intended to approach university activities from a business perspective, with the aim of facilitating knowledge transfer not just in the more technological areas of UA, but also in the social sciences and humanities (e.g. Town and Country Planning, Sociology of Education) and humanities (e.g. Didactics, History).

In addition to the growing number of departments, UA established a number of significant research centres such as Aveiro Institute of Materials (CICECO), Centre for Environmental and Marine Studies (CESAM), Telecommunications Institute (IT), Centre for Research in Higher Education Policies (CIPES), and Governance, Competitiveness and Public Policies (GOVCOPP). GOVCOPP and CIPES are social science research centres in a relatively technical university. GOVCOPP, especially, is a unit that is heavily engaged with local and regional governmental bodies and has multiple partnerships and projects in the territory. According to the Portuguese Foundation of Science and Technology (FCT), in an evaluation of research units across the country, 52% of UA's centres achieved an "exceptional", "excellent" or "very good" performance. However, it is worth noting that the FCT's evaluation solely takes into account publication performance. As Bonaccorsi (2016) argues, this is no guarantee that these research

237

centres will be as locally embedded as desired. Nonetheless, the research focus of the centres tend to align with the main productive areas of the regional economy, and data on contracts suggests there is a wide-range of projects carried out by these centres and UA's departments with industry, regional government and other sectors.

Finally, there is evidence that UA's establishment has had an economically positive impact in the region, namely in the training of highly skilled individuals in relevant industrial areas. ICT, forestry, cork industry, fisheries and sea, and ceramics are economic areas that largely benefited from UA-industry collaboration. As an example, the ICT sector, through strong cooperation with UA, has been able to consolidate itself in the region, resulting in a cluster of 60 companies with an annual turnover of about 370 M€ and attracting the headquarters of the National ICT Cluster to the region (Rodrigues & Teles, 2017). The ceramic industry has also undergone a shift from local traditional products to more advanced, high-performance materials for building applications, and its main office, the National Cluster for the Habitat Sector, can be found at UA.

Insights from the Field

The University of Aveiro has been sensitive to regional relevant issues since its creation (CIRA, n.d.-a; CIRA & UA, 2014)(UA, 2012, 2016). As a coastal, river valley region, rich in minerals like clay, it is no surprise that Aveiro would first demand of its university more specialised, scientific knowledge in environment and marine sciences and in ceramics and materials. Other early departments of UA also included electronics and telecommunications, influenced by the location of the Innovation Centre of Portugal Telecom in Aveiro. Currently, while its curriculum encompasses more varied disciplines, it remains very much defined by regional needs and development challenges, with the paradigmatic examples being agro-food, industrial engineering and tourism. Due to the character of these specialisations, and because of this sought-out synergy with the region, UA has expanded its efforts to the wider region of Centro beyond the district of Aveiro, evidenced by its multiple polytechnic schools or campuses outside of the city (figure 7.3), and the various regional engagement projects it has participated in (CCDRC, 2016; CIRA, n.d.-a; UA, 2016).

Figure 7.3 - UA's regional outreach in terms of its educational institutes and programs. Source: UA (2016)

Both the physical presence of UA in the territory and its curricula were thought by interviewees to represent a distinguishing advantage of the university in acting upon the region. They believe UA acts as a central contact point for other local agents, an intermediary between the public and private sector, and as a symbol of progress and entrepreneurship, with its multiple projects making its action visible in the territory. While typical constraints are identified regarding a *lack of absorptive capacity* of the industrial sector, with limitations for the interaction of the university with SMEs mentioned by the academic interviewees, these are still believed to profit from the university's presence, if not by integrating its research, but by hiring its highly qualified graduates, and/or by utilising its laboratories and other resources. Also, the commitment of the university in entrepreneurship, materialised in the creation of a technology transfer office and an incubator on campus, has led to the emergence of a significant number of SMEs in the region, which inevitably absorb more of the university's available resources. Nevertheless, from the side of companies and municipalities, the involvement of UA in projects is still sometimes viewed with doubt and hesitation. Especially for industry, the academic way of working is seen as slow, fragmented and bureaucratic. Policymakers, on the other hand, may find the intensity of UA's participation as a threat to their political power and visibility, as a "stealing of the stage". These different perspectives are important to factor in when a university begins working towards regional engagement.

Regarding the *institutional and organisational management* and policies of the university, several mechanisms and channels were created to promote and monitor technology and knowledge-transfer activities, as well as other forms of entrepreneurship and regional engagement. Several initiatives for this purpose emerged since the late 90s. In 1998, a vice-rector was appointed to manage the linkages between university and society, implying an institutionalisation of the third academic mission within UA. A decade later, the strengthening and transformation of these institutional arrangements and connections resulted in the establishment of the position of Pro-Rector for Regional Development, functioning as a privileged contact point between the local and regional government and UA and coordinating actions between departments to conduct related innovative actions. Other formal channels created include the Business Incubator of UA (IEUA), dating back to 1996 and UATEC, UA's technology-transfer office, created in 2006. Both allow for a facilitated knowledge exchange with the region. IEUA collaborates with other regional entrepreneurial organisations, namely through IERA (Business Incubator of the Region of Aveiro) and RIERC (Network of Business Incubators of the Centro Region). UATEC focuses more on intellectual property issues, in creating links between the university and firms, in managing UA's technological platforms and in supporting UA in its work with CIRA and other local government bodies in matters of innovation policy.

Despite growing efforts by UA in establishing a formal strategy in matters of regional engagement, interviews indicated that "*such a strategy does not exist*". Goal setting, a crucial mechanism for promoting growth and effective implementation of strategies, is referred to as absent regarding regional engagement. The accounts of the academic staff suggest there is a lack of a unified approach, partly explained by the university being a 'loosely coupled' institution with a multitude of actors, each with high degree of autonomy and *modus operandi*. There is a recognition both in university documents and interviews that not all members of staff may want to be involved in such activities. Epistemological differences in scientific disciplines and traditions, the inherent contested nature of the third mission, the impact of rankings on universities' organisation and priorities are some of the factors that influence this, ultimately affecting the university-regional development relationship. A recurrent topic was the evaluation of academics for career progression. UA's mode of assessment is carried out in an online platform called PADUA, which has been refashioned in recent years to encompass this third mission discourse. Interviewees recognised the importance in including in this tool the assessment of a regional engagement dimension, alongside teaching and research, showing UA's commitment to its entrepreneurial and place-based mission. In practical terms, however, interviewees agreed that factoring this in the evaluation is detrimental to the overall score of academics. They acknowledge the evaluation system is, in a way, experimental, allowing for revisions. But while this does not occur, they are forced to omit recording their involvement in regional engagement activities in the evaluation rather than hinder the assessment of their mandatory commitment to teaching and research.

This is especially aggravated by the fact local involvement in LDRs and international recognition still sometimes divide academics' attention rather than being complementary. Equally influential is that most of the profit (if any) obtained from such activities is sifted through the university's main administration offices, with little reaching the involved departments and academics. It is therefore unsurprising that interviewees identify individual beliefs and values as the main *motivating factors* for partaking in regional engagement activities. The statements indicate that, even though there is no great financial or career progression benefit in engaging, there is a sense of accomplishment in contributing towards the advancement of the society around them.

The incomplete journey of building institutional and innovative capacity

Given its characteristics and developmental path, Aveiro region presents an intriguing perspective on collaborative and experimental approaches to innovation. The implantation of a knowledge-intensive institution seems to have enabled a growing number of networked and collaborative initiatives between regional agents. This is especially important as in the early days of UA's creation, Aveiro region was characterised by a rather fragmented institutional landscape, with little effective interaction between regional actors, and the absence of a unified sense of direction in the development of the territory. However, with UA's establishment, collaborations emerged even beyond local industry, with partnerships also including local and regional government, third sector organisations and community associations. This has not been bilateral nor one-sided, with such partnerships often involving multiple actors in a network-type collaboration and propelling the development of new research and fields of study in the university itself. None of these partnerships was straightforward, linear nor a hassle-free journey. Each one of them entailed their own challenges. Below, some examples of these university partnerships and their role in shaping institutional-building and overall regional development will be described.

Shaping regional development networks – territorial development strategies

As already mentioned, the challenge of environmental pollution in the 80s planted the first seeds of collaboration between municipalities, with AMRIA, but also between them and the university, through the department of environmental sciences. Years later, in 2007, a national policy enabled municipalities to manage a part of the structural funds (ERDF) and encourage intermunicipal cooperation. The policy – law n.º 45/2008 – aimed at promoting municipal association at the NUTS III level. From this, the Intermunicipal Community of the Region of Aveiro (CIRA) was created, formalising a partnership between 11 municipalities to tackle common issues. The agenda moved beyond the aspect of pollution and collaboration developed on a wide range of subjects, from energy, sustainability, employment, coastal management, and regional development. Towards achieving this, CIRA has placed since its establishment a special emphasis on its collaboration with UA, developing a close partnership and co-engaging in numerous national and international projects (CIRA, n.d.-b). In the realm of governance, UA has been viewed as a preferred partner (CIRA & UA, 2014) in knowledge-intensive development policies and innovation-related initiatives.

The first interaction between UA and CIRA can be traced back to the Territorial Development Program (TDP) of Aveiro in 2007, with inter-municipal and inter-institutional cooperation in the form of joint projects emerging to enhance innovation and entrepreneurship in the region (Rodrigues & Teles, 2017). For the opportunity to manage a share of the ERDF at the inter-municipal level, CIRA was required to draft a TDP. CIRA approached UA in pursuit of technical support to develop the inter-municipal program, which developed into the partnership contract between the two institutions, signed in June 2007. This was tightly aligned with the Lisbon Agenda, that considers the incorporation of scientific knowledge of paramount importance for the effective development of regional economy. It was not a unanimous decision, however, being the first vote that ever saw such a major discrepancy of 5 against versus 6 in favour. Scepticism was ripe among mayors not accustomed to working with academia (Rodrigues & Teles, 2017; Rosa Pires et al., 2012).

After negotiations, UA assigned a small team of academic experts to lead the initiative, as well as having created the position of Pro-Rector for Regional Development to manage these interactions. Several meetings were held, both at UA, to disseminate the project and assess other academics' interest, and at CIRA and municipalities, which allowed mayors to become familiarised with researchers and voice their concerns. The initial stages of the process revealed that, on the one hand, mayors and municipal staff were not aware of the knowledge and research available at UA, and on the other, neither were researchers aware of policy demands in regional challenges. A new wave of tension and disagreement erupted when each municipality submitted their list of projects based on the previous Community Support Framework instead of the new guidelines, which required the incorporation of scientific knowledge into the development plan. In the meantime, researchers also showed discontent, which started to threaten the feasibility of the process. Individual efforts of key personalities were crucial in addressing and overcoming the disagreement. In the end, negotiations ended favourably, with those involved suggesting the university's efforts in capacity-building helped guide the project forward. This enabled the most recent strategy to develop much more smoothly.

Following the end of the 2007-2013 Structural Fund programme and beginning of the 2014-2020 programming period, the European Commission introduced a new range of mechanisms for the utilisation of ERDF between regions. These new mechanisms stipulated smart specialisation as an *ex-ante* condition in accessing ERDF. Aside from a participation of UA in the smart specialisation strategy (RIS3) of Centro region, this was an opportunity to strengthen the link with CIRA, stimulating various forms of collaboration at the municipal, inter-municipal, inter-institutional and government level. Regional institutional and innovation networks, as well as policy design efforts, have thus largely been influenced by these supranational processes (Rodrigues & Teles, 2017; Rosa Pires et al., 2012). This recent and on-going territorial development strategy of 2014-2020 attempted to adopt some of the guiding principles of smart specialisation to achieve coherence between municipalities in their development efforts, leading to the delineation of five strategic regional areas: ICT, agro-food and forest, sea and Aveiro Lagoon, and materials. These strategic areas, in turn, have influenced UA's organisational structure, partly stimulating the creation of 8 related Technological Platforms (agro-food, forest, habitat, sea, bicycle and mobility, connected communities, high-pressure, moulds and plastics) to facilitate innovation and networked interaction with actors in the region.

Significant joint initiatives resulted from the above strategies, such as the Urban Network for Competitiveness and Innovation (RUCI), now concluded, focusing on a new agenda for culture, health and wellbeing, sustainability and promotion of entrepreneurship; and the Science and Innovation Park (PCI). The latter, inaugurated in 2018, is especially relevant as it is still in its infancy. It is another example of an inter-institutionally formed organisation with multiple stakeholders, such as UA at the scientific level, the municipalities of Aveiro and Ílhavo and CIRA at the governance level, and other entrepreneurial, community and industrial associations as well as businesses. It has five strategic priorities: ICT, materials, sea, agro-industry and energy, and it receives support from the university particularly in the form of R&D and management of scientific knowledge in these. Within these joint projects, as reported in interviews, UA was seen, if not as playing a leading role, as at least the core partner, activating or intermediating relations between various institutional agents towards more effective collective action. Thus, if not completely tackling the first challenge of a *weak institutional landscape* in the

LDR, the university was at least playing a major role in capacity-building and guiding interactions.

The relationship between UA and the region is not exclusive to CIRA and has spurred some interesting initiatives throughout the broader Portuguese territory, such as with the Commission of Centro region in the RIS3, or other more distant municipalities in matters of planning. The emphasis of the UA-CIRA collaboration, however, is because it is a more direct, participative and interactive form of engagement, that reports primarily to matters of policy-making and planning while also facilitating UA's outreach to companies and other associations for the broader development of the region. Rather than approaching a consultancy firm, CIRA chose to partner with UA. The partnership is also unique in the Portuguese context in the sense that UA and CIRA both took the leadership and responsibility of the strategies, each one undertaking half of the financial costs, suggesting a co-ownership of the projects rather than a typical consultancy service relationship. It was unique for UA too as, for the first time, it was not only paid to deliver a specific service but found the opportunity to take up a more significant role in regional development affairs in Aveiro, simultaneously building its outreach to companies and other associations for the broader economic and innovation system. It therefore prepared the ground for a more civic paradigm of university-region interaction.

Shaping regional industrial networks – dynamics of entrepreneurship

One of the initiatives resulting from the development strategies mentioned above was IERA, a project that aimed at creating an incubator network throughout the CIRA region, with one incubator in each municipality. IERA is a strategic initiative undertaken by CIRA, the Aveiro District Industrial Association (AIDA) and UA, with the objective of promoting territorial

247

strategies of economic development, entrepreneurship and social innovation, through differentiating and qualifying actions, spaces (poles) and services to support the incubation of business ideas and companies. The IERA hubs benefit from a common strategy, an integrated supply of equipment and services from different agents, and the use of scientific knowledge in UA. It claims to stimulate a dynamic and interactive process that incorporates the specificities and resources resulting from municipal and regional entrepreneurship, including the aspect of social innovation.

In practice, however, IERA suffers from its organisational structure. Relying on UA incubator as manager of the process, most of the dialogue and exchanges tend to happen between each incubator and UA, and not between the incubators themselves, in somewhat of a network imbalance. Second, given the accentuated differences in development throughout the 11 municipalities, not all incubated companies are technologically based, implying they will not require UA's scientific input and that UA might not actually consider them 'incubation' material. There are different views on how an incubator should be managed, and which types of businesses should be eligible, with UA often attracting the more high-tech projects to its premises.

Nonetheless, the project is promising, and to nurture the conditions for its operationalisation, a joint promotion programme for entrepreneurship and social innovation called the Platform for Support and Appreciation of Entrepreneurship and Innovation (PAVEI) was created in a collaborative process among various regional actors. The implementation of this programme resulted from an application to the Regional Operational Programme +Centro, co-funded by the Portuguese government and the EU. It has contributed to training municipalities in the autonomous management of incubators and companies associated with IERA, and to support entrepreneurial projects resulting from the actions that integrate PAVEI. These actions, aggregated into four priority axes of intervention, strengthen the territorial articulation to explore the wide range of opportunities offered by the region and create networking references that will contribute to the implementation of other initiatives. These will be defined in the scope of the future Aveiro Region Entrepreneurship Programme, in which UA is expected to undertake a significant role.

Discussion

From the analysis of the evolution of the relationship of UA with its surrounding region, it is possible to reach certain considerations regarding the role of these institutions in overcoming some of the main challenges of LDRs. First, it is apparent that UA has spurred or contributed towards the emergence and development of several interinstitutional partnerships. Examples such as AMRIA, the CIRA territorial development strategies, IERA and the Science and Innovation Park, all including, in greater or lesser degree the participation, mediation and/or leadership of UA, demonstrate this. It is interesting as well that these initiatives seemed to emerge from a shared need to develop competitive capacity and have led towards the development of other projects in the region with the university. For instance, UA is currently developing other strategies for individual municipalities that have been pleased by its contribution to the CIRA strategies and have deemed it advantageous to work with the university rather than a consultancy office. Echoing Morgan & Nauwelaers (1999), common problems, but also a certain common vision, have brought regional agents together, contributing towards the development of innovation dynamics in this LDR. The policy framework does appear to be incentivising these types of interinstitutional collaborations, and while long-term results are difficult to discern given the volatility of mandates, in the short-term, UA-region interaction is described as based on trust, and increasingly promoted. A stronger *policy framework*, both regional and internal to the university, was built-up in support of this collective network of action in innovation. The main aim was to effectively and smoothly link the regional economy to scientific and technological knowledge, so that an interactive process of information-exchange could emerge and help UA understand the productive sector better, and firms, e.g., become more resilient and innovative. An example on the regional level, emphasised in both policy documents and interviewees' accounts, was that of the participation of the university in the design of the territorial development strategy. Given the current EU policy framework and guidelines, universities should actively engage in this process, namely in a form of entrepreneurial process of discovery, to provide a better assessment of future development tendencies in the region. The network that emerged between CIRA, UA and the industry cemented a regional, collaborative action and the importance of R&D input and was described as a unique partnership and enabled UA to be better positioned to contribute to planning and governance, and potentially shape innovation policy.

In organisational matters, UA has made efforts towards facilitating the contact with external agents. This includes its incubator and knowledge transfer offices, but also, for example, the position of Pro-Rector for Regional Development, or the Vice-Rector for University-Society cooperation. Similarly, the more recent technological platforms are an attempt not only to mirror the region's strategic development areas with the offer of the university, but to also foment this networked, clustered action with other regional public or private actors. Still, while the university claims to pursue a closer cooperation with the region, this is still limited in practical terms due to its organisational limitations and the still predominant perspective in the evaluation of academic careers that emphasises research activities and the production of scientific articles. Although regional engagement is reported as being complementary to the missions of teaching and research, drawing from the world of practical, hands-on knowledge and funneling it into the classrooms and laboratories, it is not yet viewed as quantifiable in a manner that would suffice for such an assessment. In the case of UA, while a certain valorisation of the mission of regional engagement has been tried, also as an evocative aspect associated with the university itself, in organisational terms it has been limited by the assessment tool of PADUA. In real terms, this means that whatever numbers UA may have drawn from these evaluations on regional engagement, these are significantly undervalued estimations.

Finally, and as Gunasekara (2006) states, there is a need for a unified strategy or organisational mechanism within the university that can link its various constituent 'poles' and clearly direct them in these endeavours. Optimistically, from the several interviews conducted across departments and various offices of the university, this problem seems commonly acknowledged, meaning that there is a greater possibility that change will come into effect in the next few years.

Conclusion

We have sought to shed light on the typical constraints universities face in activating regional engagement mechanisms in a less developed region and to explore how these have been and can be tackled. Previous studies have shown that innovation is a complex, multifaceted issue that is not easily stimulated in any territory, much less in an LDR that must still build the structures needed to support it. Two of the common challenges LDRs face in this quest are promoting a high-level of interaction between economic and institutional agents; and nurturing locally-based R&D activities. Not simple tasks to undertake, the region may benefit from the presence and commitment of an institutional actor widely believed to promote socio-economic development – a university. Able to nurture endogenous R&D activities and collaborative, collective action between both the public and the private sector, universities have the potential to assume a leading role in the development of lagging regions. However, they face certain common limitations: a weak institutional landscape with low levels of interaction between agents; a lack of a supportive policy framework; and, challenges in adapting their institutional and organisational approaches when integrating the third academic mission.

UA and the region of Aveiro benefit from a special connection, as the university has sought since its creation to closely respond to the needs of the society surrounding it. Consequently, given the early push for the implantation of the university in the region and the circumstances of its birth, the connection between UA and the region has been strong. Links were quickly formed with local industry and the productive sector and intensive collaboration was developed with regional governmental bodies. So, in collaborative, institutional terms, UA meet little resistance in its 'pervasive role' in regional engagement. The main needs of the region that the university focused on were not just related to scientific and technological knowledge or the training of highly qualified workers, but also the establishment and promotion of a network of innovation.

Nonetheless, while external constraints can be addressed though collective action among several actors, internal ones are more difficult to manage. UA has created several mechanisms and channels to sustain a more effective university-society link and to promote and monitor technology and knowledge-transfer activities, as well as other forms of entrepreneurship and regional engagement. Even though these have permitted the institutionalisation of the third academic mission more generally, it has not embedded this participation among all individuals. A lack of overall strategy and goal-setting regarding regional engagement, and the inability to effectively incorporate it in academic evaluation for career progression, means that tensions arise over how academic staff balance competing demands across the three missions. The questions of financial gains and local engagement/international recognition, while important factors to consider in LDRs, are here more a matter of internal organisation of the university and individual motivation.

In a world where universities have been undergoing many changes to respond to external pressures, both literature and interview findings indicate that mechanisms and indicators of regional engagement efforts have not yet adapted to the trends. The use of indicators based on commercialisation and technology transfer output are insufficient to assess overall engagement. There is an urgent need for new indicators that consider social concerns shown by academics and universities, as well as collaborative and collective action for stimulating innovation. There are many ways academics exercise their third mission without generating financial revenue but create valuable outcomes in the community. Above all, there is an absolute need to reach a consensus on what the third mission means, as there are diverse opinions between academics and within disciplinary fields, and then design and implement policies accordingly.

Finally, it is possible to conclude that, even though LDRs may present a challenging environment for an engaged university, the opportunities presented are of great value. The possibility for the university of developing closer relationships with local actors and between them, not always available in a more advanced, highly technological urban setting, is of crucial importance in supporting the highly interactive process that is innovation. And it is through this gradual process of building relationships that the appropriate structures can be built-up to create a self-sustaining innovation system.

References

Amaral, A., Correia, F., Magalhães, A., Rosa, M. J., Santiago, R., & Teixeira, P. (2002). **O ensino superior pela mão da economia**. Fundação das Universidades Portuguesas.

Amin, A., & Thrift, N. (Eds.). (1995). **Globalization, Institutions, and Regional Development in Europe**. Oxford University Press.

Arbo, P., & Benneworth, P. (2007). **Understanding the Regional Contribution of Higher Education Institutions** (OECD Education Working Papers No. 9). https://doi.org/10.1787/161208155312

Barca, F. (2009). **Agenda for a Reformed Cohesion Policy**. European Communities. http://www.dps.mef.gov.it/documentazione/comunicati/2010/report_barca_v0306.pdf

Bonaccorsi, A. (2016). Addressing the disenchantment: Universities and regional development in peripheral regions. **Journal of Economic Policy Reform**, 1–28.

CCDRC. (2016). **RIS3 do Centro de Portugal: Estratégia de Investigação e Inovação para uma Especialização Inteligente. Editorial para Consulta Pública**. CCDRC.

CEC. (2004). **A new partnership for cohesion: Convergence, competitiveness, cooperation : third report on economic and social cohesion**. Office for Official Publications of the European Communities.

Chatterton, P., & Goddard, J. (2003). The Response of Higher Education Institutions to Regional Needs. In **Economic geography of higher education knowledge, infrastructure and learning regions** (pp. 19–41). Routledge.

CIRA. (n.d.-a). **List of Projects**. Região de Aveiro. Retrieved 7 June 2017, from http://www.regiaodeaveiro.pt/PageGen.aspx?WMCM_PaginaId=29880

CIRA. (n.d.-b). **Quem Somos.** Region of Aveiro. Retrieved 4 February 2018, from http://www.regiaodeaveiro.pt/PageGen.aspx?WMCM_ PaginaId=27800

CIRA, & UA. (2014). **Estratégia de Desenvolvimento Territorial da Região de Aveiro 2014-2020.** CIRA | Universidade de Aveiro.

Clark, B. R. (1998). The entrepreneurial university: Demand and response. **Tertiary Education and Management,** 4, 5–16.

Cooke, P., Gomez Uranga, M., & Etxebarria, G. (1997). Regional innovation systems: Institutional and organisational dimensions. **Research Policy,** 26, 475–491.

Deem, R., Mok, K. H., & Lucas, L. (2008). Transforming Higher Education in Whose Image? Exploring the Concept of the 'World-Class' University in Europe and Asia. **Higher Education Policy,** 21, 83–97.

D'Este, P., & Perkmann, M. (2011). Why do academics engage with industry? The entrepreneurial university and individual motivations. **The Journal of Technology Transfer,** 36, 316–339.

Drucker, J., & Goldstein, H. (2007). Assessing the Regional Economic Development Impacts of Universities: A Review of Current Approaches. **International Regional Science Review,** 30, 20–46.

Edquist, C. (Ed.). (1997). **Systems of innovation: Technologies, institutions, and organizations.** Pinter.

Etzkowitz, H., Webster, A., Gebhardt, C., & Terra, B. R. C. (2000). The future of the university and the university of the future: Evolution of ivory tower to entrepreneurial paradigm. **Research Policy,** 29, 313–330.

European Commission. (2011). **Cohesion Policy 2014-2020. Investing in Europe's regions** (No. 40; Panorama Inforegio). European Union Regional Policy; ISSN 1608-389X. http://ec.europa.eu/regional_policy/ sources/docgener/panorama/pdf/mag40/mag40_en.pdf

Faludi, A. (2007). Territorial Cohesion Policy and the European Model of Society. **European Planning Studies,** 15, 567–583.

Feldman, M. P., & Kogler, D. F. (2010). Chapter 8—Stylized Facts in the Geography of Innovation. In B. H. Hall & N. Rosenberg (Eds.), **Handbook of the Economics of Innovation** (Vol. 1, pp. 381–410). North-Holland.

Fonseca, M. (2017). Southern Europe at a Glance: Regional Disparities and Human Capital. In M. Fonseca & U. Fratesi (Eds.), **Regional Upgrading in Southern Europe: Spatial Disparities and Human Capital** (1st ed., pp. 19–45). Springer.

Goddard, & Chatterton, P. (1999). Regional Development Agencies and the knowledge economy: Harnessing the potential of universities. **Environment and Planning C: Government and Policy**, 17, 685–699.

Goddard, Hazelkorn, E., & Vallance, P. (2016). **The Civic University: The Policy and Leadership Challenges**. Edward Elgar Publishing.

Guile, D., & Fosstenløkken, S. M. (2018). Introduction to the special issue: Knowledge dynamics, innovation and learning. **Industry and Innovation**, 25, 333–338.

Gunasekara, C. (2006). Reframing the role of universities in the development of regional innovation systems. **The Journal of Technology Transfer**, 31, 101–113.

Hirschman, A. O. (1958). **The Strategy of Economic Development**. Yale University Press.

Huggins, R., & Johnston, A. (2009a). The economic and innovation contribution of universities: A regional perspective. **Environment and Planning C: Government and Policy**, 27, 1088–1106.

Huggins, R., & Johnston, A. (2009b). Knowledge Networks in an Uncompetitive Region: SME Innovation and Growth., **Growth and Change**, 40, 227–259.

Jongbloed, B., Enders, J., & Salerno, C. (2008). Higher education and its communities: Interconnections, interdependencies and a research agenda. **Higher Education**, 56, 303–324.

Kohoutek, J., Pinheiro, R., Čábelková, I., & Šmídová, M. (2017). The Role of Higher Education in the Socio-Economic Development of Peripheral Regions. **Higher Education Policy**, 30, 401–403.

Krücken, G. (2003). Mission impossible? Institutional barriers to the diffusion of the 'third academic mission' at German universities. **International Journal of Technology Management**, 25, 18.

Landabaso, M. (1997). The promotion of innovation in regional policy: Proposals for a regional innovation strategy. **Entrepreneurship & Regional Development**, 9, 1–24.

Lawton Smith, Keeble, Lawson, Moore, & Wilkinson. (2001). University–business interaction in the Oxford and Cambridge regions. **Tijdschrift Voor Economische En Sociale Geografie**, 92, 88–99.

Morgan. (1996). Learning by interacting: Inter-firm networks and enterprise support. In **Local Systems of Small Firms and Job Creation**. OECD.

Morgan, & Henderson, D. (2002). Regions as Laboratories: The Rise of Regional Experimentalism in Europe. In M. S. Gertler & D. A. Wolfe (Eds.), **Innovation and Social Learning: Institutional Adaptation in an Era of Technological Change** (pp. 204–226). Palgrave Macmillan UK.

Morgan, & Nauwelaers, C. (2003). A Regional Perspective on Innovation: From Theory to Strategy. In K. Morgan & C. Nauwelaers (Eds.), **Regional innovation strategies: The challenge for less-favoured regions**. Routledge.

Niosi, J., & Bas, T. G. (2001). The Competencies of Regions – Canada's Clusters in Biotechnology. **Small Business Economics**, 17, 31–42.

Oughton, C., Landabaso, M., & Morgan, K. (2002). The regional innovation paradox: Innovation policy and industrial policy. **The Journal of Technology Transfer**, 27, 97–110.

Pereira, M. E., Lillebø, A. I., Pato, P., Válega, M., Coelho, J. P., Lopes, C. B., Rodrigues, S., Cachada, A., Otero, M., Pardal, M. A., & Duarte, A. C. (2009). Mercury pollution in Ria de Aveiro (Portugal): A review of the system assessment. **Environmental Monitoring and Assessment**, 155, 39–49.

Pinheiro, R., Benneworth, P., & Jones, G. A. (2012). **Universities and Regional Development: A Critical Assessment of Tensions and Contradictions**. Routledge.

Pugh, R., Hamilton, E., Jack, S., & Gibbons, A. (2016). A step into the unknown: Universities and the governance of regional economic development. **European Planning Studies**, 24, 1357–1373.

Rodrigues, C., & Melo, A. (2012). The Triple Helix Model as an Instrument of Local Response to the Economic Crisis. **European Planning Studies**, 20, 1483–1496.

Rodrigues, C., Rosa Pires, A., & Castro, E. (2001). Innovative universities and regional institutional capacity building: The case of Aveiro, Portugal. **Industry and Higher Education**, 15, 251–255.

Rodrigues, C., & Teles, F. (2017). The Fourth Helix in Smart Specialization Strategies: The Gap Between Discourse and Practice. In S. P. De Oliveira Monteiro & E. G. Carayannis (Eds.), **The Quadruple Innovation Helix Nexus** (pp. 205–226). Palgrave Macmillan US.

Rodríguez-Pose, A. (2013). Do Institutions Matter for Regional Development? **Regional Studies**, 47, 1034–1047.

Rodríguez-Pose, A., & Fratesi, U. (2007). Regional Business Cycles and the Emergence of Sheltered Economies in the Southern Periphery of Europe. **Growth and Change**, 38, 621–648.

Rosa Pires. (1986). Industrialização Difusa e 'Modelos' de Desenvolvimento: Um Estudo no Distrito de Aveiro. **Finisterra**, XXI, 239–269.

Rosa Pires, Pinho, L., & Cunha, C. (2012). Universities, communities and regional innovation strategies. **Proceedings of the 18th APDR Congress, Innovation and Regional Dynamics**, 337–343.

Rose, M., Decter, M., Robinson, S., Jack, S., & Lockett, N. (2013). Opportunities, contradictions and attitudes: The evolution of university–business engagement since 1960. **Business History**, 55, 259–279.

Scott, A., & Storper, M. (2003). Regions, Globalization, Development. **Regional Studies**, 37, 579–593.

Sterlacchini, A. (2008). R&D, higher education and regional growth: Uneven linkages among European regions. **Research Policy**, 37, 1096–1107.

Tödtling, F., & Trippl, M. (2005). One size fits all? **Research Policy**, 34, 1203–1219.

UA. (2012). **Plano Estratégico**. Universidade de Aveiro.

UA. (2016, December). **Análise Organizacional** [Promocional]. Conselho Geral, Aveiro.

Uyarra, E. (2010). Conceptualizing the Regional Roles of Universities, Implications and Contradictions. **European Planning Studies**, 18, 1227–1246.

Chapter 8

On Overcoming the Barriers to Regional Engagement

Reflections from the University of Lincoln

Rhoda Ahoba-Sam, Maria Salomaa and David Charles

Universities have been portrayed as bringing an array of benefits to their local region, no more so than in regions which are relatively peripheral and disadvantaged (Goddard and Vallance, 2013; OECD, 2007; Coenen, 2007). From simple economic multiplier effects to more transformational impacts on local innovation, culture and public services, universities are seen as a universal good which can significantly enhance a local economy (Charles and Benneworth, 2001; Huggins and Johnston, 2009; Lawton Smith, 2007). Whilst traditionally seen as providers of education, a source of research and innovation in collaboration with regional businesses, universities also support the development of civic society (Arbo and Benneworth, 2007). In peripheral regions which often lack the advantages of urban agglomeration economies and the systemic effects of innovation ecosystems, a university may offer a means of radically changing the development trajectory, enhancing skills, stimulating local innovation and connecting the region with other centres of knowledge production (Charles, 2006; Coenen, 2007). As a consequence, local interests have often lobbied for the establishment of new universities (Charles, 2016), and governments have sought to decentralise universities to promote regional development (Pinheiro et al 2016).

Whilst the UK has seen a growth in universities and campuses in rural and peripheral areas in recent decades, this process has tended to be evolutionary, with most examples either taking the form of the conversion of relatively small colleges of higher education to universities, or very small new campuses. Previous work has shown the limitations of some of these developments as small institutions which have had to specialise and hence limit the scope of their potential impact on their regions (Charles 2016). There have been very few cases since the 1960s of a new full-range university being developed in a peripheral region in the UK where none existed before.

One exception has been Lincoln, where the development of a new university since 1996 has taken an unusual course, and where the early development of the university was initiated by, and shaped by, local interests. Lincoln is a small historic city at the centre of a large rural county – one of the main centres of agricultural production in the UK. Local interests developed a new campus and invited a university to set up a satellite operation, but this then became the primary campus as the university moved away from its original site – there are very few cases of a university moving between cities, and especially to a smaller and more rural location. The genesis story of the university in Lincoln has played a significant role in the manner in which the university has sought to engage with the community. The subsequent expansion of the university and its creation of new schools, such as engineering, has involved considerable local partnership building, and is a distinctive experience within the UK. There is universal recognition that the university has changed Lincoln, as a small city, for the better, and that the university is a positive asset to the city (Regeneris, 2017), and an exemplary case of a successful campus based in a small city in a rural region that has to cope with significant economic, social and environmental diversity. During its twenty years of existence, the University of Lincoln has grown from a branch campus to a full-range university, currently responding to regional economic needs by collaborating with local businesses and employers, such as Siemens, and serving the large food manufacturing sector in the region through the National Centre for Food Manufacturing (NCFM) at the Holbeach campus in the south of Lincolnshire.

There remain substantial challenges though. Although the University of Lincoln is now a medium-sized university with 14,000 students, and with a smaller second university in the city (Bishop Grosseteste University with 2000 students), Lincoln remains a small labour market for academics and is relatively peripheral. The university seeks to continue to grow and increase the value it can add to the community, requiring an ongoing transformation (UoL, 2016). The wider region, beyond the city of Lincoln still has considerable weaknesses as an agricultural area with relatively low-income levels and seasonal industries. The regional business environment is dominated by micro-enterprises, and the whole region struggles with a relatively weaker skills base than the rest of the UK (Lincolnshire Assembly, 2008; DCLG, 2017). Since the turn of the millennium, the region has sought to build on local strengths such as its traditional engineering and agricultural base to encourage regional entrepreneurship, working in collaboration with the university to both increase the number of SMEs and respond to their particular needs (Lincolnshire Assembly, 2008).

The absorptive capacity of both the city and region for university services and outputs is limited, and a challenge for the university is to help develop that capacity. The future of the region requires joint development to realise mutual benefits – how can local engagement help the university enhance its position in the national university hierarchy? What are the challenges in developing an engaged university in a rural region meeting the expectations of local stakeholders, whilst also moving up the university rankings and attracting international students? This chapter examines how universities in a rural area can overcome the challenges in engaging with its region. Through the case of the University of Lincoln, we will illustrate the ways in which the university collaborates with its local partners and businesses thus fostering innovation and engaging with the local community.

A brief overview of universities' engagement in rural regions is outlined in the next section, after which the method employed for collecting empirical data is reviewed. This is followed by a description of the local context and the story of the origins of the university. An overview of how the University of Lincoln fosters regional innovation, and the challenges involved in doing so, is presented highlighting three cases that demonstrate the university's regional engagement efforts. Subsequently, a discussion of findings that synthesises empirics and theory is presented, and ultimately the reflections and conclusions drawn from the case.

Universities engagement in rural regions

The UK government has focused much effort on encouraging the economic engagement of universities (e.g. BIS, 2013). It is thus widely recognised that universities should contribute to regional development, through the so-called third mission – also referred to as outreach or community service – which goes beyond the traditional core functions of teaching and research (Jongbloed *et al.*, 2008). Encouragement of the third mission is particularly concretised in policies and research funding instruments (Vorley and Nelles, 2009), in which higher education is expected to take actions to facilitate entrepreneurship, technology transfer and interactive learning, building the third mission around their interaction with regional industry and society (Arbo and Benneworth, 2007).

Over the past two decades the UK has been a leading player in the shift from a more traditional approach to higher education, leading to new models of collaboration for innovation, such as science parks, incubators, increased contract research, consultancy services, access to state-of-the-art-laboratories, and strategic alliances with non-academic partners for joint R&D activities (Jongbloed *et al.*, 2008). Under the Labour government of the 2000s, a number of new funding schemes for academic entrepreneurship and wider business and community engagement were introduced, including the Higher Education Innovation Fund as an annual addition to the university block grant focused on supporting external engagement activities (third stream funding). Regional development agencies provided considerable funding for regional innovation activities, and although subsequently abolished and replaced with Local Enterprise Partnerships, some of this activity has continued, especially with support from the ERDF. More recently the development of a national industrial strategy (UK Government, 2017) and preparations for Brexit have stimulated the creation of a number of new programmes to encourage universities to work with business, especially through new local industrial strategies currently under development (BEIS, 2018).

Universities' engagement is mainly influenced by two factors, namely the type of university and the type of region, which together determine universities ability to work together with local

263

stakeholders and engage with regional systems (Boucher *et al.*, 2003). In the UK there are substantial differences in the scale and research intensity of universities, affecting the scale of intellectual and financial resources available for engagement with business and the community. Specialist institutions such as creative arts-based universities play a very different role in their region than science-based or generalist universities. Universities have also taken different stances on their mission and regarding regional engagement. The type of region also has a significant impact on universities' ability to foster economic development: if the other local key players' capacity to absorb knowledge is limited, it is more difficult for universities to become central drivers of regional development just by themselves (Breznitz and Feldman, 2012). Therefore, universities in a rural environment have to consider even more carefully how and to which local needs they are capable of responding, though their ability to determine the type of institution they are may be limited for several reasons. First, most universities are mainly urban institutions, and a more rural location limits some of the external partnerships and interactions on offer to them (Charles, 2016). Second, the role of universities in building a strong civic society by creating a space for debates and exchanging of ideas (UUK, 2014) may be even more important in rural areas; the most engaged universities are typically *"single, relatively large universities located in peripheral regions"* (Boucher *et al.*, 2003, 984–896). Third, the university is faced with the tension between meeting local needs, reinforcing existing traditional industries and potentially locking-in to past development paths (Hassink, 2010), or bringing new ideas and technologies to the region as part of smart specialisation strategies (Kempton et al 2013).

Many universities in recent years have taken on a degree of responsibility for working with regional partners for the collective good of their local area, seen in various ways as engaged universities (Bridger and Alter, 2006; Uyarra, 2010), civic universities (Goddard et al, 2016, CUC, 2019) or anchor institutions (Harkavy and Zuckerman, 1999; Taylor and Luter 2013). In these cases universities recognise some mutual interests with regional partners in promoting economic and social development, although as an active rather than a passive partner, playing a full role in the development of regional strategies, and not simply responding to regional demands.

Although universities' regional roles include the attraction of talented people, providing study opportunities and supporting both the local economy and the community, these goals can be more difficult to achieve in rural areas, in which the universities must deal with a more diverse economic base, very small-scale businesses and a lower presence of other knowledge institutions (Charles, 2016). In particular the SMEs may not be able to articulate their needs for knowledge, which hinders interaction and potential knowledge transfer between universities and businesses (Jongbloed *et al.* 2008). This also decreases innovation potential in rural areas, in that the potential for innovation is likely to increase with the size of the business (GLLEP, 2014). However, for university-industry collaboration, location is indeed important: when partners are located in the same area, the networking opportunities increase (Jongbloed *et al.*, 2008).

Common drivers for rural universities are typically fostering greater student participation in higher education, responding to local educational needs – as generic as they may be – as well as developing research fields linked to local industries. Responding to all these expectations at the same time is especially demanding for smaller rural campuses, and they often lack the scale to meet both the educational needs and create true collaboration with local industry at the same time (Charles, 2016). The type of research collaboration is also very much reliant on the disciplines in

265

question, and the universities should seek mutually beneficial exchange, so that the collaboration is a response to the expectations of both parties (Jongbloed *et al.*, 2008). This may again, be more challenging to achieve with the more limited disciplinary base of smaller rural campuses.

In the case of Lincoln this context raises some interesting challenges. A new university was brought into a rural region with considerable local expectations. As the university grows how does it meet local demands as an anchor institution yet also develop capacities to compete within a national higher education system?

Research methods

The case study of Lincoln was developed as qualitative study with empirical data obtained through interviews with both university and external stakeholders. A qualitative approach was preferred in gaining more insight into the topic for a case study of this explorative nature (Yin, 2002; Hammarberg *et al.*, 2016). Interviews, which were typically semi-structured, were valuable for obtaining deeper understanding into the chosen case (Yin, 2002; Hammerberg *et al.*, 2016; Wilson, 2014), as this type of interview structure allows the investigator to probe more deeply. Interviews with staff members of the University included those working in the Research and Enterprise services, the Engineering School and at the National Centre for Food Manufacturing. These choices were guided by the involvement of these departments in on-going university engagement and impact efforts. A County Council officer in charge of innovation support processes was also interviewed, the choice based on the active collaboration between the university and the County in regional innovation support services. Industry contacts presently 'engaged' with the university were also approached. Attention was paid to 'engaged' firms in particular as these were deemed better placed to comment on the challenges faced while engaging with the University of Lincoln.

In addition, three former graduates from the university were interviewed, especially to probe the 'issue' of graduate retention. Altogether, 11 interviews were undertaken from the University, County Council and industry. Given the research question, interviewees were essentially asked questions relating to their experiences of links between the university and local industry, the challenges involved and how these challenges were being managed. As a means to triangulate, data from policy documents, company websites and reports were also utilised. This was advantageous for the development of 'converging lines of enquiry' as suggested by Yin (2016, 87). The interviews were complemented with the experience of one of the authors in sitting on university committees for enterprise and employer engagement.

The framework method (Gale *et al*, 2003; Ritchie *et al*., 2003, 256) was useful for analysing the qualitative data collected, allowing for a similar logic to flow through the entire scope of the study. Collected data was transcribed and coded. Emerging themes were analysed between and across data sets (e.g organisational types) to make meaningful interpretation. Empirical data was also compared with secondary sources such as documents and ultimately to the relevant literature. Validity and reliability of research was enhanced by having investigators swap sections of focus, in order to critique the work in its entirety and ensure that a similar logic flows through.

The need for a university in Lincolnshire

The UK has seen a gradual process of filling in the gaps in the map of higher education provision over a period of many decades. From an initial group of universities in the major cities (plus Oxford and Cambridge), successive rounds of development have diversified the locations of campuses, both in the form of main campuses and satellites. In the 1960s a new set of 'county' universities were set up in smaller cities – York, Canterbury, Guildford etc. The polytechnics, to become universities post 1992, were mainly based in the larger cities and industrial towns, but some of these also had campuses in more rural settings – Staffordshire for example. A later round of new institutions from the late 1990s onwards have included some more specifically focused on rural areas –Cumbria, Highlands and Islands – and smaller cities – Chester, Winchester.

Lincolnshire as a county had missed out on the earlier rounds of university development prior to 1992, with Lincoln overlooked during the development of county focused universities in the 1960s even though it shared some similar characteristics with cities such as York and Canterbury which were selected at that time. Lincolnshire perhaps suffered more from its relative peripherality though, both in terms of its access to transport networks, but also through its perceived parochial nature.

Lincolnshire is known mainly as an agricultural county, with a primary focus on arable farming and related food processing. Much of the county is relatively flat with rich soils and moderate rainfall, and is devoted to large scale arable farming of cereals and vegetables. With the exception of Lincoln and an area to the north, the settlement form is largely of small villages and market towns, with an economic base of very small firms. The Northern strip of the county along the Humber Estuary is somewhat different with Scunthorpe as an industrial town built around its steelworks and Grimsby as a port and fisheries centre. These areas of North and North East Lincolnshire have the character of old industrial areas with concomitantly high levels of unemployment. Another distinct area is the coastline with a strip of low-budget holiday resorts, focused on Skegness, areas with relatively low paid seasonal jobs around a limited set of tourism-related sectors.

As a result, Lincolnshire has experienced continual low levels of GDP. In 2005 the per capita GDP figure was €29,100 compared with €39,030 for the UK. Only 7 NUTS II regions in the UK were lower: areas such as Tees Valley, Cornwall and Northern Ireland, and several of these had experienced Objective 1/ Convergence status in the Structural Funds at some point, recognising them as some of the weakest economies in the EU. Calculated on a purchasing power per capita basis Lincolnshire is at an equivalent level to the Algarve, or sits between the Italian Mezzogiorno and the poorest North Italian region (Eurostat, 2017).

Despite the agricultural nature of the county, the city of Lincoln has a long tradition of engineering, although this saw considerable decline from the 1980s, after dominating local employment for around 100 years. The wider East Midlands economy has also been highly dependent on manufacturing, which shows in its high share in GDP: for example, in 2001 the share was 29.4 %, compared with an average of 21.3% in the UK. However, the relatively low level of R&D investments in manufacturing within the region, suggested that this sector was unlikely to grow rapidly in the future (UUK, 2001), and by 2015, the share of manufacturing had indeed fallen to 16.9%, which is still the highest percentage level of any region in the UK. In Central Lincolnshire, the key sectors for economic growth remain agri-food, manufacturing and tourism. The city of Lincoln has also been aiming for growth in retail and knowledge-intensive business services with support from the University, for example in the Science and Innovation Park. (Greater Lincolnshire LEP, 2016.)

The business environment in the wider East Midlands is dominated by micro-enterprises. In 2015, the region had 133,055 businesses employing only 0-9 workers corresponding to 87.7% of the area's employers. Small businesses (10-49 employees) share was significantly lower, 15,445 (10.2%) but still ahead of the national average (9.6%). Though there are only 605 large businesses (250+ employees) in the region, their share of 0.4% corresponds to the UK as a whole. This also limits the innovation potential in rural areas, as the potential for innovation is likely to increase with the size of the business (GLLEP, 2014).

The whole East Midlands struggles with a relatively weaker skills base than the rest of the UK. At the beginning of the 21st century, the region was 3-5% behind of the rest of the country (UUK, 2001), and there has not been any significant improvement since: only 31.8% of the East Midlands population has a degree qualification, compared with 36.8% in England as a whole. The lack of a highly skilled workforce has even led to difficulties in finding suitable candidates for open vacancies (DCLG 2017). According to a 2014/2015 graduate destination survey of University of Lincoln, 42.7% of graduates stayed in the East Midlands and 13.4% in the adjacent East region of England. The East Midlands breakdown shows that Lincoln is the most popular destination (40.5%), followed by the neighbouring district of North Kesteven (10.0%) and then Nottingham (8.0%). The survey's results also demonstrate that University of Lincoln's graduates have good prospects after completing their studies: 95% of the graduates had either employment or pursued their studies after 6 months of finishing their degrees (UoL 2016a), even though the region is struggling to retain the graduates.

Since 2004 Lincolnshire has experienced a wave of immigration from central and Eastern Europe which was unexpected but built upon a previous round of Portuguese migrants in the 1990s (Barnes and Cox, 2007). These flows illustrate the weakness of the Lincolnshire economy, with migrants taking up seasonal positions in the food and agriculture sector, occupying jobs which are poorly paid by UK standards and are not seen as desirable by

UK workers. The continued flow of such migrants into an area unused to migration stimulated considerable tensions, leading to a high Brexit vote in 2016.

Despite the recent growth of the city of Lincoln, many regional problems remain from health issues to problems in the living environment, the rising number of student and migrant workers causing pressure on the infrastructure to keep up with the fast growth (Greater Lincolnshire LEP, 2016). Lincoln's role as the major centre of employment in Lincolnshire needs to be supported with policies aiming to foster a wider range of employment opportunities, and to support both existing and new companies in order to attract new investments to the area. The policies should also reinforce Lincoln as provider of innovative employment possibilities (Greater Lincolnshire LEP, 2016). Thus, the universities' role as key drivers of economic growth and providers of further development (OECD, 2011) is acknowledged also in Lincolnshire, and the County Council express their support for further university growth to maximise their economic impact to Central Lincolnshire (Greater Lincolnshire LEP, 2016).

Lincoln as an embedded anchor institution

The University of Lincoln is an unusual case as its origins do not lie in the rural environment of Lincolnshire, but in the urban location of Hull. The university started as several colleges based in Hull which came together to form the Hull College of Higher Education in 1976. It briefly became Humberside Polytechnic before achieving university status as the University of Humberside in 1992. The move to Lincoln was thus a very unusual development in the UK context and emerged from local demands in Lincoln during the 1990s.

Lincoln had long aspired to having its own university. In the early 1990s the local branch of the Confederation of British Industry

(CBI) produced a forward-looking document 'Towards the Year 2000'[42]. This presented the views of local industry on the regeneration of Lincolnshire and specifically identified the need for the county to have its own university. Previous attempts had apparently been made, unsuccessfully, since the Robbins expansion of the 1960s[43], but were allegedly frustrated by the 'commercial jealousy' of other universities in the East Midlands (GOA Ltd, 2001, 12).

The university idea was then backed up by Lincolnshire County Council and Lincolnshire Training and Enterprise Council (TEC) which sought the possibility of a university college in Lincoln as a satellite to an existing university from one of the surrounding cities. The TECs had been established from 1990 by central government to develop local partnerships for training, skill development and wider regeneration. Each local area had a TEC with a local board responsible for developing a plan focused on the needs of the locality. In the case of Lincolnshire, the TEC identified the idea of a University for Lincolnshire in its initial business plan, and was in a position to support the idea with direct funding. The County and TEC did not have a statutory duty to develop a university, but argued that they had a statutory power to support the process on the grounds of economic regeneration, and were able to persuade government to allow them to make a grant toward the establishment of a university presence in Lincoln. A project company was thus established to hold a grant of £10 million and to negotiate with a university on the establishment of a campus. Local businesses, including the

---

[42] This account of the development of the University of Lincoln has been informed by an unpublished paper from David Rossington, the former chief executive of Lincolnshire TEC.

[43] The Robbins Committee report of 1963 identified a need for new universities to meet growing demand for graduates and set out locational criteria leading to the designation of a number of new greenfield universities such as York, Essex, Surrey and Kent in smaller cities in rural counties.

Lincolnshire Co-op, Jackson Building Centre's, GEC-Alsthom (later Siemens) and Cargill seed merchants, became involved in the process and raised additional funds towards the project. It was decided that the County should approach universities to see if they would be willing to establish a University College in Lincoln and in April 1991 the Director of Education approached six institutions in the Yorkshire and East Midlands areas. Following discussions with each in late 1991, four were asked to make formal presentations on the support they could offer. An initial agreement was made with Nottingham Trent University, and a site identified in central Lincoln on derelict railway lands beside the Brayford Pool, an old canal harbour near the city centre (Rossington, 2016).

As construction of the first building began in 1995, Nottingham Trent was forced to withdraw as they were unable to secure quota for additional funded student numbers and were presumably unwilling to transfer quota from their Nottingham site. The new University of Humberside was however very willing to step in, as it is reported they were unhappy with the local context in Hull and felt under pressure to merge with the University of Hull. They would operate a full university presence on the site, would change their name to the University of Lincolnshire and Humberside (ULH) and would transfer existing student allocations to Lincoln through relocating departments. They even suggested that the vice-chancellor's office be moved to Lincoln. The campus opened in 1996.

Over time the university consolidated its position in Lincoln, including acquiring two former colleges of art and agriculture in Lincoln. These two specialist colleges had been in Lincoln for many years and had been absorbed by De Montfort University of Leicester as part of their expansion as a regional university in the East Midlands. De Montford had then decided to retrench to

Leicester and were willing to pass the two colleges on to ULH. At the same time ULH gradually transferred departments from Hull to Lincoln and eventually renamed itself the University of Lincoln and sold off its campus in Hull.

The origin of the university in Lincoln was thus the culmination of active lobbying and funding from the County Council and local business interests and the university has always responded to this in terms of its mission as an anchor institution (Birch *et al.*, 2013), supporting the local economy. In a sense this is ironic as the university is only in Lincoln because it was footloose in the first instance, but having invested heavily in the new campus in Lincoln it is clear that the university has sought to embed itself in the locality and take on that anchoring role.

The University has also had a major impact on the physical form of the city. In the early 1990s the Brayford Pool area, close to the centre of the city, was a large area of derelict land, with old industrial property and railway yards. The Pool itself was an ancient port originally developed by the Romans and subsequently linked by canal to the wider English waterway system. The Brayford site was the preferred site for the University, the other considered being a former mental hospital in a village on the outskirts of the city, so the decision to build the University in the centre of the city has been an important factor for its physical regeneration. Initially one building was erected on the south side of Brayford Pool, and land was transferred to the University surrounding this. From this point the campus has developed to the south and now occupies a large area removing almost all signs of the former industrial blight, now gradually spreading west with the building of a science park on yet more derelict land. The emergence of the University as a major employer and source of students has led to the north side of the Brayford Pool also being developed with hotels, bars and

274

restaurants, creating a major leisure destination of regional significance.

Given the anchor institution philosophy adopted by the university (UoL, 2016) it has sought to develop broad and deep relationships with the city and region. On the one hand this can be seen in the links with business and entrepreneurship which will be explored in the next section, but this is only one dimension of its engagement. There are also collaborations around the cultural and creative industries in Lincoln, around nursing and future medical training, in social care, sport and not least through educational opportunities for disadvantaged students. However, universities' engagement is typically a peripheral activity, and unless it is successfully linked to a broader institutional change, the activities will remain "peripheral to the core" (Benneworth & Sanderson, 2009). Partnerships are one of the key elements in linking regional engagement to universities core functions. Partnerships in Lincoln operate at three main levels. There are some strategic relationships involving the university, public sector and business, notably through Greater Lincolnshire LEP and the implementation of the EU Structural Funds. These strategic relationships, notably with the public-sector, steer the university's other regional partnerships through varied policies and funding instruments. A second layer of partnerships link the university with individual large organisations such as the County Council, or Siemens and are focused around specific objectives and relatively long-term projects. A third level of partnerships concern shorter term links with a wider range of businesses and organisations including SMEs and the voluntary sector and across a wide range of topics.

Examples of these partnerships are examined in the next section. Two collaborations which have been highlighted nationally as good practices in recent higher education policy documents are the link with Siemens and the Sparkhouse incubator (BIS, 2013). The Siemens collaboration demonstrates how a long-term, strategic university-industry partnership can have multiple benefits to both parties. The Sparkhouse case portrays how the incubator, initially launched by the County Council, has become part of the university's business support services, and how it can concretely support local start-ups and graduate entrepreneurship. Finally, the University has also been developing a new science park project with the Lincolnshire Co-op to build on the experience of Sparkhouse, and also the Think tank incubator.

The case of the Siemens collaboration

Siemens are the largest local manufacturer in Lincoln, with 160 years of history as an engineering business in the city under a variety of different ownerships and names. The company had experienced difficulties in recruiting and retaining engineers, to the point where they were considering company relocation. Discussions with the university led to a proposal for a collaboration agreement and the formation of a new engineering school. As a result of the collaboration Siemens made a long-term commitment to produce turbines for industry and power generation in Lincoln, and expand its R&D and product innovation processes. The systematic collaboration required more highly skilled workforce and enhanced the region's R&D capacity (University of Lincoln, 2010). One of the major outcomes is the establishment of a new school of engineering in 2009 (Charles, 2016), the UK's first purpose-built engineering school in 25 years. The school received significant financial investment of £7.3 million from Siemens Industrial Turbomachinery limited (SITL), EMDA, Lincolnshire County Council and £4.3 million from HEFCE (University of Lincoln, 2010). What is innovative about the school is not just the joint research agenda between the school and the company, but that Siemens placed their Training and

Competence Institute in the new university engineering building, a unique development for the company. This is used by Siemens employees and customers to learn how to operate and maintain Siemens machinery safely.

The Siemens-University of Lincoln partnership has stimulated a number of collaborative research projects on themes of interest to the company. According to the Wilson Review (BIS 2012), the partnership resulted in the generation of six times the turnover cited in the original business plan, provided major business benefits for the company as well as research outcomes for the university all while protecting IP and observing commercial sensitivities.

A key benefit for Siemens was a much higher retention rate for their graduate engineers, increasing from around 40-50% to 90%. Also, due to Siemens involvement in the curriculum at Lincoln, they have been able to reduce the additional training needs for new graduates from 18 months to just 9 months (Deloitte, 2017). Overall, the student employment rate of the School of Engineering in the Graduate Destination Survey 2014/2015 is significantly better compared to the whole university. The graduate level employment for the School for Engineering is 90.91% compared with 71.89% at the overall university level. Siemens is also the most frequently mentioned employer of graduates (UoL, 2016a). The partnership has also spread beyond the engineering school, and now the Business School also places a number of students in non-engineering functions in the local Siemens business in areas such as marketing and procurement.

The Sparkhouse case

Lincoln, like many other HEIs, has recognised how important and beneficial it is to strategically support student entrepreneurship (Gibb and Hannon, 2006). So, student and graduate entrepreneurship has been identified as a strategic goal in the new university strategy (UoL, 2016) and the university has established structures to provide incubation support for start-ups. The University of Lincoln's Sparkhouse, first launched in 2002, is an award-winning business incubator, based on the Lincoln campus, originally designed to foster student entrepreneurship in the creative sector and to help retain graduates, that has supported over 230 new and growing businesses in the region and has created over 370 new jobs (Sparkhouse, 2017). At first, the incubator was run by the Lincolnshire County Council, and it mostly provided entrepreneurial services to students and graduates, especially in the field of arts and creative industries. This was at a time when there was a gap in fostering entrepreneurial skills in the East Midlands' universities. Helping students to start up their own businesses was a way to try to retain more graduates in the area (staff member, UoL).

Since establishing Sparkhouse, the University's role has grown in supporting local SMEs. Besides the targeted outreach activities, there are beneficial experiences from providing a single point of entry for local businesses (BIS, 2013), and Sparkhouse currently offers a variety of services to both students and businesses (University of Lincoln, 2010). The business support services include business planning advice, mentoring, finance services, training and access to specialist support and also networking opportunities among tenants (Sparkhouse, 2017). Sparkhouse still offers support to students from entrepreneur skills training to small grants to start their own businesses with ERDF funding.

All services combined, the incubator's role is to shape the local economy, but also makes Lincoln more attractive as a city (staff member, UoL). Though facilitating networking is not a part of Sparkhouse's core functions, the sharing of facilities with other start-ups creates a sense of community.

278

Fostering regional innovation in Lincoln

The benefits of the University of Lincoln's role in the local economic regeneration of Lincolnshire are most visible in the city of Lincoln.[44] A major channel for the UoL in fostering innovation in local businesses is the Lincoln Science and Innovation Park, established in collaboration with the Lincolnshire Co-operative Society as a hub for investment in science and technology. The Co-operative Society owns the main tranche of land on which the park is based but has been a long-term supporter of the university since its foundation, also involved in the development of a pharmacy degree. Currently consisting of the Think Tank Innovation Centre, the Joseph Banks Laboratories and the newly opened Boole Technology Centre, the Science Park is the sole science, innovation and R&D dedicated site for private and public sectors in Lincolnshire. The interviewees thought that the Science Park will eventually attract larger companies, strengthening links with the university:

> '[...] We are getting new businesses to relocate here just because of the university. I think the Science park, Boole Technology Centre and Think Tank, is really gaining momentum.' (employee, County Council)

> '[...] Facilities attracting big companies might even influence the curricula, which links between research and business.' (staff, UoL).

The Science Park has required the County Council and the University of Lincoln to work together closely, something which builds upon a rather successful history of collaboration dating

---

[44] In 2000–2009 the number of business grew 23% in Greater Lincoln, which is a significantly higher percentage compared to the rest of the county (17%) and East Midlands (17%).

back to the origins of the University. Adjacent to the science park site but part of the wider vision of the park, UoL is also managing an existing incubator called the Think Tank on behalf of Lincoln City Council under a management contract, combining commercial tenants and university activities.

In addition to the science park, the UoL has also been developing training and support for SMEs through externally funded programmes, notably through the ERDF supported Innovation Programme for Lincolnshire. The university was invited to bid for the management role as well as the delivery of innovation support as a key strand of the 2014-20 European Structural Investment Funds programme for Lincolnshire, and coordinates the whole innovation expenditure on behalf of Greater Lincolnshire LEP.

The 'challenge' of engagement

The challenges faced by the University of Lincoln, in its quest to engage with its local community can be said to be both internally and externally generated.

A 'cultural gap' exists between the university and its industry collaborators especially bordering on issues of inadequate marketing observed through a lack of information on 'engagement' opportunities on the university's website, and a 'relatively' slow response time. Industry partners who are used to a quicker response time than experienced from their university partners find this to be a challenge with engagement. This challenge as exemplified below, calls for better understanding between collaborating partners and a sense of urgency from the side of the university when industry is concerned.

> '[...]You get a referral come in, or a question that could have led in a lot more, but we did not respond quick enough, it went to the wrong people, somebody didn't understand it...I think the understanding that has to take

280

place between industry and academia takes a lot of time and experience to navigate your way through it. If you look at a relationship like Siemens and the school of engineering that's a very good example where it's worked well because there is that level of understanding between academia and commercial aspirations' (staff, UoL).

Besides engaging with local businesses, this gap hinders collaboration with local authorities, and promoting the university's regional role:

'[...] so how can we help to promote these offices, it's really about knowing who is the right person to go to, what's the structure of each school,[...] it's just that for us it's important to know who's the 'go to' person in which school, which are the offices wanting to work the businesses, just to be clear so we can provide routes.' (employee, County Council).

Some internal barriers exist between academic staff focused primarily on teaching and research and staff employed to engage with business. The need to support university aims around teaching excellence and improved research performance in some cases leave limited time available for wider business engagement.

Issues of intellectual property pose a challenge where the *'University academic is interested in publishing a finding, whereas his Industry partners are more interested in patenting it'* (staff, UoL). The issue here lies in finding a good balance between the industry's 'money-making' ambitions and the University's 'knowledge dissemination ambition', which may be challenging to always achieve in practice. This is also symptomatic of tensions between local engagement and the research excellence objectives in which publication is a central theme.

281

For University staff actively engaged in community outreach within the food sector of the county, having enough staff who could engage in training efforts to the locals remains an issue suggestive of the need to invest in more 'outreach staff' and to further develop internal mechanisms to link researchers and businesses:

> '....... I am expected to know the entire breadth of qualifications and curriculum because you have to do that, because you can't go to a company and say, well I'll get somebody to get back to you...' (staff, UoL).

Government interventions and policies, such as the 'apprenticeship levy'[45] which require effective communication and informing of the local businesses on the changes, and 'Brexit' for instance were found to be significant challenges with regional engagement efforts by the university. This is seen for example in the sense that

> 'when Brexit was announced, some of our clients lost 20% of their workforce over-night and you know the shock waves that happened [...] those sorts of things impact on us hugely because we have to be proactive in trying to find solutions with them [...] our challenges are externally-driven, political challenges' (staff, UoL).

---

[45] The UK government is committed to boosting productivity by investing in human capital, for example, through the Apprenticeship Levy, introduced in 2017. It is a levy on UK employers to fund new apprenticeships: it will be charged at a rate of 0.5% of an employer's salary costs and each employer will receive an allowance of £15,000 per apprentice to offset against their levy payment.   https://www.gov.uk/government/publications/apprenticeship-levy/apprenticeship-levy 14th of August 2017.

'Brexit' has also raised worry concerning the funding for business support and R&D in the future:

> 'Brexit, when the vote was out, many of our businesses thought that the European tap is closed at once, and they have been really pleased that we have still been able to run our programmes until the end of their life cycles. For us, there is a real worry that there's going to be a huge gap [...]' (employee, County Council).

A local infrastructural deficit, relating to the road network to access very rural parts of the county is a challenge for broadening engagement efforts. This, as expressed by an enterprise partner of the University working in the food sector made it challenging to 'share advancements in the food sector in the county' (industry partner, NCFM).

The rural, geographically diverse environment of the county also makes it more difficult to reach businesses outside of Lincoln, and many of the businesses are not aware of their possibilities. '-- getting to those business that are hidden away, which are very busy with production and actually haven't got chance to lift up their head and see what support is out there: how do we reach those and make them aware of what's available and that's our biggest challenge' (employee, County Council).

Though Greater Lincolnshire's economy is relatively stable, its large group of land-based businesses does not embrace innovation as it is more challenging to release resources for investment. The area has many family businesses, which typically are looking for lower risk and long-term investments '[...] there is a lot of family businesses in Greater Lincolnshire [...] that lends itself to the degree of stability, because those family-based businesses look for long term investments, they have an eye in the future giving the business to their children, so they tend to be a little more risk-

aversive and there's this link between risk and innovation, it is an interesting one.' (staff, UoL).

A low educational status of people in the county was found to be affecting aspirations of people in the county. This issue was found to be generational and requiring careful management.

> *'[...] we have low skills aspirations for those who do stay in the county [...] we have a university academy and if you look at the 11 year olds that are coming into our academy [...] we hear stories where they have never picked up a book before because their families don't have any books at home, very low aspirations [...] you have 3 generations now of families who were land workers, factory workers,....and you now want first generation people who might be dreaming of going to university one-day'* (staff, UoL).

Interviewees described that there is a large innovation potential in Lincolnshire, but also lack of ambition hinders economic growth *'[...] the challenge of the Greater Lincolnshire is the ambition [...] and I think we have the key role in driving ambition in Greater Lincolnshire as a whole and there are many (businesses) that are very innovative but don't recognise their potential.'* (staff, UoL).

Generally, a problem with graduate retention in the county was re-echoed in interviews. This was found to be the case for various reasons including lack of jobs and the graduate's dream to live in the big city. For example, *'[...] well there are no jobs, some who could actually get jobs just have the big cities like London on their minds'* (graduate, UoL). It was also noted, that the University of Lincoln has already taken actions to support graduates to stay in Lincolnshire, such as work placements at Siemens that might lead to employment after graduation, and discount schemes for post-graduate studies. Also, a more employer-led curricula design was seen as one of the solutions:

> 'Tailored curricula is an example on how universities can respond to the changing needs of the markets, by combining [...] teaching material and practices from the right businesses to basic degree programmes' (graduate, UoL).

But despite these initiatives and possible job opportunities, the personal situation of a student – especially family relations – often steers their choices to stay in the local region.

All these constraints were observed to be interrelated and somewhat overlapping, especially the graduate retention and cultural gap between university and businesses, which were identified to be both internal and external barriers hindering the university's regional engagement and contribution to economic development (see figure 8.1)

Figure 8.1: Internal and external constraints hindering engagement in Lincolnshire

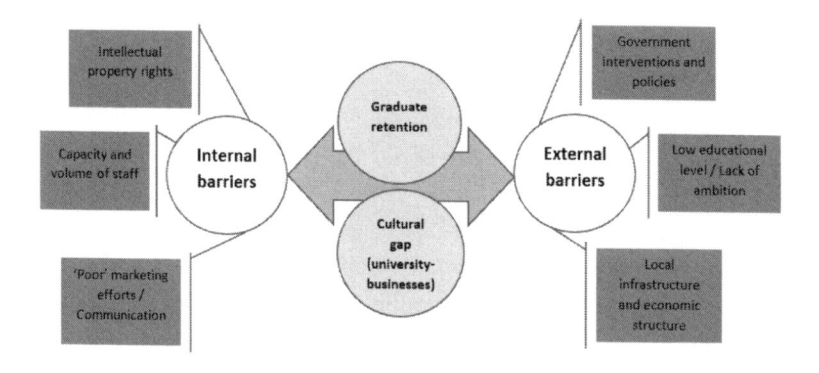

Overcoming challenges to regional development

Universities are constantly pushed to reassess their role and relationship with their main stakeholders and communities. Understanding and managing the diverse partnerships as well as avoiding undesirable consequences of adopting new collaboration models requires considerable strategic planning (Jongbloed *et al.*, 2008).

A key role of universities in facilitating economic growth is defined by their cutting-edge research capability in their respective fields, innovation expertise and wide collaboration with businesses (BIS, 2013). They are in a unique position due to their capability to bring together external knowledge and research links with local students, actors and ventures, enabling global knowledge exchange in local processes, and thus increasing the innovation capacity of rural areas compared with relying solely on internal knowledge processes (Charles, 2016). This lends very well to the case of the University of Lincoln, which actively engages with its local community, through various partnerships based on competence and leading research.

The University of Lincoln's rapid growth and expansion of a range of degree programmes demonstrates that a full-range, multi-disciplinary university is more likely to be able to cater for different local needs from education services to research collaboration, and the organisation is capable of adapting rather quickly to the emerging local needs. This is not, however, a typical set-up for a rural campus, despite the university's brief history of being a smaller branch campus. It seems that the fast growth of the organisation has allowed the University of Lincoln to surpass the common dilemma of smaller campuses to either specialise in a region's vocational needs or focus on fewer disciplines linking teaching and research activities to the region

(Charles, 2016). Indeed, the university is actively doing both of these.

The regional innovation support services have become somewhat dependent on the university, especially in incubation support (Sparkhouse, Think tank), but also providing training for SMEs (e.g. Innovation Programme for Greater Lincolnshire[46]) or engaging with regional innovation policy (GLLEP's Innovation Council). The University of Lincoln's major role in the regional innovation processes, especially for start-ups, makes it easy to forget, that universities are not the only providers of high-level research and innovation support services for the business sector (BIS, 2012), though as is typical for rural regions, there are fewer knowledge institutions in Lincolnshire. Thus, the University has managed to secure this position in addition to the County Council as a key driver for regional innovation in just twenty years.

Universities tend to be considered as fairly "fixed" institutes in the regional development literature, with a weak capability to adapt to the changes of the external world. Despite being a hub of highly skilled people, their organisational capacity for strategic planning is seen as rather limited. At the same time the growing diversity of partnerships makes universities more integrated with society, also demanding more from management so that the HEIs do not become overburdened by the claims of the stakeholders (Jongbloed *et al.*, 2008, 308). This poses even further challenges to rural campuses, which are typically expected to respond to the needs of the local economy. These demands may be more diverse and complex than presumed, varying from more traditional sectors such as agriculture, tourism and services to high-technology manufacturing (Charles, 2016).

---

[46] http://lincsinnovation.co.uk/

The University of Lincoln's strategy aims to conduct research that contributes to local challenges which can also have global significance. The university's 'living lab' approach strives to find solutions for regional problems that can be transferred multi-nationally, especially in personalised health, agri-food technology, creativity, digital arts and archives and rural communities. (UoL, 2016b). It is, however, a big challenge to balance research excellence and relevance and to find a profitable combination of the local and the global (Benneworth and Arbo 2007, 30, Rip 2000). This is especially the case when the challenges in doing so are not all within the university's reach to solve (e.g. externally-generated challenges created through new government policies and initiatives) and the specific elements of operational environment, such as local infrastructure or economic structure, which hinders university's regional engagement.

Government policies and interventions play a major role in developing business-university collaboration, but in the end it comes down to the collaboration and actions between individual universities and businesses to determine whether the partnership is successful (BIS, 2012). In the case of the University of Lincoln-Siemens collaboration the success is a result of committing to a long-term strategic collaboration, which is equally beneficial for both parties and building the partnership solidly on university core functions, education and research – though a wider impact on the local industry and innovation is typically harder to achieve and also identify. It is also worth noting, that a deep employer collaboration may, especially in curriculum design, steer research orientation. The anticipation of the future development of national policies in the post-Brexit era may change the present approaches to innovation support services and university-collaboration patterns, for which more hands-on strategising is expected; especially in the area of communicating with, and educating the local businesses on what to expect, and how to apply themselves to expected changes.

Despite the University of Lincoln's rapid transformation from a branch campus to a full-range university, the surroundings remain rather rural, and as typical for such regions, they rely heavily on small and micro businesses and lack knowledge based businesses (Charles, 2016). The ongoing expansion of the university is without a doubt a challenge also for its management. The University of Lincoln's strategy 2016–2021 addresses the issue with the concept of a "tough leader", which refers to the spirit of innovation and experimenting new practices in teaching, research, partnerships (UoL, 2016b). It goes without saying however that with the ongoing expansion, the university would need to attend to the requirement for more staff especially in support of ongoing engagement efforts that require outreach into the rural community.

In the light of the actions the university presently employs to foster engagement and the identified challenges involved in doing so, it remains a question of, what it would take for the university to overcome these challenges, and from a cost-benefit perspective, which strategies would be worthwhile. The coming years will reveal how the university will continue to combine innovation support with the university's core functions in other emerging sectors beyond engineering and food manufacturing, such as business services and visitor economy (Greater Lincolnshire LEP, 2016), but also if the region will manage to retain more graduates who are essential for knowledge transfer from the university into the local businesses. It will also remain to be seen if the university is able to maintain their rather dominant role and cater for changing regional innovation support needs or if other major innovation support providers emerge in the area in the future.

References

Arbo, P. and Benneworth, P. (2007). **Understanding the Regional Contribution of Higher Education Institutions: A Literature Review, OECD Education Working Papers, No. 9**, Paris: OECD Publishing.

Barnes I. and Cox, V. (2007). EU migrants as entrepreneurs in Lincolnshire: Exploiting the enterprise culture, **Entrepreneurship and Innovation**, 18, 209-218

BEIS (2018) **Local Industrial Strategies: Policy Prospectus**. London: Dept for Business, Energy and Industrial Strategy.

Benneworth, P. & Sanderson, A. (2009). The regional engagement of universities: Building capacity in a sparse innovation environment, **Higher Education Management and Policy**, 21, 123-140.

Birch, E., Perry, D.C. and Taylor, H.L. (2013). Universities and anchor institutions, **Journal of Higher Education Outreach and Engagement**, 17 (3), 7-15.

BIS (Department for Business, Innovation and Skills) (2012). **A Review of Business-University Collaboration: The Wilson Review**. London: BIS.

BIS (Department for Business, Innovation and Skills) (2013). **Encouraging a British Invention Revolution: Sir Andrew Witty's Review of Universities and Growth**. London: BIS.

Boucher, G., Conway, C. & Van der Meer, E. (2003). Tiers of Engagement by Universities in their Region's Development, **Regional Studies**, 37, 887–897.

Breznitz, M.S. & Feldman, M.P. (2012). The engaged university, **Journal of Technology Transfer** 37, 139–157.

Bridger, J.C. and Alter, T.R (2006). The engaged university, community development and public scholarship, **Journal of Higher Education Outreach and Engagement**, 11, 163-178.

Charles, D and Benneworth, P (2001). **The Regional Mission: The Regional Contribution of Higher Education: National Report**, London: Universities UK.

Charles, D. (2006). Universities as key knowledge infrastructures in regional innovation system, **Innovation: The European Journal of Social Science Research**, 19, 117–130.

Charles, D. (2016). The rural university campus and rural innovation – conflicts around specialisation and expectations, **Science and Public Policy**, 43, 763–773.

Civic Universities Commission (2019). **Truly Civic: Strengthening the Connection Between Universities and their Places**, London: UPP Civic Universities Commission.

Coenen, L (2007). The role of universities in the regional innovation systems of the North East of England and Scania, Sweden: providing missing links? **Environment and Planning C: Government and Policy**, 25, 803-821.

Committee on Higher Education (The Robbins Committee) (1963). **Higher Education, Report of the Committee appointed by the Prime Minister under the Chairmanship of Lord Robbins**. London: Her Majesty's Stationery Office

DCLG (Department for Communities and Local Government) (2017). **Midlands Engine Strategy**, available at: https://www.gov.uk/government/uploads/system/uploads/attachment_d ata/file/598295/Midlands_Engine_Strategy.pdf (accessed 15th April 2017).

Deloitte (2017). **Catalyst Fund Economic Impact Study: Summary Report for the Higher Education Funding Council for England**, Bristol: Higher Education Funding Council for England.

Eurostat (2017). **2015 GDP per capita in 276 EU Regions**, News Release 52/2017, 30th March.

Gale, N. K., Heath G., Cameron, E., Rashid, S., & Redwood S. (2013). Using the framework method for the analysis of qualitative data in multidisciplinary health research. **BMC Medical Research Methodology**, 13, 117.

Gibb, B. & Hannon, P. (2006). Towards the Entrepreneurial University? **International Journal of Entrepreneurship Education** 4, 73–110.

GOA Ltd (2001). **The Impact of Lincoln University Campus on the Economy of Lincolnshire**: Final report to Lincolnshire TEC Group.

291

Goddard, J. and Vallance, P. (2013). **The University and the City**, London: Routledge.

Goddard, J., Hazelkorn, E., Kempton, L. and Vallance, P. (eds) (2016). **The Civic University: The Policy and Leadership Challenges**, Cheltenham, UK: Edward Elgar

Greater Lincolnshire Local Enterprise Partnership (2014). **Innovation Research Report**. Lincoln: GLLEP.

Greater Lincolnshire Local Enterprise Partnership (2016) **Strategic Economic Plan 2014-2030, Refresh Spring 2016**, Lincoln: GLLEP.

Hammarberg, K., Kirkman, M. & De Lacey, S. (2016). Qualitative research methods: when to use them and how to judge them. **Human Reproduction**, 31, 498–501.

Harkavy, I., & Zuckerman, H. (1999). **Eds and Meds: Cities' Hidden Assets**. The Brookings Institution Survey Series, 22. Washington, DC: The Brookings Institution, Center on Urban & Metropolitan Policy.

Hassink, R (2010). Locked in decline? On the role of regional lock- ins in old industrial areas, in Boschma, R. and Martin, R. (eds) **Handbook of Evolutionary Economic Geography** (pp 450-468), Cheltenham: Edward Elgar,.

Huggins, R and Johnston, A. (2009). The economic and innovation contribution of universities: a regional perspective, **Environment and Planning C: Government and Policy**, 27, 1088-1106

Jongbloed, B., Enders, J. & Salerno, C. (2008), Higher education and its communities: Interconnections, interdependencies and a research agenda, **Higher Education** 56, 303–324.

Kempton, L., Goddard, J., Edwards, J., Hegyi, F.B. and Elena-Pérez, S. (2013) **Universities and Smart Specialisation** S3 Policy Brief Series No. 03/2013, JRC Scientific and Policy Reports, Sevilla: European Commission Joint Research Centre, IPTS.

Lawton Smith, H (2007). Universities, innovation and territorial development: a review of the evidence, **Environment and Planning C: Government and Policy**, 25, 98-114.

Lincolnshire Assembly (2008). **Lincolnshire Economic Strategy 2008-2012, Turning the Corner**, Lincoln: Lincolnshire Assembly.

292

OECD (2007). **Higher Education and Regions: Globally Competitive, Locally Engaged**, Paris: OECD Publications,

OECD (2011). **Reviews of Regional Innovation Regions and Innovation Policy**. Paris: OECD Publications

Pinheiro, R., Charles, D. and Jones, G. A. (2016). Equity, institutional diversity and regional development: a cross country comparison, **Higher Education**. 72, 307–322

Regeneris, (2017). **The Social, Cultural & Economic Contribution of the University of Lincoln**, Manchester: Regeneris Consulting.

Rip, A. (2002). Regional innovation systems and the advent of strategic science, **Journal of Technology Transfer**, 27, 123-131.

Ritchie, J. & Lewis, J. (2003). **Qualitative Research Practice: a Guide for Social Science Students and researchers**. London: Sage.

Rossington, D. (2016). **The University of Lincoln: A Story Worth Telling**, private paper.

Sparkhouse (2017). website, available at: http://www.sparkhouselincoln.co.uk/ (accessed 15th April 2017).

Taylor, H. L., & Luter, G. (2013). **Anchor Institutions: An Interpretive Review Essay**. Buffalo, NY: Anchor Institutions Task Force, University at Buffalo.

UK Government. (2017). **UK Industrial Strategy: Building a Britain fit for the Future**. London: HMSO.

Universities UK (2001), **The Regional Mission - the regional contribution of higher education. East Midlands: Innovation through diversity**. London, Universities UK.

Universities UK (2014), **The Economic Impact of the East Midlands Higher Education Sector** (2014). London, Universities UK.

University of Lincoln (2010), **Community Engagement. Impact of the University of Lincoln**.

University of Lincoln (2016a), **Graduate Destination Survey 2014/2015**.

University of Lincoln (2016b), **Thinking Ahead 2016-2021. University of Lincoln Strategic Plan**.

Uyarra, E. (2010) Conceptualizing the regional roles of universities, implications and contradictions, **European Planning Studies**, 18, 1227-1246.

Vorley, T. & Nelles, J. (2009), Building entrepreneurial architectures: a conceptual interpretation of the third mission, **Policy Futures in Education,** 7, 284–296.

Wilson, J. R. (2014), **Essentials of Business Research, A Guide to Doing your Research Project**, London: Sage.

Yin, R. K. (2002), **Case Study Research - Design and Methods**. London: Sage.

Yin, R. K. (2016), **Qualitative Research from Start to Finish** (2nd edn). New York: Guilford Publications.

Chapter 9

Conclusion

The Entrepreneurial University from a
Regional Innovation Perspective

Rhoda Ahoba-Sam, Sergio Manrique & David Charles

The cases presented in this book have examined the role universities can and do play in the regional innovation process highlighting the uniqueness of universities' offerings to their stakeholders. In that way, by focusing on both internal and external issues related to universities' entrepreneurial outlook, the cases present an end-to-end exposé of universities' contributions to regional engagement. Altogether, the cases highlight the nature of impact entrepreneurial universities can exert on the development of their regions.

From the cases, it is evident that beyond their engagement in teaching and research, these universities have met a diverse set of further needs in contributing to the economic and social development of their cities and regions, especially emphasized by their involvement in the ECIU and participation in the RUNIN project. Across varied fields of knowledge and through interaction and engagement with businesses, government and citizens, among other regional stakeholders, the seven institutions have, in different ways, played a key role in regional development.

Whilst the various chapters captured the nature of each university and their unique approach to regional impact, they collectively highlight the following:

i)   Certain systemic challenges constrain universities' efforts in delivering their role as significant contributors to regional innovation

ii)   Though challenged in scale and scope, universities in peripheral, rural or less developed regions are significant players in facilitating regional development

iii)   The contributions of universities usually need to be tailored to meet the specific requirements of their respective regions

iv)   A broad stakeholder involvement is required to address the challenges and tensions inherent in regional development

In this closing chapter, we employ the concept of *regional innovation systems* (RIS) as a lens to analyse the findings from the case studies. The RIS theory finds its origins in the conception of national systems of innovation, pioneered by Lundvall (1985, 1992), Freeman (1987) and Nelson (1993) following an evolutionary economics view (Schumpeter, 1942), and was further developed with a regional level focus by Cooke (1992), and Cooke, Uranga, & Etxebarria (1997). The theory claims that the innovation process in regions follows a systemic nature given the relevance of different economic, political and social relationships that generate collective learning; such interactions support the creation, diffusion and use of new and economically useful knowledge within a geographic area. Subsequently, the RIS is placed at the intersection of the research streams of economic geography, innovation studies and regional studies.

Applying a regional innovation perspective

The case studies included in this book are theoretically founded in a range of concepts closely related to the innovation systems approach, such as the roles of universities in regional development (Uyarra, 2010), the triple/quadruple helix of innovation (Etzkowitz , 2003; Arnkil *et al.*, 2010), university-firm collaboration (Perkmann & Walsh, 2007), localised capabilities (Maskell *et al.*, 1998), industrial transformation (Lester, 2005) and universities' engagement in [rural/peripheral] regions (Boucher, *et al.*, 2003), among others. At the intersection of these theories, we project that a regional innovation perspective is relevant for analysing the role the universities play in innovation and regional development.

Figure 9.1 The Regional Innovation System Framework (source: Stuck et al 2015)

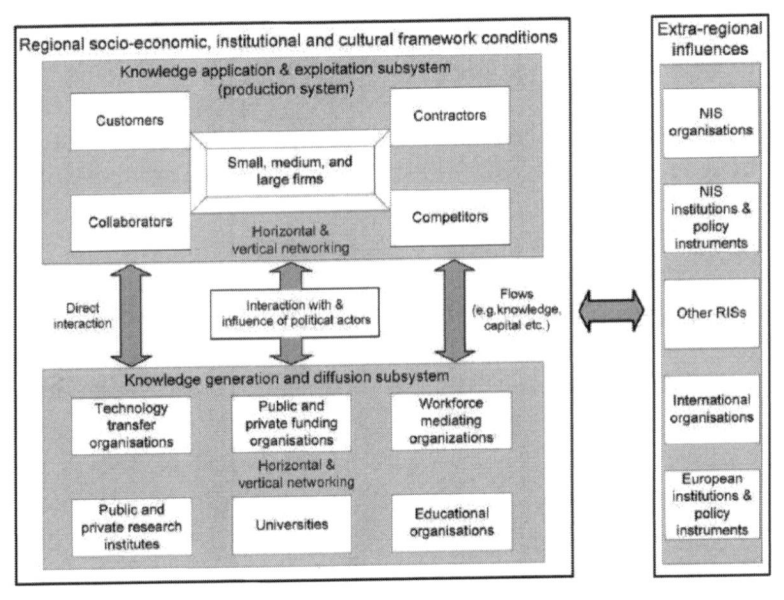

Creating a university as a response to regional needs

First it is important to acknowledge that these universities were all established specifically to address regional needs in the last half of the twentieth century. So compared with many other universities in the same countries these institutions have a very distinct history and internal culture which is linked strongly with the interests of their regions. Most were the result of deliberate lobbying on the part of their local regions and local groups of representatives of government and industry played a key role in their establishment. We note the attempts by groups in Lincoln, Aveiro and Aalborg for example to establish universities over some time, in some cases raising funds to help initiate the university. Other cases had a stronger national dimension – UAB was one of two autonomous universities created in the two largest Spanish cities, but was done through engagement with local communities.

So, in terms of the regional innovation system there was a direct action on the part of members of the local innovation system to fill a major gap by adding the university as a key knowledge institution in the region. In several of the cases it was the absence of other major knowledge institutions that was the driver, notably in Aalborg, Lincoln, Twente and Aveiro, whilst in others it was the need for a university to work alongside industry that was needed, in Linköping, Stavanger, and Barcelona. Furthermore the university was in several cases designed to address the needs of a specific industry, where there were skills shortages or need for technical support and the university was built around certain specialisations such as oil and gas in Stavanger. In Twente the challenge became how to help the region transition from an old innovation system based on textiles to a new one, with the presence of the university opening up new opportunities in high technology which would not have been possible otherwise. These transitions have not always been successful, as seen in the case of biotech in Aalborg, and it is the localised capability across the innovation system as whole that matters as the ICT sector, also in

298

Aalborg, demonstrates. It is the promise of additional capabilities and the contribution to the development of localised skills resources though which has encouraged regions to demand universities, and the call for them to play a central role in local innovation.

As a consequence, all of the universities in this study acknowledge in their mission the need to support the local industry and the wider community. It is a responsibility they accept and helps to shape both the disciplinary configuration of the university, but also its culture and its identification as an entrepreneurial university meeting the characteristics of the Burton Clark (1998) model. However there are tensions between this local mission and the international research mission. As ambitious institutions which want to grow and succeed they also look to develop a strong research base even if the local region has limited demands for that discipline or lacks a related industrial cluster. Universities need an international profile to succeed within their own peer groups at national level in order to attract high quality staff and students. So there is an apparent paradox here: by focusing purely on local needs a university may neglect its wider competitiveness and limit the quality of contribution it can make to the host region. But by looking to research excellence in order to attract the best possible staff, then it may become more oriented to national and international partnerships and neglect the local region. The balance between these tensions is difficult to strike and this is an ongoing dynamic in all of these universities: being both global and local, and ensuring that their research excellence also contributes to the regional innovation system.

Global knowledge networks are important to regions and hence the presence of an internationally connected university in a region helps to connect the regional innovation system to wider industry and knowledge networks. Universities are a key part of the global pipelines (Bathelt et al, 2004) which facilitate the flows of codified knowledge between regions. This role has many aspects whether it be in the form of libraries, conferences and managed knowledge exchange, or in the informal networks that develop between academic staff and local industry partners. So whilst there are tensions between the global and local roles there are also important interdependencies, as long as these are recognised by the university and reflected in its investments and culture.

Promoting entrepreneurship

A second major theme is entrepreneurship and all of these universities have, to varying degrees, developed entrepreneurship programmes, incubators and science parks to stimulate the development of new firms, partly through academic spin outs but more significantly through student and graduate enterprise. Indeed some of the universities, notably Twente and Linköping, have international reputations for their success in stimulating entrepreneurship. In part such programmes are a response to some of the local contexts in terms of relatively low levels of new firms and the need to replace old declining industries, and support has often come from local partners for these schemes. As a heightened level of entrepreneurship is an outcome, the input from the universities has been the adoption of an entrepreneurial culture and investment in the components of an entrepreneurial architecture. This builds on the Burton Clark model of the entrepreneurial university, as well as the meeting the objectives of the ECIU.

Key elements of the entrepreneurial architecture of universities (Vorley and Nelles, 2009) can be seen across the case studies: structures, systems, strategies, leadership and culture. Structures include formal organisational mechanisms which are adopted across all the institutions including science parks and TTOs, organisations such as LiU Innovation, specialist research centres and dedicated engagement campuses such as Lincoln's National Centre for Food Manufacturing, but also structures within the central administration to support and encourage commercialisation and entrepreneurship, such as Aveiro's Vice rector for Regional Development. In the case of Twente, through

Kennispark and the Twente Technology Circle the university participates in structures which incorporate many regional partners, and most university entrepreneurship initiatives involve external partners to support and mentor new businesses. Systems relate to the networks and processes within the institutions that support entrepreneurship, and which sit within strategies developed by the universities in which entrepreneurship, and regional engagement are core themes. Leadership for these activities comes strongly from university rectors and presidents, and also from individuals in key departments and faculties, but also from outside the university in terms of building shared localised capabilities. And finally the culture of the university as an entrepreneurial university is a common theme across all, encouraging external engagement and rewarding entrepreneurial behaviour.

The results so far have been varied between institutions: for some the incubators are still relatively young, but Twente and Linköping have demonstrated dramatic success in numbers of startups. Lincoln also has seen the formation of over 200 new businesses, whilst for Stavanger these are still early days, but the new incubator is already showing results. Time and local contexts matter here in reshaping the innovation system.

Modes of engagement in the regional innovation system

There are some distinct forms of engagement with the regional innovation system displayed across these seven universities which shape and characterise the ways in which they support regional innovation. Whilst all seek to develop research excellence and build research collaboration with local industry, they all engage in a variety of other distinctive patterns of interaction which enriches their collaborations and meets the specific needs of their regions, embracing both teaching and research-related activities.

301

One particular form of engagement is around problem based learning (PBL), where the students work on projects in which a problem, which might have emerged from a local business, is a trigger for the learning process. PBL originally emerged in medicine, but both Aalborg and Linköping have adopted it more widely across a number of disciplines as a core form of pedagogy within their universities. The particular strength or opportunity is that it both offers potential solutions to the businesses offering the problems as well as instilling greater problem-solving capabilities in the graduates emerging from the university. Developing links with the businesses through teaching projects also helps develop deeper relationships across the regional innovation system. A related development is Twente's science shop which connects students with societal partners with specific problems

The other universities have also developed a variety of interactions involving students, and placements are a key part of many teaching programmes. Lincoln for example through its strategic alliance with Siemens provides placements and project-related student collaboration in order to help provide future employees for the company, but this was only the start of the wider collaboration which now includes a shared space in the engineering building, used by Siemens for delivering training to its industry partners as well as university teaching, and a variety of research collaborations and projects involving staff. This collaboration is also being extended beyond the engineering school to include the business school and others. The benefits of such collaboration work in two directions as not only does the company benefit, initially from a ready supply of graduates who want to stay and live in Lincoln, but the partnership and Siemen's support enabled the university to create the first completely new engineering school in the UK for over 20 years. UAB has developed hackathon programmes with many local employers in which students address problems and present their results back to the company.

These universities also seek to collaborate across the regional innovation system through externally focused research centres, often in collaboration with regional partners. UAB's COREs as strategic research communities focus together researchers from different disciplines to address key challenges in partnership with regional organisations. Stavanger's Centre for Oil Recovery (COREC) links the university with a number of key local firms, and even predated the university being an actor in its formation. These centres act as important nodes within the RIS linking together actors, playing the role of intermediary and also making the external linkages to other related regional clusters elsewhere.

A final central role for the universities in the RIS is their role as the provider of human capital and skills. Whilst engagement with employers in the educational process as observed above helps to ensure students are well prepared for work with local employers, the proximity and interaction between university and firms helps in introducing graduates into the local labour market, and particularly convincing graduates that there is a local future for them. This was especially the case in Lincoln where the collaboration with Siemens was driven by the difficulty Siemens had in attracting and retaining graduate engineers, a problem much reduced following the development of new engineering programmes. Part of the challenge is to retain local students who would otherwise migrate to central regions, something which remains an ongoing issue in Northern Denmark, and Linköping – graduates need to be aware of local opportunities. The other challenge is to attract in talent from other regions, something which is probably best achieved by the attraction of students who then decide to remain.

Underpinning all of these mechanisms by which universities contribute to their regional innovation systems are intermediaries which can make the connections and here the story is more mixed. In the cases of Lincoln and Twente there is a problem reported for local business and organisations to find the correct academic partner within the university. This is a common issue for

303

universities with multiple disciplines, especially when problems are defined as multidisciplinary 'mode 2' (Gibbons et al 1994) problems when it is unclear where a local academic with relevant intersts might be located. To some extent, high profile, externally funded, research centres may address this issue by offering an obvious gateway for firms from a particular industry. For firms outside of major clusters or with more obscure interests there remains a problem of finding a way to the right person. The key entry point would therefore be the technology transfer office or related initiative, and staff with extensive experience of the university and its faculties. However such technology transfer staff require time to acquire knowledge of their university faculties and are difficult to replace when they move on. Multiple routes to developing contacts are therefore vital to developing deep relationships.

The campus as a shared space

Regional engagement for these universities is not just about what they do off campus with regional partners, but also the way the campus itself is used as a means of facilitating interaction. This may not have always been the case: Twente initially sought to isolate itself and its students from local society, but there seems to be a general trend across this group of universities to open up the campus for partner activity as a kind of shared space. While this thinking began perhaps as the idea of a science park as special campus space for businesses to be located in, the approach has gone further to recognise that campuses can be shared by multiple organisations as public spaces, in a way reversing the shift on the part of universities from being embedded in city centres to the out of town single use campus. Traditionally, city-based universities started as a small number of buildings near the centre of a city and gradually expanded by annexing buildings and spaces around them. This results in a campus which has a core that is usually pure university activities, but with a penumbra consisting of mixed university and non-university uses. There is an advantage in terms of engagement of the university being close to various other partners, and little need to actually house such partners on the core campus. For the group of universities in this book though, as younger institutions, they were all established on dedicated blocks of land as new campuses which they have gradually been building up. All but Lincoln are in suburban locations some way from the centre of the city and so are largely being developed from green fields. Lincoln is the exception in that a brownfield industrial site was available near to the centre of the city which gives a combination of a campus location with proximity to key partners.

So a challenge for this group of universities has been how to use the campus as a means of developing close links with partners, and one approach has been to attract partner activities onto the campus, using spare space to build new non-university buildings, or creating shared spaces where multi-partner teams can collaborate. The case of Siemens in Lincoln and their shared use of the new engineering school has already been mentioned. UAB not only has a research park on campus, but as part of their campus of excellence initiative there are a variety of government and private organisations sharing the campus. By providing additional services to companies on campus UAB can assist their development.

Participation in regional governance

A final theme emerging from these cases is the importance of the university participating in and contributing to regional decisionmaking and governance frameworks, working with partners and networks to reshape the regional innovation system. This activity takes a number of forms: leadership activities, expert roles, project partnering and developing visions and understanding.

In terms of leadership, senior members of universities are often asked to sit on regional boards and committees, representing their institutions and providing validation for regional strategies. In

305

Lincoln, for example, the Vice-chancellor sits on the board of the Local Enterprise Partnership whilst Linköping has been active in establishing regional consortia such as GrowLink which brings together many public and private partners to support economic development. The success of such bodies in developing coherent strategies depends however on the coherence of the boards with universities struggling sometimes when regions establish multiple bodies with constantly shifting agendas and strategies. This problem of complexity is seen in Twente region where various regional level boards have been established in addition to Kennispark at the local level. Governance structures evolve over time, sometimes new structures being set up whilst old ones still exist. Understanding who does what and how these structures interact requires considerable local knowledge outside of the usual university domain, and often universities recruit from the public sector to bring that knowledge in house. However, in the absence of clarity over the mission and responsibilities of regional structures many participants may hold back from commitment and fail to make the key strategic decisions.

As experts, many university staff also provide specialist advice to regional public bodies through a variety of forms of contractual and informal knowledge exchange. Often such advice is delivered alongside other connections through research centre collaborations or specific projects. Many connections are relateivly invisible as individual level links develop through research or teaching activities, or even through social connections outside of the university. Here the embeddedness of the university and staff in the region is crucial.

All of this comes together in considering how the presence of the university changes the overall vision and understanding of the region, and the options for the future. Through formal partnerships and individual experts, universities contribute to the development of future visions, analysing and creating narratives of the current problems, and proposing new policy responses. But more than this, the university opens up new potentials and creates

306

opportunities which would not have existed otherwise, stimulating new thinking and allowing the region to rethink the nature of its regional innovation system.

Conceptualisation

The case studies have also contributed to the way in which we can conceptualise the university engagement in the regional innovation system, illustrating a number of key issues and challenges.

As already noted there is the challenge of addressing the tensions among regional stakeholders for managing the innovation process in the region and building a regional innovation culture in a social knowledge economy (Benneworth & Ratinho, 2014). Four main types of tensions were identified in the case of Twente. First, the proliferation of strategic bodies led to a misalignment of stakeholder interests and a reluctance to commit to alignment. For the university this led to particular tensions between an international research mission and local engagement, which was exacerbated by the absence of a clear regional strategy. A second problem was the absence or invisibility of intermediaries to connect regional partners to the university. Third was the consequences of a dependence on key individuals in maintaining relationships, and the vulnerability of networks when those individuals moved on. Finally, there were asymmetries across knowledge communities in the region, which were seen as intractable problems in understanding the complexity and workings of the regional innovation system, and therefore hindered effective coordination and collaboration.

Together these tensions pose conceptual and practical challenges for the characterisation of the innovation system and for system-building. Whilst the university may be a central actor in the RIS, there are limits to which partners can identify and articulate how best the university can contribute, and limits to their ability to evaluate the performance of the university in meeting objectives around regional engagement. Each of the tensions identified relate to problems of complexity, indicating the limitations of relatively simple models of the regional system, and stressing the importance of continual dialogue to try and overcome the asymmetries of information. Regional innovation systems cannot easily be described but are best enacted through dialogue and interaction.

Alongside the RIS framework there are a number of other models of conceptualising the university engagement as demonstrated by Uyarra (2010). Although some such as the triple helix conceptualise the innovation system differently, it is clear that some of these models present a form of progression of greater breadth and more sophisticated forms of engagement. The analysis of the transition of Linköping University from a systemic to an engaged university over time illustrates how some of these models might be used alongside the innovation system concept to capture the evolution of the third mission for an individual university, or indeed a national higher education system.

Similarly the process of developing an innovation system can be seen as the application of localised capabilities (Maskell *et al.*, 1998) with university support. Whilst the notion of the innovation system is rooted in evolutionary economics, most studies of innovation systems focus on the form of the system at a particular point in time. The Aalborg case study illustrates some of the different mechanisms behind the more or less successful development of such capabilities, with evidence from two industries with different outcomes in North Denmark region. Such longitudinal studies of particular regions examining the roles of particular organisations are valuable in building an understanding of the dynamics of such systems.

The case study of Stavanger and the energy industry provides an applied analysis of Lester's industrial transformation model

(2005) and illustrates the dynamic role of the university as the industry has evolved and the transition pathway has progressed from industrial transplantation to a more mature process of upgrading. In this the university is responding to the evolution of the cluster, but is also an actor in that maturation process. Different industries and different transition pathways will require different university responses. In the same case study Tödtling and Trippl's (2005) RIS failures typology is also used to highlight the high risks of failure due to lock-in as a result of the domination of the oil and gas industry.

The diversity of regional impacts from universities in the studied cases highlights the need for differentiated regional innovation policy approaches among European regions (Tödtling & Trippl, 2005), both in empirical and conceptual terms. While chapters 2, 4 and 6 are broad in their theoretical backgrounds, combining different conceptual approaches to look deeply at the roles these entrepreneurial universities have played in regional innovation, chapters 3, 5 and 8 refer to more specific contexts (e.g. peripheral regions) and conceptual developments (e.g. Uyarra's university modes, localised capabilities) in order to explain more specific challenges and phenomena that universities face in their regional engagement activities. What all these case studies have in common is the recognition of the university as a key knowledge infrastructure in their regions (Charles, 2006), being then crucial in the framework of regional innovation systems.

Looking to the future

The universities in this study are not typical, but set the trend in terms of support for business and engagement within their regions, looking to be thought leaders within their national systems. They will presumably continue to do this even as other universities seek to imitate their actions and learn from their experience. There remains much to do though in their regions, and even within the universities there are lessons that can be transferred from one discipline area to another. In Lincoln the lessons from working with Siemens are being applied in the health sector, and the success of running incubators used as a basis for the new science park. New societal challenges require new responses and new opportunities for activities to support clean growth in a post-COVID world.

Looking beyond the innovation agenda, these universities display many of the characteristics of civic universities as anchor institutions, not just rooted in the place but of the place (Goddard et al, 2016) As such the challenge in the future is supporting the wider economic, social and cultural development of their regions, and particularly in facing new problems which emerge. Since 2020 we have all seen the consequences of the COVID-19 pandemic and universities globally have responded to the challenges of their cities and regions through their contribution to health systems, the development of new tests, treatments and vaccines and in providing business support to firms that have struggled through lockdowns. Universities have not been immune to the impacts of the pandemic with the loss of international students (and fees where applicable), the loss of income from services to students such as accommodation and meals, and the additional costs and reduced productivity from working and teaching online.

The experience of the pandemic though has reinforced in many minds the importance of the university in the region and highlighted what can be expected. Looking forward it would be expected that there will be continued pressure for universities to increase their engagement and intensify their collaboration. The Linköping case demonstrated the transition from the systemic to the engaged model, and we would expect such transitions to continue, especially as networks such as the ECIU promote good practice across the university sector.

In all the universities though there is a heavy dependence on key individuals as institutional entrepreneurs, making the links with the regional partners, developing and running key research groups, immersing themselves in community activities. Much of the tacit knowledge involved in these relationships and trust with the local community is tied up with individuals and when they move on to new positions or retire there are risks of a loss of knowledge and an erosion of relationships. Often these people may not be the ones participating in strategic meetings and with senior management roles, and it can be easy for them to be overlooked by the university management. Recognition of their contribution and recording their knowledge and networks is an important step in building continuity in engagement.

Experimentation and design will continue in the formation of new systems and initiatives to better support knowledge exchange, and ensuring that the right connections are made with local partners, and mismatches between supply and demand are at least managed even if they can never be truly removed. A key trend is the adoption of greater engagement with the wider population and the principles of responsible research and innovation. By bringing a greater variety of perspectives to bear, including those usually excluded from an input into research, the university can deliver innovation that is closer to the needs of the region and socially responsible. Tools such as living labs, already in use in several of the cases here, can be expected to be adopted more widely as a means of bridging the gaps between university researchers and the users of research.

It is likely therefore that these universities will continue to enhance their support for regional innovation, and their wider engagement with their regions. The trend internationally is for universities to make claims that they are becoming entrepreneurial, or engaged, or civic universities, building local and regional partnerships for mutual benefit. This particular group examined here have extensive experience which is often offered as national exemplars, and this book has attempted further to draw out these lessons, demonstrating some of the common approaches, but also illustrating the importance of local specificity and the use of appropriate institutions in different regional and national contexts. Success is never guaranteed, but the commitment is to try to make a difference, and in these cases enough difference has been made to their regions to reward those that argued for universities to be created there, and those that have laboured to build the partnerships.

References

Arnkil, R., Järvensivu, A., Koski, P., & Piirainen, T. (2010). **Exploring the quadruple helix. Report of quadruple helix research for the CLIQ project**. Tampere: Work Research Centre. University of Tampere.

Bathelt, H., Malmberg, A. & Maskell, P. (2004). Clusters and knowledge: local buzz, global pipelines and the process of knowledge creation, **Progress in Human Geography**, 28, 31-56.

Benneworth P., & Ratinho, T. (2014). Regional innovation culture in the social knowledge economy. In: Rutten, R., Benneworth, P., Irawati, D., & Boekema, F. (eds). **The social dynamics of innovation networks**. London: Routledge.

Boucher, G., Conway, C. & Van der Meer, E. (2003). Tiers of Engagement by Universities in their Region's Development. **Regional Studies**, 37, 887–897.

Charles, D. (2006). Universities as key knowledge infrastructures in regional innovation systems. **Innovation. The European journal of social science research**, 19(1), 117-130.

Clark, B. (1998). **Creating Entrepreneurial Universities: Organizational Pathways of Transformation**. Oxford: Pergamon/IAU Press.

Cooke, P. (1992). Regional innovation systems: competitive regulation in the new Europe. **Geoforum**, 23(3), 365–382.

Cooke, P., Uranga, M. G., & Etxebarria, G. (1997). Regional Innovation Systems: Institutional and Organizational Dimensions. **Research Policy**, 26, 475-491. DOI: https://doi.org/10.1016/S0048-7333(97)00025-5

Etzkowitz, H. (2003). Innovation in innovation: The triple helix of university-industry-government relations. **Social Science Information**, 42(3), 293-337.

Freeman, C. (1987). **Technology and Economic Performance: Lessons from Japan**. London: Pinter Publishers.

Gibbons, M., Limoges, C., Nowotny, H., Schwartzman, S., Scott, P. & Trow, M. (1994) **The New Production of Knowledge, The dynamics of Science and Research in Contemporary Societies**. Thousand Oaks, California: Sage Publications.

Goddard, J., Hazelkorn, E., Kempton, L., and Vallance, P. (eds) (2016). **The Civic University: The Policy and Leadership Challenges**. Cheltenham: Edward Elgar.

Lester, R. (2005). **Universities, innovation, and the competitiveness of local economies**. A summary Report from the Local Innovation Systems Project: Phase I. Massachusetts Institute of Technology, Industrial Performance Center, Working Paper Series.

Lundvall, B. Å. (1985). **Product Innovation and User- Producer Interaction**. Aalborg: Aalborg University Press.

Lundvall, B. Å. (1992). **National Systems of Innovation: Towards a Theory of Innovation and Interactive Learning.** London, England: Pinter Publishers.

Maskell, P., Eskelinen, H., Hannibalsson, I., Malmberg, A. & Vatne, E. (1998). Localised capabilities and the competitiveness of regions and countries. In **Competitiveness, Localised Learning and Regional Development. Specialization and Prosperity in Small Open Economies**. 50–71. Taylor & Francis.

313

Nelson, R. R. (1993). **National Innovation Systems: A Comparative Analysis**. Oxford: Oxford University Press.

Perkmann, M., & Walsh, K. (2007). University–industry relationships and open innovation: Towards a research agenda. **Journal of Management Review**, 9(4), 259-280.

Schumpeter, J. (1942). **Capitalism, Socialism and Democracy**. New York: Harper and Brothers.

Stuck, J., Broekel, T., & Revilla Diez, J. (2016). Network Structures in Regional Innovation Systems. **European Planning Studies**, 24, 423-442.

Tödtling, F. & Trippl. M. (2005). One size fits all? Towards a differentiated regional innovation policy approach. **Research Policy**, 34, 1203-1219.

Uyarra, E. (2010). Conceptualizing the Regional Roles of Universities, Implications and Contradictions. **European Planning Studies**, 18(8), 1227–1246.

Vorley, T. & Nelles, J. (2009), Building entrepreneurial architectures: a conceptual interpretation of the third mission, **Policy Futures in Education,** 7, 284–296.